OBAN HIGH SCHOOL

THE FIRST HUNDRED YEARS

Edited by
Robert A Reid

Published by Oban High School
1993

First published 1993
Oban High School, Soroba Road, Oban.
© Editor and Contributors 1993
ISBN 0 9521080 0 3

Set by Oban High School
Printed by Oban Times Limited

Contents

Preface   v

1   Introduction *Robert A Reid*   1

2   The Beginnings and the Rectorship of James Beattie
      Ian D S Thomson   12

3   From 1919 to World War II   67
      Appendix. Angus MacLeod - Gaelic Scholar   80
      Dugald MacArthur

4   World War II to 1950 *Lake Falconer*   83

5   The Fifties: a Campaign for Academic Success and
      Technical Innovation *Coll MacDougall*   100

6   The years 1960 - 1972 *Ann McCulloch*   123

7   The years 1972 - 1981 *Neil A MacIntosh*   145

8   Impressions of the Eighties   174

9   The Glasgow Branch of Oban High School Former
      Pupils' Association *John MacFarlane*   192

10   The Future *Brian R Mitchell*   199

      School Captains   202

      Dux Medallists   204

      Indices   207

NOTES ON THE CONTRIBUTORS

Robert A Reid MA, PhD was Dux of the School in 1955 and Captain in 1955-56. He formerly lectured in Greek at St Andrews University.

Ian D S Thomson is a teacher in   the School's History, Economics and Modern Studies Department.

Dugald MacArthur BSc, FLA was Dux in 1928 and is married to the Dux of 1929. He was formerly St Andrews University Librarian.

Lake Falconer attended the school during the war years of the 1940s. He has retired from legal practice in Oban.

Coll MacDougall MA attended the School in the 1950s. He is well known as a journalist and award-winning Shinty correspondent of *The Times*.

Ann McCulloch (née Naismith) MA was Dux in 1965. She taught Classics in the School between 1974 and 1979.

Neil A MacIntosh MA attended the School in the 1970s. He now works in industry in the south of England

John MacFarlane BSc was Captain in 1967-68. He now teaches at Blantyre High School and is Secretary of the Glasgow FP Association.

Brian R Mitchell BSc came to the School as Principal Teacher of Physics in 1969. He has been Rector since 1989.

PREFACE

Oban High School has provided a common element in the life and experience of the larger part of the population of Oban and the surrounding area: education, in every sense of the word, has been received, teachers enjoyed or endured, games played, exams sat, lifelong friendships formed. While the catchment area of the School has diminished in recent years, feeder schools in Oban and the district around, which once extended as far north as Ullapool, have passed their children to Oban High School for the imbibing of a secondary education.

"Johnnie is at the High School now." That statement has been made by generations of parents in north Argyll. Oban High School has, for them, been synonymous with secondary education and the granite building in Soroba Road. However, perhaps surprisingly, the title of the book, *Oban High School - The First Hundred Years*, requires explanation. The name "Oban High School" was conferred on the school at Rockfield Road in July 1877, just shortly after its opening in May of that year. The Soroba Road building was constructed as an extension to the existing High School at Rockfield Road. It was opened in September 1890 and only in February 1959 did the Rector of Oban High School cease to be head of Rockfield. It was in 1892 that secondary education began at Oban High School. The reference of the book's title is therefore to the centenary of secondary education at the School, in accordance with common usage. The background is explained fully in Chapter 2, which tells of the beginnings of the School and carries the history through to the end of the Rectorship of James Beattie in 1910.

Yet, while it is intended that the main events in the life of the School should be chronicled and the principal changes in educational attitudes, trends and practice recorded, the remainder of the account of the school is not meant to be a systematic academic history. That fact should be emphasised. A E Housman, in addition to being a poet, was Kennedy Professor of Latin at Cambridge (where one Rector of Oban High School, John Maclean, attended his lectures). To classicists the pungency of Housman's criticism is well known. In the Preface to his edition of Manilius I he refers to the text published in 1679 by the unfortunate Michael Fayus or du Fay, "which," he says, "seems to have composed itself without the help or knowledge of the editor". Perhaps such virulent criticism of my own work on the text of the present book may be preempted if it is recognised that Chapters 3 to 8 are intended to evoke the atmosphere of the School by providing the personal impressions and reminiscences of the authors, who either are Former Pupils or are intimately associated with the School. Each of these Chapters should, apart from a few obvious cross-references, be regarded as a self-contained essay and, since personal impressions may differ, total consistency between them is not to be expected. It is hoped that the personal approach will add to the attractiveness of the book, but if this approach is deemed worthy of censure, let it be in the spirit of Rector Terence Twatt's "Thought for Today" which appears on page 170.

The editor and contributors have executed their task as a labour of love and wish to record their thanks to the following:

To Murdo MacDonald, the Archivist of Argyll and Bute District Council, for providing the School Board Minute Books and other sources, to the late Donald MacKechnie, Bridge of Douglas, Inveraray, for the use of his booklet, *Education in Argyll, 1872-1972*, and for other material, to Duncan Campbell for researching the period of 1900 to 1910, to *The Oban Times* and to Elma MacKillop for her helpfulness and to many friends and associates who jogged memories and provided inside information, including Ishbel Banks, Ellis Carmichael, Iain Kennedy, Isa MacInnes, Farquhar Macintosh, Kenneth MacIntyre, Carol MacLaren, Jackie MacLaren, Lorna MacMillan and Anne MacPhail.

To Iain Crichton Smith for translating the poem on pp 115f and to Mainstream Publishing for permission to reproduce on pp 121f part of John MacLeod's poem and its translation, which appear in *The Highlands* by Calum I Maclean.

To Ian Gowdie, of the School's Art and Design Department, who designed the cover, to Robert McCulloch who provided some of the photographs and assisted in the preparation of the photographic section, and to the many Former Pupils and friends of the School who so readily submitted for selection photographs in their possession.

To Anne Stewart of the School's Business Studies Department for her stalwart work in preparing the text for the printers, together with her assisting band of typists, Gemma Cummins, Moira Lang, Catherine MacKechnie, Karen Mackie, Christine Mason and Betty Moncrieff, and to Arthur Gillies and Andrew Mathieson of *The Oban Times*.

To Donald Skinner, Coll MacDougall, Ian Thomson and the School Young Enterprise Company for marketing the book.

For financial assistance to Argyll and the Islands Enterprise Company, to Argyll Education Trust, to the Governors of Catherine McCaig's Trust, to Communn na Gàidhlig and its Director, Allan Campbell, and to the Glasgow Highland Society.

Oban, February 1993   Robert A Reid

CHAPTER 1

Introduction

ROBERT A REID

(i)

In April 1911 the Congress of the Educational Institute of Scotland was held in Oban, the President being James Beattie, who had recently resigned as Rector of Oban High School. In an article in the Handbook for the Congress[1] Dr W J Watson wrote, "The Celt has always, and I believe rightly, been credited with a nimble wit. He is appreciative, ready to take on culture; appropriative, quick to seize an idea, make it his own and give it his own turn". As evidence of his statement Dr Watson pointed to the Gauls, who "soon learned the use of Greek letters from the Greeks of Massilia. Within a hundred years after their conquest by Caesar, they competed, not unsuccessfully, with the Romans for the prize of eloquence."[2] Of the Gauls, the "scissors and paste" Greek historian Diodorus says in the 1st century (5.31) "... they are quick of mind and with good natural ability for learning".

The Roman evidence supports Dr Watson's view of the Celtic character generally. As part of the policy pursued by the governor, Julius Agricola, of encouraging the Romanisation of the Celts of Britain, his son-in-law, Tacitus, tells us that about 79-80 AD " ... he educated the sons of the chiefs in the liberal arts and he expressed a preference for the abilities of the British over the trained abilities of the Gauls, so that those who had recently found the Latin language distasteful were fired with passion to attain eloquence in it".[3] In 96 AD the Roman epigrammatist Martial wrote of Britain singing Roman verses[4]; and, writing at some time after 127 AD, Juvenal expresses the view that by that time the entire world had the culture of Greece and Rome, and he says "... eloquent Gaul has trained the advocates of Britain, now Thule talks of hiring a teacher of rhetoric"[5]. Thule (used by Tacitus probably to mean Shetland[6]) was the name used by the Romans to denote the most distant known land to the north.[7]

However there is a complete lack of archaeological evidence for Roman interest in the West Highlands. The people living in what is now Argyll would not have been given the benefit of the Romans' policy of diffusing their language and ideals. The history of Highland education really begins with the introduction of Christianity from Ireland in the sixth century. For the next thousand years or so, first the monks of the Celtic Church were the sole teachers and then education was in the hands of the Church of Rome. Before the Reformation Ardchattan was a centre of instruction, as were also, in the Highlands, Kingussie, Kinloss, Fearn, Rosemarkie and Beauly. There were scholars from the Highlands in the time before

1

the Reformation. In 1307 Walter, son of the Earl of Ross, was a scholar at Cambridge. In 1316 there appears on record Magister Felanus Rector Scholarum de Invernes. Later, the Master of Lovat, who fell at Blar Leine in 1544, had studied at Beauly and then in France.[8] As early as 1496, in the reign of James IV, the Education Act, in theory at least, obliged the eldest sons of Scottish gentry and freeholders to attend school at the age of eight or nine. This Act has been described by Alastair Cherry as "a brave piece of educational pioneering which may be the earliest example of compulsory elementary education in Europe".[9] In Scotland as a whole before the Reformation there were probably less than a hundred schools and most of them were in burghs, though some of these burghs, such as Kirkwall, were quite small. Very few were in the Highlands.[10]

In January 1561 John Knox and other preachers presented to a convention of nobility and lairds a draft of a national programme of reform. *The Book of Discipline* aimed at organising the whole nation in accordance with the will of God and included in this declaration of intent was a national system of education. The expansion of education was emphasised because by Protestant theology every man was responsible for his own salvation without the mediation of the Church. Since it was thought that children were born wicked, a programme of godly training was needed, and provision was made for primary, secondary and university education. The aim of the early reformers was that every person should receive at least a minimal education. If possible every parish was to have a school and all children were to be compelled to attend.

However lack of finances meant that education did not advance immediately. As Professor T C Smout has written, "It is hard to believe that there was much advance in educational standards over the country as a whole before 1600 ..."[11] While it may not immediately have had any significant impact, the Knoxian idea of education as a necessity for everyone was of the greatest importance. Moreover, from the time of the Reformation until 1872 education was conducted mainly under the auspices of the Protestant church or churches.

In 1616 the state supported the Church with an act of the Privy Council which ordered the establishment of a school in every parish "where convenient means may be had". The purpose was "that all his Majesty's subjects, especially the youth, be exercised and trayned up in civilitie, godliness, knowledge and learning; that the vulgar Ingleesh tongue be universallie planted, and the Irish language, which is one of the chieff and principal causes of the continuance of barbaritie and incivilitie among the inhabitants of the Isles and Hylandis, may be abolishit and removit."

A loophole had been provided in the 1616 act in the provision that a school was to be established in every parish "where convenient means may be had". An act of 1633 added the provision that landowners should be taxed in order to furnish the necessary endowment, though the phrase of the 1616 act still allowed a loophole by which payment could be avoided. However in 1646 an act forced the landowners to pay for the parish school.

In 1661 the position reverted to that of 1633, but in 1696 an act restored the provisions of the 1646 act and that act of 1696 regulated Scottish elementary education until 1872. In Scotland generally between 1616 and 1661 many parish schools had been established. But, to quote Professor Smout, "The northern and north-western Highlands may have had no parish schools at all, though the foundation of isolated schools in such burghs as Inverary and Dingwall was satisfactorily accomplished and children came even from the Macleod lands in the western isles to attend the grammar school at Rosemarkie."[12]

Thus in the 17th century, while the educational system in Scotland was more advanced than in England or in most other European countries, there were only a few schools in the Highlands. In fact, the parochial system of education was not suited to the Highlands. Most of the Highlands had only comparatively recently come under the control of the state and there was no tradition of schooling on which to build. Moreover, the Highlanders spoke Gaelic and there were almost no Gaelic books. Most importantly, Highland parishes were very large. Professor Smout gives among his examples that of Glenorchy, which was sixty miles long and twenty-four miles wide. He writes, "Given that parishes were often more or less evenly populated and without any major village concentrations, it was almost impossible for a single fixed conventional parochial school, the minimum that heritors [landowners] were obliged to finance, to make any impression at all on the massive problem of illiteracy."[13]

It was realised in some large parishes that one school was of little use. At Inverchaolin in Argyll in 1755, "There is no *parochial* school, nor would such a school if we had one be of use to above a fifth of the parish ... hence it has come about that usually we have had five little schools kept about six months in the year."[14] According to Professor Smout, Inverchaolin "was a parish with a populous coastline twenty miles long and the rest of the people lived in inland glens separated by high mountains". One solution therefore was to have the landowners pay for the maintenance of several small schools.

By 1755 charity schools had moved into the Highlands. Near the beginning of the century the Catholics had been successful in winning converts. A group of gentlemen in Edinburgh, motivated by the ignorance and superstition of the Highlanders and concerned at their Jacobitism, made representations to the General Assembly of the Church of Scotland. The latter appointed a committee, which published proposals for propagating Christian knowledge in the Highlands and Islands of Scotland and in foreign parts. The gentlemen had been impressed by information from London concerning the work of the English Society for the Propagation of Christian Knowledge, which had been founded in 1699 and which believed in charity schools as the way to cure social ills. In 1709 the Scottish SPCK was founded as a non-profit-making concern, Presbyterian in belief. The General Assembly provided financial backing and the state gave it legal backing on the understanding that its moral teaching would include support for the Hanoverian succession.

The aim was to found schools in which reading, writing and arithmetic would be taught together with religious instruction. Since a knowledge of Gaelic was considered to be a cause of ignorance and superstition, its use was forbidden until 1766. Always in the Highlands charity schools were schools for learning English and the Highlanders realised the advantage gained by their children in the outside world if they could understand English.

Concerning the parish schools, Professor Smout writes, "The Church of Scotland and the heritors [landowners] did in fact make considerable efforts to meet their responsibilities. There is reason to believe that by the middle of the eighteenth century less than a fifth of Highland parishes were without some kind of school supported by a tax on landowners and that fifty years later virtually all the parishes had such a school."[15] Shortly after the middle of the eighteenth century the solution to the problem of parochial size such as the one testified at Inverchaolin was given up and the provision of additional schools was left to charity.

The number of Scottish SPCK schools increased rapidly. Their importance and success can be judged from the fact that the schools supported by the Society rose in number from five in 1711 to twenty-five in 1715, to 176 in 1758 and to 189 by 1808. The number of pupils taught in them rose from almost 6,500 in 1758 to 13,000 in 1808.

The SPCK was not however the only provider of schools outside the parochial system. In 1811 the Gaelic Society of Edinburgh was formed because of alarm felt at continuing illiteracy in remoter parts. This Society was followed shortly after by the founding of the Gaelic Societies of Glasgow and of Inverness. These Societies also established schools in the north, which usually moved from place to place round a parish after some of the children had been taught elementary reading.

In 1826 the Gaelic Society of Inverness published a survey carried out in 1823-24 of educational establishments in the Highlands and Islands (which were held to include Orkney, Shetland and the shores of the Moray Firth). It was found that nearly 500 schools were in existence, teaching almost 25,000 children. About one third of the schools were parochial schools, a quarter were SPCK schools and the remainder were schools of the Gaelic Societies.[16] Later there were other benefactors of education. From the time of the Disruption in 1843 the Free Church of Scotland supported schools over the Highlands; the Ladies' Society of the Free Church supplied over 140 schools. Moreover, in 1869 the Rev Dr James Calder Macphail inaugurated a scheme to provide bursaries for Gaelic-speaking young men. The funds were raised by Dr Macphail's own efforts, and under his scheme there were 264 bursars in all, the greater majority of whom went to university.

Yet by the first quarter of the nineteenth century the success of the educational endeavours must be considered only partial. Professor Smout writes, "The general picture of Highland education ... appears to be of a steadily increasing number of school places, of which much the largest proportion was consistently provided by charity schools. Against this must be set the fact that population, too, was increasing very fast, especially in the remotest areas where there were still fewest schools. Charity tried hard, but it is doubtful if it did much more than keep abreast of this increase after about 1780."[17] In 1824 officers of the Educational Scheme of the Church of Scotland visited every Highland and Island parish and found that 90,000 people between the ages of six and twenty could read neither English nor Gaelic.[18] The Gaelic Society of Inverness survey published in 1826 showed that in general only one half of those over the age of eight could read. There were regional variations: for example, in Argyll and highland Perthshire seven in ten could read, whereas in the Hebrides, Wester Ross and western Inverness-shire only three in ten could do so. An interesting finding of the survey was that literacy in English was poor in Gaelic-speaking areas and good in others (eg Orkney and Shetland), where there was no greater provision of schools.[19] In 1856 out of 400 people married in the county of Inverness, 370 could not sign their names. In 1865 Sheriff Nicolson reported that in Lewis out of 11,065 persons over sixteen years of age only 5,385 could read in any language.[20]

The position up to 1830 is summed up thus by Professor Smout: the effort of the charity school movement "had been a brave one, and it had been much better than nothing. But the results fell far below that of the parochial system in the rural Lowlands".[21] The achievement of the schools in the Lowlands, on the other hand, he sums up as "the construction of a literate peasant society ... that was not merely able to read but apparently loved reading".[22]

(ii)

A school had been founded at Glenshellach Terrace in Oban by as early as 1780. In an article written in 1792, which is contained in the *Statistical Account of Scotland* published in 1794, the Rev Peter McDonald, minister of the parish of Kilmore, said that it was a very good schoolhouse, built by the Duke of Argyll and the inhabitants, who made up a salary of £20 a year to the schoolmaster, who also had other emoluments. The number of scholars was at an average between forty and fifty through the year.

But what was Oban at the end of the eighteenth century? In 1772, the historian and topographer Thomas Pennant speaks of "the Bay of Oban, where are the Customs House and Post Office". [23] The Custom House, a white building which had been constructed about 1765 and which stood at the southern end of Shore Street,[24] was occupied also as his home by the Collector of Customs, who in 1773 was Colin MacVicar. MacVicar was visited for eight days that year by his niece, well known as the writer Mrs Grant of Laggan, author of *Letters from the Mountains.* From her letters it appears that at that time Glenshellach was studded with cottages. She also refers to "the spot where the joint wisdom of the Duke and the collector have projected a future village, the rudiments of which already begin to appear".

That last remark reflects the optimism felt by those in command of Highland society in the last forty years or so of the eighteenth century. There was an expectation that a change for the better was about to take place.[25] In the period after Culloden there was a weakening of the clan system and with it a growth in the number of landowners enthusiastic for "improvement". The threat of disorder had been removed and the government's policy of road-building considerably opened up the area. Moreover, a rising demand for Highland products changed the economic climate in favour of the Highlands and brought the promise of material reward to anyone able to exploit their resources. Oban is one of the towns which Professor Smout lists as "monuments to the hopes of this generation", towns which he describes as "designed by Highland landowners in the same spirit of economic zeal and moral reformation that characterises their Lowland counterparts".[26]

It is well known that on their visit to Oban in October 1773 Dr Samuel Johnson and James Boswell "found a tolerable inn". The same was not true of Thomas Newte Esq, a gentleman from Tiverton in Devon, who, on arrival in Oban in July 1785, "put up at the only public-house there, which is one of the very worst kind".[27] He goes on in his account, "There are but two or three tolerable houses in this village, but they have a few boats intended chiefly for the herring fishery." In his article in the *Statistical Account* Peter McDonald says that the first house of any consequence, and the only one before the Custom House, was built about 1712 by a trading company from Renfrew. They used the house as a store room, "Oban being considered even then, as one of the most convenient situations for trade". He says that after trade increased in the period following the building of the Custom House "the attention of the Duke of Argyll, Mr Campbell of Dunstaffnage, and some other persons particularly interested in the prosperity of the village was attracted". Oban had been "reckoned a proper place for clearing out vessels for the herring fishing". In fact prospects for fishing had been revived all down the west coast as far south as Kintyre and McDonald says that about 1772 there had been twenty to thirty vessels registered at Oban, chiefly employed in fishing, and although that trade had decreased, he says (bemoaning the lack of a proper quay) that there were in 1792 still "fifteen to twenty sloops employed in the fishing and coasting business, and one vessel from 250 to 300 tons is employed in the Baltic trade".

At this time the land belonging to the Duke of Argyll was divided from the land of Campbell of Dunstaffnage by the water which ran from Loch a'Mhuillin to the sea. (McDonald describes Loch a'Mhuillin as "a shallow lake of some extent, with sloping banks, which are cultivated for hay, corn, and garden stuffs"). McDonald says, "About the year 1778 the spirit of building arose in this village and has been gradually increasing until the present time. It was on that side of Oban which belongs to the Duke of Argyll that these buildings were first erected. But now Mr Campbell of Dunstaffnage has feued out part of his property for the same purpose on the other side, and the demand for lots daily increases."

It was in that year, 1778, that the carpenter John Stevenson took over a lease at Glenshellach and proceeded to set up business there. Two years later his brother Hugh obtained a lease at Glencruitten and the two brothers entered upon a shipbuilding venture. In 1785, Newte, who had a very favourable view of Oban's potential for development "under the fostering hand of the Duke of Argyll, and the numerous gentlemen of the name of Campbell in that county", referred to the Stevenson brothers as "the only men of enterprise in the place". He went on, "They have built several vessels from 100 to 150 tons, which they employ in the coasting trade; and I find their exertions are attended with success." McDonald wrote in 1792, "Oban ... may look on them as its founders", and he adds that over and above the shipbuilding business "the younger brother [a stonemason to trade] employs also many artificers in house-building". They also built a tannery and other commercial properties. Their enterprise attracted other craftsmen to the village and thus there arose an increasing demand for housing.[28]

So Oban was growing. According to Mrs Grant of Laggan, in 1773 the combined populations of Oban, Kilmore and Kilbride stood at little more than 400, the focal point of the area being Kilmore. In 1791 the figures are for Kilmore 700, for Kilbride 600 and for Oban 586.[29] The population of Oban is reported as 700 in 1797. It was in this context of optimism that the Duke's school was founded.

As is well known, in the Highlands generally the optimism proved for various reasons to have been misplaced. But Oban was one of the places which flourished and prospered. The government's demand for Scots beef was greater than ever in the Napoleonic period, and Oban, being situated at the western end of the drove road over the Monadh Meadhonach (the drove road leading to the markets in the south), saw huge herds of cattle (and sheep too) being driven to the Lowland trysts. The opening of the Crinan Canal in 1801 brought sailing ships in numbers to the harbour, their passengers being added to those people who had long come overland en route to the islands.[30]

The census of 1841 showed the population of Oban to be 1,398. In the early 1840s there were several schools in the town, including the following: Miss Rankin's ladies' school, Cawdor Place; Miss Campbell's, George Street; Miss Cameron's, Combie Street; Mr William Stevenson's, Cowan's Land, High Street; Mr Dugald MacCorquodale's, High Street; and the Secession School in Tweeddale Street.

(iii)

The Education (Scotland) Act of 1872 is the source of Scotland's modern education and it avoided the social divisiveness which resulted from the English system introduced in 1870. But the Scottish act was a long time coming.

A government survey of 1834 showed that about one in nine of the whole population of Scotland was at school, about one in six of the population could read or was learning to read at school and about one in twelve could write or was learning to write. There were regional variations: in Glasgow only one fourteenth of the population was at school and only one twenty-fifth in Old Aberdeen.[31] While the figure of one in nine placed Scotland high on a notional European league table - at the top was Holland with a fifth of the population at school and Prussia with a sixth - all was not well.

A pamphlet was published in 1835, written by the Rev George Lewis in 1834, entitled *Scotland, a Half-Educated Nation, both in the Quantity and Quality of her Educational Institutions.* This pamphlet has been interestingly shown by Donald J Withrington[32] to be a partisan statement made on behalf of the Established Church at a time when it was under severe attack by seceders and dissenters after the passing of the Test and Corporation Acts in 1828 and Catholic Emancipation in 1829. Yet Lewis used data that had been made available by investigations carried out over the previous fifteen years. After reviewing the evidence, Professor Smout writes that "... it is difficult to avoid the conclusion that provision for elementary education deteriorated for most members of Scottish society in the half-century beginning around 1780, and that was primarily due to the shift in the distribution of population away from a rural environment where ... the parochial system still provided the major channel of education towards an urban environment where illiteracy, or semi-illiteracy, was widespread and the public authorities chose to ignore the evil. The Achilles heel of the national system of education had been its failure to provide means for making town councils provide the good cheap schools like those that still determined the general character of the countryside."[33]

From the 1820s to the 1850s there appeared in public statements, in journals, newspapers and pamphlets and in debates in the General Assembly complaints that adult criminality and juvenile delinquency were increasing, as were pauperism, immorality, prostitution and illegitimacy. The problem was viewed as stemming from a lack of moral instruction in childhood and the answer appeared to lie in attendance at school and church. Much effort in various directions was put into encouraging parents to send their children to school, including the "ragged school" movement, whereby poorer children received free elementary schooling. Feeling grew in favour of a system of national schooling based on the Bible and the Shorter Catechism with Protestant religious teaching.

In England schools were either profit-making concerns or endowed by charity. There was no compulsion to build a school or to provide for its continued existence. In England there was opposition to state intervention in education and in the 1830s and 1840s governments, having only slim majorities, did not dare to promote intervention by the state. Scotland, however, in the parish schools had a state system, at least in embryonic form, and any opposition to state intervention was more muted. In the 1840s people of different religious affiliations were arguing that a national system of education was needed in Scotland. There was a succession of bills in Parliament aimed at extending the system of parochial schools under the direction of local management committees, which would supervise the existing schools and build new ones where necessary. In 1854 and 1855 the government actually sponsored two bills, which were introduced by James Moncrieff, the Lord Advocate. These bills were supported by majorities of the Scots MPs who voted, but they were defeated thanks to the votes of English MPs, who did not want to see a dangerous precedent set.

Nothing could be done for Scotland until after 1870, when an act was passed allowing the state to provide elementary education for those of the poorer classes in England who were not already in private, Church or endowed schools. This act was socially deeply divisive, for the state only saw to the elementary education of the most deprived children.

The Education (Scotland) Act of 1872 was quite different. It proclaimed that it would provide "education ... to the whole people of Scotland". Unlike the English act, it introduced compulsory attendance at school. While compulsion could not be wholly effective until free schooling was made possible in 1893, a start was made towards the ideal of universal education. The system was truly national. A temporary Board of Education in Edinburgh supervised school boards, which were elected in every parish. The great majority of voluntary schools joined with the existing public sector. A special committee of the Privy Council, called the Scotch Education Department, both controlled government grants and had responsibility for the activities of Inspectors. When the Scotch Education Department introduced the Leaving Certificate on a national basis in response to the threat posed to its domination by the universities' offering local examinations, that Certificate was highly instrumental in confirming central control over the schools.

Thus the Education (Scotland) Act achieved common schooling in neighbourhood schools and it avoided the social divisiveness of the English system. How it operated in Oban will be shown in the next chapter.[34]

NOTES

1   W J Watson, MA, Ll D, *Highland Education Past and Present* in the Handbook of the Congress of the EIS, 18-19 April, 1911, pp 47-60

2   The value put on eloquence in Gaul is noted by Tacitus at *Histories* 4.73.1. Cf Juvenal 7.147-9

3   Tacitus *Agricola* 21.2: iam vero principum filios liberalibus artibus erudire, et ingenia Britannorum studiis Gallorum anteferre, ut qui modo linguam Romanam abnuebant, eloquentiam concupiscerent.

4   Martial 11.3.5: dicitur et nostros cantare Britannia versus.

5   Juvenal 15.110ff:
nunc totus Graias nostrasque habet orbis Athenas
Gallia causidicos docuit facunda Britannos,
de conducendo loquitur iam rhetore Thule.

6 This was the opinion of Professor R M Ogilvie in his note on Tacitus, *Agricola* 10.4

7 In his note on Tacitus *Agricola* 21.2 Professor Ogilivie wrote, "The failure of Latin to survive as the native language of Britain shows that it was not deeply rooted in the country." It was only the sons of chiefs whom Agricola set about educating. For those interested Professor Ogilvie pointed to K H Jackson, *Language and History in Early Britain* (Edinburgh, 1953) pp 94-105. Cf also Glanville Price, *The Languages of Britain* (London, 1984) esp pp 158-169.

8 The information is given by W J Watson, *art cit* pp 49f.

9 Alastair Cherry, *The Renaissance King* in *The Story of Scotland* (Glasgow, 1984) p 236. The man behind the Education Act of 1496 may have been Bishop William Elphinstone, whose most celebrated achievement was the foundation of Aberdeen University in 1495.

10 Private tutors might be used by the nobility. The Highland chiefs who signed the Band of Icolmkill in 1608 could read and write.

11 T C Smout, *A History of the Scottish People 1560-1830* (London, 1969) p 87.

12 T C Smout, *op cit* p 88.

13 T C Smout, *op cit* p 461. Professor Smout gives an excellent account of education in Scotland in the 18th and early 19th centuries in Chapter XVIII. His account of the Highlands is on pp 461-6.

14 Cited by T C Smout, *op cit* p 462, who acknowledges the quotation in D J Withrington, *The SPCK and Highland Schools in Mid-Eighteenth Century* in *Scottish Historical Review* xli (1962) p 26.

15 T C Smout, *op cit* p 462.

16 *Moral Statistics of the Highlands and Islands of Scotland* (Inverness, 1826).

17 T C Smout, *op cit* p 464.

18 W J Watson, *art cit* p 51.

19 *Moral Statistics of the Highlands and Islands of Scotland* (Inverness, 1826). Cf T C Smout, *op cit* p 466.

20 The figures, quoted by W J Watson, *art cit* p 52, are derived from Rev W M Macgregor, *Our Church in the Highlands*.

21 T C Smout, *op cit* p 466.

22 T C Smout, *op cit* p 460.

23 Thomas Pennant, *A Tour of Scotland and Voyage to the Hebrides in 1772* (ed London, 1790)

24 The Custom House was removed in 1880 to make way for the Callander and Oban railway.

25 See T C Smout, *op cit* pp 343-351.

26 T C Smout, *op cit* pp 346f.

27 Thomas Newte, *Prospects and Observations on a Tour in England and Scotland, Natural, Economical, and Literary* (The accuracy of the picture of Oban which appears in the book is to be doubted as too heavily reliant on the artist's imagination.)

28 About 1793 David Dale, whom Professor Smout (*op cit* p 346) describes as "the doyen of the early Scottish cotton manufacturers", was attracted to introduce a small branch of cotton manufactures into the Kilmore area, but there were problems caused by a lack of fuel.

29 This is the figure given in the *Statistical Account*. According to Edward Daniel Clarke, who visited Oban in 1797, a list of inhabitants was made in 1791 by John Stevenson at the request of the Duke of Argyll and they amounted to 659. Much of Clarke's journal is embodied in Rev William Otter, *Life and Remains* (1825).

30 An excellent readable account of early Oban is provided in Màiri MacDonald, *Oban and its Environs from Earliest Times* (Oban, 1985), No 8 in the West Highland Series.

31 The latter figures, with others, were quoted in a speech in the Commons by J C Colquhoun on 17th June, 1834 (Hansard vol. xxiv, cols 514-8).

32 Donald J Withrington, *"Scotland Half-Educated Nation' in 1834? Reliable Critique or Persuasive Polemic?* in (ed) Walter M Humes and Hamish M Paterson, *Scottish Culture and Scottish Education 1800-1980* (Edinburgh, 1983) pp 55-74.

33 T C Smout, *op cit* p 472.

34 This section relies heavily on an article by Donald Withrington, *'The Schoolin' of Your Weans'*, which appears in *The Story of Scotland* (Glasgow, 1984) pp 1182-5.

CHAPTER 2

The Beginnings and the Rectorship of James Beattie

IAN D S THOMSON

From *The Edinburgh Evening Courant* of Monday, April 1, 1822:-

"CATECHIST AND SCHOOLMASTER WANTED FOR THE VILLAGE OF OBAN

"The Committee for Managing his Majesty's Royal Bounty for Reformation of the Highlands and Islands, having agreed to establish a SCHOOL in the village of OBAN in ARGYLL-SHIRE, are desirous of obtaining a proper Teacher for the situation. The Committee therefore request Candidates to appear at Edinburgh, on Thursday the 25th of April 1822, to undergo a comparative examination before the Committee, as to their knowledge of the Greek and Latin Languages, the rules of Arithmetic, Writing, and reading English, and the principles of Christian Religion. Besides teaching the above branches of education, the person appointed must Catechise the parishioners, in the church or elsewhere, as shall be found most convenient.

"The encouragement is considerable. The salary given by the Committee is £35, and nearly as much by the Heritors, and if the Master be faithful and industrious in performing the duties of his office, from the thriving state of the village of Oban, and the neighbouring country, he may expect a numerous school. He will also enjoy the usual accommodation which the Heritors furnish to all the Missionaries under the Committee. Candidates must produce certificates of their moral character.

"Recommendations and certificates may be forwarded to Mr Murray, W S agent for the Church of Scotland, Bank Street, Edinburgh, to whom candidates may apply for farther particulars."

This was not the earliest school in Oban, one having been founded by the Duke of Argyll as early as 1780, but it shows that, in the first quarter of the nineteenth century, there was concern that the young people in the district should be offered a sound education. The Duke's school, like so many of the time, was small; it occupied a site in Glenshellach Terrace, continuing to operate until 1850, by which time it was known as "the ragged school", presumably because by then it served the poorer children of Oban, other schools having come into existence to attract children from the better-off homes. Some of these schools, such as Selma Villa, were run privately by an individual and took only a handful of pupils; others were larger and were the responsibility of the churches: the Free Church with a boys' school in Combie Street and a girls' school in High Street, the Church of Scotland with a school at Blantyre House, the

Episcopal Church with a school in Stevenson Terrace (now Stevenson Street) and the Secession Church with a school in Tweeddale Street. In addition, there were schools in Kilmore and on Kerrera.

Then, in 1872, there was passed the Education (Scotland) Act which made schooling compulsory for all children between the ages of five and thirteen. Responsibility for the schools in each district of the land was put in the hands of a school board which was elected every three years by those in the community who owned or occupied property valued at £4 per annum or over. The minimum number of members of the school boards was five, the maximum fifteen, and for the first twenty four years of its existence the burgh of Oban managed with the minimum. By 1897 it was judged that there had become too much work to be done properly by five and the board membership was raised to seven. At the time when the Education Act became the law of the land, there was a wide variety of educational establishments for the young, the principal ones in the county of Argyll being parochial (public) schools, Church of Scotland schools, Free Church schools and non-denominational schools and it was one of the tasks of the new school boards to rationalize this educational provision.

Elections in Oban were held triennially in the month of March, the first being in 1873, and the first Oban School Board meeting was held, as they were until the opening of the Rockfield Road school building in 1877, in the Court House in Argyll Square. The five members of the first Board were Messrs Gregorson, McCaig, Brown, Cumstie and Hunter with Gregorson elected Chairman; when he died in the middle of the year, Cumstie was elected in his place. In addition to the elected members, the Board had to appoint a Secretary (or Clerk to the Board), a Treasurer and a Board Officer, the two former positions soon being amalgamated. In the first thirty years of the life of the board there were only three Clerks to the Board - two solicitors, Robert Lawrence and Martin Brydon Lawrence, and William Jolly, who worked in the office of the town clerk. The first Board Officer was John Carter and he had to combined his duties in this post with those of school janitor.

The first main task of the school boards was to take an educational census of the district so that it could be ascertained how many children, male and female, were between the ages of five and thirteen and how many of these were already attending a school of one kind or another. The Oban Board also sought to ascertain how many children, residing in the area, were between the ages of four and five. At the end of 1874, there were 396 children within the burgh and 81 in the outlying parts who were aged between five and thirteen. The census figures for the earlier years of the Board are not recorded in the Board's minutes but they do make an appearance from the mid 1880s onwards and at the end of 1889 the figures were:

The Board's School (Rockfield Road)	623
St John's Episcopal School	78
Roman Catholic School (St Columba's)	55
Oban Academy	24
Miss Mackay's Seminary	13
Miss McDougall's Seminary	10
Dunach School (Kilmore)	4
Not known what school to be attended	10
Total	817

By September, 1895 the number of children of school age in the burgh was 990.

The School Board was required to establish a fund for the running of the schools in the area, the sources of revenue for this being a government grant, a local rate levied on the householders in the district and fees paid by the pupils for, in those days, parents had to pay for the privilege of having their children educated as well as for the purchase of books and other materials. The scale of fees was set by the School Board and the local rate by the parochial board after the School Board had indicated how much it would require to make good the deficit of expenditure over income once the other sources of income had been calculated. The local rate varied from one place to another across the country as, indeed, did the teachers' salaries which were paid by the boards. The Oban School Board estimated that, in its first year, it would require £180 from the rates to fund it with sufficient total revenue to provide elementary education in the town and this would result in a rate of four pence in the pound on those liable to pay. The following year the rate was increased to five pence in the pound and this further increased as time passed.[1]

Clearly the boards were often under pressure to keep the local rate and the fees as low as possible and this obligated them and the School to maximize the annual grant coming from the government, this being determined, *inter alia*, by the quality of education being provided and the average pupil attendance throughout the session. The fees exacted from parents in the first session were, in the words of the minute book:
"For scholars under seven years of age, two shillings per quarter; scholars in Standards 1 and 2, three shillings per quarter; scholars in Standards 3 and 4, four shillings per quarter; scholars in Standards 5 and 6 five shillings per quarter and specific subjects, viz. Mathematics, Latin, Greek, French etc. one shilling and sixpence per quarter."

These fees were payable in advance: until April 1884, they were paid by parents quarterly; for just over a year thereafter, they were paid monthly and then, at the beginning of the session 1885-6, they were payable weekly on Mondays. In the early years of the Board's school, the fees were collected by the Treasurer, who reported regularly to the Board those in arrear, but in November 1882 it was decided by the Board that the fees should be collected by the teachers who would account to the Treasurer for the fees collected. This procedure was adopted until September 1885 when responsibility reverted to the Treasurer. At the beginning of that month, the Board decided how the fees should be collected:

"The meeting considered the subject of the collection of fees and directed the clerk to commence with the infant department, taking next the junior department and finishing with the senior department and the teachers are requested to give what assistance may be necessary to facilitate the collection."

It appears from this that the fees were brought to the school by the children who paid them directly to the Treasurer. Whatever the method used, the collection of the fees was a constant headache for the School Board because many parents were reluctant to pay and in some cases they simply could not pay. Parents who were too poor to pay the fees were able to apply for help from the parish relief fund and, for a number of years, from the inspector of the poor; with these parents the Board would have their children's books bought with money from the school fund, it being the responsibility of the parents in general to provide these materials from their own pockets. As further assistance to the poor families in the town, in 1893 a collection of cast-off clothing was started so that the poor children could be better clothed. Certainly, insufficient clothing was among the reasons given to the Board for the non-attendance of some children at school. One difficult case the Board had to deal with was that of Peter Thomson who, in spite of pressure, had declined to send his children to school. It is evident from the following entry in the minutes of the School Board that he was in financial straits. It is dated 1st February, 1875:

"The officer of the board, being in attendance, gave explanations as to the children in the burgh who are not attending school. The clerk is directed to bring the case of Peter Thomson before the parochial board as it appears to be impossible to get his children to attend school unless the fees are paid for them and they are provided with suitable clothing."

A good deal of the Board's time was devoted to summoning defaulting parents to appear before the Board to try to obtain payment of the overdue monies. This was reluctantly backed up with the threat of prosecution before the Sheriff or the Justices of the Peace but before cases came to court the names of the defaulters were given to the Sheriff's Officer who endeavoured to collect the money. Prosecution was used with the recalcitrant parents and in the later 1880s the Board started the practice of publishing the names of the non-payers with the Board's annual statement of accounts as a way of pressing the defaulters to pay what was owed. It seems to have met with some success, perhaps in part because the annual statement was published in the local newspapers.

In 1889, fees were abolished except in Standard VI and Ex VI and four years later they were abolished altogether, the loss of this source of income being made good by an additional government grant paid to each school.

If the Board was concerned with the non-payment of fees, it was equally concerned with non-attendance or irregular attendance of pupils at school. This was partly through its belief in the value of education for the children, partly because it had a statutory duty to see that all children between the ages of five and thirteen received elementary education and partly because high attendance would bring more money for the provision of education through the fees and through the annual government grant. Parents of children who were not attending school were summoned before the Board accused of failing to carry out their legal obligation, again with the threat of prosecution if they continued to fail to do so. The Board was reasonable in its handling of parents who did not have their children attend school regularly and it was common for them simply to admonish those who promised to send their children to school in future. Even with parents who failed to appear before them, the School Board adopted a generally tolerant line with the parents being summoned to present themselves at the next Board meeting, these initially being held normally once a month. Perhaps this generosity of spirit was partly attributable to the costs of prosecution, an indication of which is given in the minutes of 4th September, 1876 which reveal that the Treasurer was directed to pay the Procurator Fiscal in Inveraray the sum of £3.75 for prosecuting defaulting parents in 1874.

Sometimes the blame for a child's non-attendance was placed on the School as in the following cases which date from 7th January, 1889. The words come from the Board minutes: "James McIntyre, tailor, Soroba Road, for failure to educate his child, Archibald. Mr McIntyre appeared and complained of undue punishment having been inflicted on his child by Mr Faichney, assistant master. Mr Faichney, having been heard in reference thereto, Mr McIntyre was cautioned and promised to send the boy to school without delay.

"There was read a letter from Alexander Lang, Drimvargie Cottage, dated 6th ultimo, complaining of his son, Alexander, having been ill-treated out of school in consequence of having been set to watch the other scholars in his class and report cases of misbehaviour to the teacher. The headmaster was heard in reference thereto and stated that the practice of setting one scholar to watch the others had been discontinued and the clerk was directed to inform Mr Lang thereof."

Sometimes parents admitted that they had insufficient control over their children as is revealed by the following two entries in the Board's minute book, the first for 22nd October, 1889 and the second for 13th January, 1890:
"She [the mother] stated that she had done all she could do to induce her son to attend school. She promised to compel his attendance and, if necessary, bring him."

"He [the father] appeared and stated that he had lost control over the boy."

Even when efforts were made by the family to have a child attend school, these were not always blessed with success as in the case which was reported in the School Log Book under the date 20th November, 1895:
"Boy, brought up to the school this morning by elder brother, refuses to enter. After a struggle with the elder brother, the boy escapes minus hat and coat."
The resolution of the matter was revealed in the entry for 25th November, 1895:
"Boy mentioned above has been sent to evening school, his books having been purchased from him for the sake of relieving his father."

The Board was prepared to take a firm line with the more recalcitrant parents. For instance, at the meeting on 16th March, 1896:

"The clerk reported that he had had James McKinnon, Parkgate Cottage, brought before the sheriff for non-compliance with an attendance order as to his child, Jessie, and that McKinnon had been convicted and fined 10s 6d with the alternative of five days imprisonment.

"The board had before them the following case:

"Mrs Mary Jane Balfour, 10 Combie Street whose children, Willie (11), Duncan (6), Agnes (12) and Emily (8) had not been attending school sufficiently well. Mrs Balfour failed to appear and the clerk was directed to write to her intimating that, unless the children were sent to school on Monday and attended regularly in future, application would be made to the sheriff to have them sent to an industrial school."

At the beginning of February 1880, the Board had to deal with a complaint from a parent that his child had been unjustly punished and this complaint was considered at the next meeting of the Board when, after an investigation, it was decided that the punishment given to the child had been justified. However, the case did prompt the Board to make clear its policy on corporal punishment:

"The meeting are of the opinion that corporal punishment should not be inflicted in the school unless in cases of grave offences and then only when there is clear evidence. It should be administered with due solemnity and deliberation. In all cases of this kind where the teachers are in difficulty they are directed to consult the board."

On 12th May, 1885 the School Board issued detailed regulations on the subject of corporal punishment and these were:

"1 The board absolutely forbid any pupil teacher, ex-pupil teacher or temporary teacher (male or female) to inflict corporal punishment of any form whatever. When any such teacher shall be proved to have done so, he or she shall be liable to instant dismissal. The master and mistresses of departments are hereby instructed to report at once to the board any violation of this rule.

"2 No teacher shall use any instrument except a tawse supplied by the board for the infliction of corporal punishment. It is considered unseemly that such instruments should be in the hands of a teacher when he or she is engaged in teaching.

"3 Punishment for grave offences, such as lying, swearing, stealing, or the use of indecent language, shall always be inflicted by the head teacher of the department to which the offender belongs and to whom all such cases must be reported. The assistant shall enter in the Punishment Book all the particulars of any such case reported to the head of his or her department.

"4 It is absolutely forbidden to strike any scholar on the head or elsewhere than on the palm of the hand; and no scholar is to be asked to place his hand on a desk, table, form or any other hard substance in order to receive the necessary stripes. Teachers are requested to take special care not to inflict corporal punishment on any nervous, delicate or infirm child.

"5 It shall be the duty of every teacher to enter in the book furnished for the purpose all cases under Rule 3 and all cases in which it has been found necessary to inflict more than four stripes, particulars of the case, including the name of the scholar, a statement of the nature of the offence and the nature and amount of the punishment inflicted. The entry must be made immediately after punishment. In the case of assistants this book shall be handed once a week to the head of the department who will sign the same after due inspection. All entries must be made in ink."

In September, 1901, it was decided that girls in the earlier stages of the elementary division of the School should not be given corporal punishment, although the older ones still faced this sanction on their conduct.

The Board became especially defensive of their right to provide education for the young of the district when there was the prospect of another school opening in the town. In October 1877, a new venture (privately run) school, known as St John's Boys' School, applied for a government grant. This school was additional to, and separate from, St John's Episcopal School which had already provided education for the children of Episcopal parents since 1872. The Board was quite direct in their response to the Scotch Education Department on the matter of the rival school receiving a government grant:
"The clerk is directed to inform the [Scotch Education] Department that this board cannot see any connection between 'St John's Episcopal School' and 'St John's Boys' School' as they are of the opinion that no children of Episcopal parents are taught in the latter and as the board has provided accommodation for all the children in the burgh except those attending 'St John's Episcopal School' and as the ratepayers are assessed for such accommodation this board think it is unfair that a new and purely venture school should be receiving government grant."

It is evident that the Board's main concern with this development was that the new school would attract pupils from the Board's school in Rockfield Road with the consequent loss of revenue it would entail for their school. This concern, as well as one of a more religious nature, was manifested also with the proposal to open a Roman Catholic school in the town. The School Board meeting of 16th January, 1882 discussed the matter and, responding to a letter from the Scotch Education Department asking the board's view of the proposed school receiving a government grant, had the following entered in the minutes:
"The meeting after deliberation now record their decided opposition to the application [for a grant] which has been made as they view the giving of grants to denominational schools as objectionable and not in accordance with the spirit of the Education Acts - and further they are of the opinion that there exists no necessity for the establishment of the school proposed. The clerk is directed to communicate these views to the Scotch Education Department."

By the time of the next meeting of the Board nine days later, the new Roman Catholic school had been opened and the Board had something more to say on the matter:

"The board unanimously resolve to adhere to the views expressed at the last meeting and they now add that the Conscience Clause is duly observed in the board's school, religious instruction being given at a separate hour and it being in the power of any parents who object to such instruction to withdraw their children at that hour. Children of Roman Catholic parents have hitherto attended the board's school and no complaint has been made to the teachers or the board of due regard not being paid to their religious belief. The meeting are convinced that great injustice will be done to the public and ratepayers by giving the grant asked to the Roman Catholic school inasmuch as their school will withdraw children from the board's school, diminish the fees of the latter and may seriously affect the amount of the government grant to be earned. The clerk is directed to communicate these views to the [Scotch Education] Department."

These efforts to deny the new Roman Catholic school a government grant were to no avail: the Clerk of the Board presented a letter to the members of the Board at their meeting on 1st March, 1882. It stated that the Scotch Education Department "cannot refuse to place the Roman Catholic school recently established in Oban on the list of those schools to which annual grants are conditionally made".

Perhaps the School Board's anxiety to maximize the numbers in the school in order to maximize income was one reason for a decision taken at the meeting of 5th March, 1888: "It was resolved to petition the House of Commons in favour of the bill which has been introduced to provide for the registration and regulation of travelling vans or other vehicles used as temporary abodes; and the clerk was directed to have the necessary petition written and signed by the chairman and thereafter forwarded for presentation."

The school boards were responsible for the school buildings in their districts and for providing accommodation for the teachers in the schools. To obtain a government grant to help with the costs of renovating or extending existing buildings and of erecting new ones, the proposals had to be submitted to, and approved by, the Scotch Education Department in London who would give a Proportion Grant if the work was completed within a set time and a certificate of completion was produced. It was, therefore, of importance to the board that the contractors kept to their building time-schedules. If insufficient money was available through the government grant and the board's other sources of income, the board could, with approval from the Scotch Education Department, borrow money from the Public Works Loan Commissioners or elsewhere, these loans normally being repayable over a long period at a low rate of interest.

The history of school building under the Oban School Board began soon after its inception. At the time there were two Free Church schools in the town, one for boys in Combie Street - or 'Comby' as it was then spelt - and the other, for girls, in the High Street. The girls' school building, which stood opposite the junction of High Street and Campbell Street, still exists as a private dwelling but the boys' one, which lay opposite the Parish Church and beside the junction of Combie Street and Glencruitten Road has long gone. (The Roman Catholic St Columba's school began its days there.) Hugh Skinner was the schoolmaster in the boys' school and Miss Davidson the schoolmistress in the girls' which was also known as the industrial school and offered subjects of particular use to girls. The Deacons' Court of the Free Church Congregation intimated to the board that these schools would be discontinued at the end of session 1872-3 and urged the board to employ Mr Skinner and Miss Davidson who had been "faithful and diligent servants in their profession in Oban, the former for ten years and the latter for two". The Board was concerned to know if the Free Church was willing to rent its school buildings to the board. The High Street School and Schoolhouse were made available for a rent of £20 per annum and the Comby Street school for a rent of eight pounds per annum. Skinner was employed at an annual salary of £120 and he continued to teach in the building in Comby Street while Miss Davidson was offered employment in the school in the High Street at an annual salary of £60, there being no equality of pay for males and females in those days. The sticking point was her continued occupancy of the Schoolhouse, with which she was unhappy owing to its damp condition which she said was hurtful to her health. She asked for an additional £20 per annum if she found her own accommodation but the Board was willing to offer her only £10, which she declined and, after the post had been advertised, Miss Mary Mackay from Appin was appointed at the original salary of £60. It is not known if she lived in the damp house but it is to be presumed that she did. Mr John Macmillan was appointed assistant teacher in the Comby Street school at an annual salary of £40.

It was never intended that the use of the schools in Comby Street and the High Street would be other than a temporary provision which would cease once a new school had been built. First, ground had to be bought and this was found, in the words of the minutes of 22nd September, 1873, "in Thomas' Park, north of the new road leading to the Free Church, and in the plot extending from the old bleaching green on the south to the old road leading to the Free Church on the east". It was land, adjacent to Rockfield Road, which had been the property of the late Mr Gregorson, first Chairman of the School Board, and his wife accepted the offer of £450 made by the Board. The conveyance of this land was approved by the Scotch Education Department, who were then approached for a grant to assist with the costs of building the school.

It was agreed with the Board of Education in Edinburgh and the Scotch Education Department in London that the new school should be built to accommodate four hundred pupils, this being one hundred places fewer than the School Board had estimated as necessary in their proposals which allowed for some expansion in the child population in the burgh and the surrounding area. In this regard, the Board proved itself to be rather more prescient than the government departments. In order to attract a number of architectural plans for the new school from which the most suitable would be chosen, the School Board decided to offer a prize of £10 to the architect of the one selected. Several entries were received and these were judged by the Board without the members knowing the names of the firms which had prepared them. At the Board meeting on 26th April 1875, it was unanimously resolved "that the prize of £10 be awarded to Design A No 1 and the envelope with this motto, having been opened, it was found that the design was from Mr Alexander MacQueen, Architect, 37 West Nile Street, Glasgow, and the clerk is directed to communicate this decision to Mr MacQueen accordingly."

Some modifications were required to the plans but these were made without difficulty and MacQueen's fee (which included travelling expenses) was £150. The new school consisted of six rooms and the dimensions of these were recorded by Hugh Skinner in his school log book. There were two infant rooms, one being 30 feet long, 24 feet wide and 15 feet high, the other 19.6 feet long and 15 feet both wide and high. Four rooms were 19.6 feet long, 16 feet wide and 14 feet high while both of the other two were 36 feet long, 25 feet wide, one with a height of 15 feet, the other 14 feet high. Tenders were invited for the construction of the school and two were received, one from McDougall and McColl for £3,051 and the other from J and A McDougall for £3,320, and the contract was given to McDougall and McColl after they had agreed to reduce their offer by £31. Together with the price of the land, architectural and legal fees and extras, the total bill for the building of the new school came to £3,700. Towards the cost of this, the Scotch Education Department made a grant of £400 while a loan of £3,300, repayable in fifty annual instalments at a rate of interest of three and a half per cent was obtained from the Public Works Loan Commissioners.[2]

The contract with McDougall and McColl stipulated that the building would be ready for occupation on 15th December, 1876 but, as it was to transpire, there were delays and the school was not opened until 14th May, 1877. It was soon decided by the Board that the new school required a new name more in keeping with its status and in the school board minutes for 10th July, 1877, there is the following entry:

"The meeting having taken into consideration the amalgamation of Schools A (Comby Street) and B (High Street) and that those names are now inapplicable resolve that the future name of the new school be 'The Oban High School' and the clerk is instructed to intimate this change to the Education Department."

After the opening of the new school the duties of Mr Skinner and Miss Mackay had to be defined and this was set out as follows in the minutes of the board dated 20th August, 1877:

"1 Mr Skinner shall have the charge of the whole school and be responsible to the board for the proper conduct of the whole.
"2 Miss Mackay shall have charge of all pupils under the standards [ie infants] and all pupils in Standard I and the teaching of music and industrial work and in her work she shall be assisted by two pupil teachers.
"3 Mr Skinner shall have charge of Standards II and III and all above these and in his work he shall be assisted by an assistant teacher and two pupil teachers."

Although he was the senior teacher in the School, Hugh Skinner was not made headmaster; however, from 2nd January, 1884 he was designated "headmaster" in the minutes so that there must have been an unrecorded meeting at which the decision was made to offer him the headmastership of the school.

There was a move by the Board as early as the beginning of August 1880 to enlarge the size of the school building as it was already too small for the number of children in the town between the ages of five and thirteen who were in fairly regular attendance at the school. Additional accommodation was "absolutely required" and it was decided that the most efficacious way in which this could be achieved was "to enlarge the present building by adding two halls on the north end in communication with the existing classrooms, these halls having separate entrances to them for boys and girls; and that the buildings thus enlarged should be so divided that two schools might be conducted in them under separate masters, School No 1 being devoted to elementary work whereas in School No 2 special attention should be given to higher subjects in addition to the standard work".

By 1894, the Rockfield Road building had again become too small for the number of its pupils in spite of the opening of the Soroba Road building in 1890 and it was decided that an addition should be made to it. The bulk of the contract went to D and J McDougall and the estimated total cost of the work came to £828 5s.

This extension to the Rockfield Road building did not solve the problem of overcrowding there and on 4th April, 1898 the Board decided to remit to the Management Committee for its consideration a scheme "for the erection of a new school at Drimvargie", the idea being that the building and grounds at Rockfield Road should be "utilised for dwelling houses etc." On 3rd October the Board instructed the Clerk to insert an advertisement in the press stating that it was prepared to receive offers. Approval of the plan to sell the Rockfield Road property and to build a new school was sought and apparently obtained from the Scotch Education Department; but then the Board had a change of heart, for the minutes for 9th October, 1899 record that the Board unanimously agreed to enlarging and altering the Rockfield Road building. Thus the proposal to replace the Rockfield Road building with a new structure was at an end and the overcrowding was to be resolved by a further extension to the existing school.

The beginning of the events which were to lead to the erection of the Soroba Road building is to be found in the minutes of the Board meeting of 4th April, 1887 which reported that the Board was asked to consider the necessity of extending the existing school accommodation. On 16th June, 1887 the Board appointed a committee of three of their number "for the purpose of looking out for a site for a new school and also where premises can be leased for temporary accommodation". The meeting of 11th July, 1887 discussed the matter of a site for the new school fairly fully as the minutes of the meeting showed:
"The meeting resumed consideration of the question of school accommodation and the members having expressed their sentiments thereon individually and the matter having been fully discussed it was resolved that it is necessary to have additional school accommodation and that the new buildings should be erected at a different part of the town from the present buildings. Mr Livingston dissented from this resolution on the ground that the board had in their own possession, and beside the present school, sufficient land to erect new buildings. The former committee, the chairman, Messrs McLean and MacKinnon are reappointed with

instructions to enquire into available sites and the cost of the ground and to report to the next meeting of the board. The committee were also directed to enquire where temporary accommodation can be got and the cost thereof."

The next stage of the search for a site for a new school was the meeting of the Board on 5th September, 1887 when the committee appointed to look out for a site reported offers which they had received from various parties to give ground for the proposed new school. After discussion, it was resolved that the members of the Board should visit the various sites the following Friday and consider the position at their next meeting. The same committee reported offers for temporary accommodation and it was agreed that these would also be visited. Temporary accommodation was accepted from Robert Macfarlane at 18 and 20 Stevenson Street (by then called Stevenson Street, not Stevenson Terrace) for a rent of £24 per annum on condition that "water be introduced in a jawbox at the back window, suitable grates be installed and the woodwork painted". Macfarlane was also expected to put a coal bunker into the premises, the Board being liable for any damage done from inside and out by the school children during school hours, provided Macfarlane put wire netting in the windows above the shutters. In addition to this accommodation in Stevenson Street, the Board was allowed to use the Free Church lower mission hall, also in Stevenson Street, at an annual rent of £15. The whole of the infant department and Standard I were to be housed in the buildings thus acquired; however, the lower mission hall was used for only a short time. On 7th September, 1888, the Board indicated that the hall would no longer be required as school accommodation, the infant department returning to its proper rooms in the school.

By 7th October, 1887, there was a development in the search for a site for the new school. As the Board minutes of that day stated:
"The meeting resumed consideration of the matter of a school site and Mr McLean moved that the board should now proceed to consider the comparative merits of the sites which are now within their choice with a view to a decision, which motion was seconded by Mr Craig and agreed to. After discussion, it was moved by Mr Mackinnon and seconded by Mr McLean that the board confer with Miss McCaig with the view of acquiring from her ground to the south and east of the bowling green and what will be her terms, which motion was agreed to, and Mr Mackinnon and Mr McLean are appointed to a committee to wait upon Miss McCaig accordingly and to report to the next meeting of the board."

The required information was laid before the Board on 21st November as the minutes said:
"Messrs McLean and Mackinnon now reported that Miss McCaig was disposed to feu a site for a new school on the north and west side of the bowling green at the rate of £30 per acre; but did not meantime incline to feu for a school on the south side. On consideration the meeting resolve to postpone the decision of this question till after the election of a new board."

The new Board was elected in March 1888 and the Board meeting on 9th July of that year discussed the matter of the new school at some length. One member proposed that they did not add to the present school building and this motion was seconded by another member;

another member proposed that they resolve the problem by adding to the existing school building but his motion to this effect did not find a seconder and so it "fell to the ground", as the minutes put it. The minutes of 9th July continued:

"Mr Craig then moved, that the site on the hill which is understood to be available be selected, which motion was seconded by Mr Mackinnon. Mr Hutton moved as an amendment, seconded by the chairman, that the site referred to be not selected. Motion and amendment having been put to the meeting, there voted for each the proposer and seconder, Mr Livingston declining to vote, and the chairman thereupon gave his casting vote in favour of the amendment which was therefore carried. Mr Hutton then moved, that the site at Soroba Road, offered by Colonel McDougall, be selected, which motion was seconded by the chairman. Mr Craig moved as an amendment, that the site in Glencruitten Road, belonging to Mr Caddow's trustees, be selected, but this amendment not having been seconded, fell to the ground and there being no other amendment, the motion was declared to be carried. It was resolved accordingly that the site in Soroba Road be selected for the proposed school, subject to the sanction of the Scotch Education Department with whom the clerk was directed to communicate with a view to such sanction being obtained. It was resolved further to invite competitive plans for a school to be erected on the proposed site, the building to be of one storey and capable of accommodating 400 children and of being added to; and the clerk was directed to advertise accordingly."

Colonel McDougall offered to feu the land at £16 per acre and this was accepted by the Board. The competition to find an architectural design for the new school was duly held and the Board was divided on which of two plans to adopt. One had been code-named 'Utility' and the other 'Simplex'. The chairman voted for 'Simplex' to give it a three to two majority; it was prepared by Mr J Fraser Sim, an Oban architect.

Sim's plans for the new school had to be submitted to the Scotch Education Department for their approval and they had some criticism to make of them. In an interesting comment on education at the end of the 19th century and beyond, the minutes of the School Board of 15th October, 1888 stated:

"The clerk submitted a letter from the Scotch Education Department, dated 5th inst., returning Mr Sim's plans for the proposed new school, upon which the Department's architect reported as follows, viz.: 'The plan would permit the sexes to mingle in the corridor. The minimum class room is 18 feet by 15 feet.' " It continued:

"The meeting had also before them an amended plan prepared by Mr Sim, giving effect to these modifications, along with a letter from him explanatory thereof, dated 10th inst. Further consideration of this matter was delayed in the meantime."

Some further changes were requested by the Board and these were implemented by Mr Sim. As with the rooms in the Rockfield Road building, Hugh Skinner recorded the dimensions of the rooms in the new school in his School Log Book. There were five rooms, all 22 feet wide and 17 feet high. The central room was 62 feet in length, two class rooms were 48 feet long and the other two were 16 feet long. In addition there were a boys' shed and a girls' shed with lavatories at the end of each. At the Board meeting of 7th January, 1889, the revised plans were accepted by the Board but Mr Craig moved "that the resolution of the board to build on the site in Soroba Road should be rescinded and that a plebiscite be taken of the electors on the question whether the school ought to be built on that site or on the hill; but this motion not having been seconded fell to the ground and the meeting instructed the clerk to take the necessary steps for the acquisition of the site in Soroba Road". It was decided that a sum of £3,500 should be borrowed for the erection of the new school, although this decision was made before tenders had been submitted. Approval for the loan had to be secured from the Scotch Education Department and, with this in view, an application was made, accompanied by the revised plans and specifications drawn up by Mr Sim, and in the meantime the tenancy of the rooms in Stevenson Street was renewed until the following Whitsunday.

Although the Board had resolved to build the school on the Soroba Road site, there was clearly debate in the town over whether it should be built there or whether the existing school should simply be extended. On 25th March, 1889, there appeared before the Board two deputations consisting of people of standing in the burgh. The first to appear requested that the plan to erect a new building should be abandoned in favour of an addition to the existing school and the second supported the decision to use the Soroba Road site. Since the Board, conscious of their responsibility to represent the opinions of their electors, decided that they themselves could not decide which of the two proposals to adopt, although they were in favour of a new school on Soroba Road, they wrote to the Scotch Education Department asking them to make the decision. This the Department did and came down in favour of Soroba Road after consultation with John Boyd, the Inspector with responsibility for the schools in Argyll.

Remaining problems with the architectural plans were resolved as the result of a visit Mr Sim, the architect, made to the architect of the Scotch Education Department in London. The latter had suggested certain alterations and Mr Sim had produced sketches giving effect to these alterations which were approved by the Board and these were then submitted to the Scotch Education Department for final ratification. Towards the end of May 1889, advertisements were placed in the newspapers asking for tenders for the construction of the school and those firms interested were given only a week to submit their tenders.

On 12th August, 1889 the Board had before it the tenders which had been received. The contract was awarded to McDougall and McColl with the exception of the plaster work, which was awarded to James Gorrie from Callander, who was sub-contracted to do the work by McColl and Graham, whose bid of £61 was the lowest for the plaster work. McDougall and McColl's costing for the remainder (ie mason work, carpentry and joiner work, slater work, plumbing, gas-fitting and painter work) amounted to £2,676 1s 5d. Under pressure from the Board, the firm was prepared to reduce their offer for the carpenter and joiner work by £10. The meeting which decided to accept McDougall and McColl's offer also signed the feu contract with Colonel McDougall and the plans and specifications were sent to the Scotch Education Department for their seal to be affixed and their sanction sought to the Board's raising a loan of £3,000. This sanction was given, provided that the loan was repaid within fifty years. After some difficulties, a loan was arranged through a Liverpool firm of mortgage brokers, Messrs Stanley and Macara, with the Royal Liver Friendly Society of Liverpool. It was repayable by way of annuity in fifty years at three and five eighths per cent interest, the brokers' fee, which included their costs, being one per cent.

The Board considered that it would be wise to try to secure some additional ground adjacent to the Soroba Road site and they approached Colonel McDougall to feu them an extra quarter of an acre along Soroba Road at the same rate as the ground which had been already feued. He agreed to feuing them the extra ground for a feu duty of £4.00, the southern boundary of the additional ground being four feet from the Dalintart Farm road. The new school was insured against fire with the Union Assurance Society up to a maximum of £2,500. As with the school built in Thomas' Park, the construction of the new school fell behind schedule and it was discussed at the meeting of the Board on 16th May, 1890, by which time Mr Sim had died and his architectural practice had been taken over by Alexander Shairp. The minutes of this meeting recorded:

"The meeting had under consideration the state of the new school building which Mr Shairp reported would not be ready for occupation by the 28th instant when the board's tenancy of the Stevenson Street schoolroom terminated. The clerk was directed to inform Messrs McDougall and McColl that the board are very much disappointed that the building is so far behind and request that they will put the whole of their men on the work and have the north wing ready for occupation by the 2nd proximo. Mr Shairp was requested to prepare a specification and obtain offers for the heating apparatus for the new school."

The contract for the installation of the heating apparatus was awarded to Messrs Henry Walker and Son, Newcastle-on-Tyne whose tender price was £8.

The meeting of 8th September, 1890 looked ahead to the opening of the new school and discussed the arrangements of the staff once it was in operation. As the minutes recorded:

"The meeting then proceeded to consider as to the arrangements of the staff in view of the opening of the new school and the transfer to it of Standards IV, V and VI and upwards but after discussion it was resolved not to make any alteration in the present arrangement, except that the headmaster should have such additional assistance as might be required, leaving Mr Faichney in charge of Standard IV.

"On the motion of Mr Hutton, it was resolved that the principal teachers should hereafter be paid fixed salaries in full of all emoluments, Mr Craig dissenting for reasons to be given in, and the amounts were fixed as follows, viz. Mr Skinner £175, Miss McDougall £85, Miss Fraser £85. The meeting also increased Mr Faichney's salary to £100 and Miss Strathern's to £50."

Before it was opened, some problems had developed in the Soroba Road building: the windows were not watertight and the bell was not properly hung. These faults were brought to the attention of Mr Shairp for rectification. Then, on 1st December, 1890, the Board discussed a report from the janitor that the bars of the furnace were burning out and the furnace door was cracked. The Clerk was instructed to write to Messrs Walker and Son saying that the Board were disappointed at this and expected they would send bars to replace the present ones. These problems were exacerbated by the breaking of glass in the WCs at the new school and the Clerk was directed to bring the matter under the notice of the police with a view to the protection of the premises.

The opening of the Soroba Road building on 15th September, 1890 was almost unmarked in the annals of the burgh, to the evident disappointment of Hugh Skinner who referred to the matter in his Log:
"19th September, 1890. Opened school on Monday after a long holiday of seven weeks. Assembled in old school. All the staff present. On Tuesday began work in the new building on Soroba Road. The numbers present [in both schools] for the week are as follows:

Monday	362
Tuesday	366
Wednesday	368
Thursday	370
Friday	354

No demonstration at the opening of the new school and not a member of the school board present."
There was no reference to the opening of the Soroba Road building in the School Board minutes and virtually nothing in the local newspapers.

If there had been a continuing problem of overcrowding in the Rockfield Road school building, it was not to be long before consideration was being given to enlarging the new school in Soroba Road. Indeed, as early as August 1893 it was proposed by Mr Munro, one of the members of the Board, that immediate steps should be taken to arrange for the erection of additional class rooms, a laboratory and gymnasium - as well as securing a park, adjoining the school, for boys' games and providing a swimming bath. Two years later plans for an extension to the existing building were well in hand. There was also the need for additional playground space and it was recorded in the minutes of the board of 25th November, 1895:
"The meeting had under consideration the necessity for additional playground accommodation in connection with the proposed new building at Soroba Road and it was reported that the members of the board with the exception of Mr MacKinnon had met on 16th inst and inspected the ground lying between the present feu and the Lorn Combination Poorhouse. It was resolved to ask Colonel McDougall to feu to the board the ground referred to extending to 1.6 acres and also another piece of ground extending to 0.9 of an acre on the opposite side of the Dalintart Farm Road and it was further resolved to offer for the two pieces of ground, extending together to about 2.5 acres a feu duty of £20, being at the rate of £8 per acre. The clerk was directed to obtain from Mr Shairp a sketch of the ground and thereafter to write to Colonel McDougall."
The colonel was unable to provide all the land wanted by the Board but he was able to give them sufficient for their purposes.

The extension to the Soroba Road building, which abutted the original building on the north-east, included a cookery room, a music room, two art rooms, a lecture room, a laboratory and an adjacent scullery, two other classrooms, a Rector's room, a male staffroom, a female staffroom and two indoor cloakroom lavatories, one for the boys and one for the girls. In addition, a gymnasium and a workshop with three benches were provided in a separate block. After some alterations were made to the plans drawn up by the architect, Mr Shairp, they were approved by the Scotch Education Department.

The meeting of 4th May, 1896 had before it the offers for the building and other works to be undertaken at Soroba Road. The levelling and laying out grounds and the building of boundry walls, D and A Munn costed at £555. The erection of the gymnasium and workshop was costed at £627 17s 6d, by far the major contractor being again D and A Munn (mason, joiner and slater work) and the minor contractors being Anderson and Nisbet (plumber work), James Gorrie (plaster work), Andrew Calderwood (gas-fitting) and John Kilgour (painter work)

As with the other building projects undertaken by the Board, there were delays in completing the contract. It was originally hoped that the extension would be ready for occupancy in August 1896 but on 27th October of that year, "Attention having been called to the slow progress being made with the new school building, the clerk was instructed to write to Mr Shairp asking him to urge the contractors to push on with the works in order that the building might be ready after the Christmas vacation."

As it was to transpire, the extension was not to be opened until the end of April 1897. It had been hoped that either Lord Balfour or Sir Henry Craik, secretary to the Scotch Education Board, would conduct the opening ceremony and when they indicated that they would be unable to do so Lord Rosebery and Sir Donald A Smith of Glencoe were considered. However these efforts failed and in the end the new buildings were opened by Mr Macfie of Airds and Oban. The occasion was recorded in the School Log under the date 28th April, 1897:
"Opening of the new buildings for the Secondary Department today at 12 noon. The ceremony was performed by Mr Macfie, the younger, of Airds and Oban in the presence of all the school children of the Soroba building, all the teachers of the school (both buildings), all members of the board, Mr Boyd, HMI, the Reverends Duff, Brown, Macleod, Hutchison, Rosling, Martin, MacKenzie (of Maryburgh), Gladstone, Reid and Begue, Provost Cooper, Mr Watson, Mr Bruce Robertson, Mr William Sutherland, Mr J D Sutherland, Surgeon-Major MacDougall of Dunollie, Mr Mitchell, Dr Campbell and a large number of other parents and friends.

"The gathering took place in the hall of the new building. The proceedings opened with a half hour's concert by the pupils. Thereafter, the audience united in singing the 'Old Hundredth' and Rev A Duff offered up a prayer. Mr Munro, chairman of the board, then explained why the new rooms had been built and introduced Mr Macfie who declared the new rooms open. Mr Shairp presented Mr Macfie with a gold key. Mr Boyd, HMI, spoke as representing the

Education Department. Mr Robertson proposed a vote of thanks to Mr Macfie whereupon the rector proposed a vote of thanks to the school board and to Mr Boyd and Mr Hutton [the late chairman]. The proceedings closed about 2.30 pm with the singing of 'God Save the Queen'.

"The afternoon was given as a half holiday."

In 1901, another extension was made to the Rockfield Road building and eight years later the Soroba Road building had its last extension until 1933. The first indication in the School Board minutes that a further enlargement at Soroba Road was being earnestly considered appeared in the minutes of 2nd March, 1908 when it was recorded that "... the board resolved that it be remitted to the Attendance Committee to enquire and report without delay as to the congestion in the Higher Grade Department and the question of additional accommodation referred to in the communication from the [Scotch Education] Department of date 2nd November, 1907." On 4th June, 1908 the Board was sent a letter by the Scotch Education Department asking what steps the Board intended to take "to remedy the serious defects in accommodation pointed out in the report of HM Inspector on his recent visit to the Higher Grade School" and the Board responded by asking the Buildings Committee to ascertain the cost of implementing the plans prepared by the architect, J A Carfrae, for extending the school. Tenders for the work were invited for the various works involved and the best of these amounted to £6,938 14s. Thereupon, the Board applied to the Scotch Education Department for its sanction to the Board's raising a loan of £8,800 to cover the costs to be repaid over a period of forty years and this was granted, the money being borrowed from the Savings Bank of Glasgow at a rate of interest of 3.5%.

The 1909 extension was achieved by adding a floor to the original single-storey building of 1890 which was itself altered internally. The ground floor of the extension comprised a Central Hall, five classrooms, two boys' cloakrooms, a girls' cloakroom and a girls' lavatory, while the first floor contained a large art room, a classroom/demonstration room, a chemistry room, a physical laboratory, another classroom, a small room and a store room. These additions to the school caused some changes of use in the rooms of the 1896 extension: with the opening of the new large art room, the two 1896 art rooms became ordinary classrooms, a similar fate befalling the lecture room while the 1896 laboratory was combined with the scullery to form a single classroom. The reopening of the school after the summer holiday was delayed until 20th September, 1909 to allow the new building to be completed and on 23rd September, in his School Log Mr Beattie recorded the attendance that day as 837 out of 929 for the whole school and for the higher grade department 221 out of 248. It is clear that many were still enrolling because the total roll that afternoon in the higher grade department was 254. In anticipation of the completion of this enlargement of the school, the Inspector made comment upon it in his report of 1909:

"The work at this centre under the able supervision of the skilled and scholarly headmaster is carried on with marked ability. The cramped conditions in respect of accommodation under which the staff have for some years had to work will now disappear as the large addition to the premises nearly approaching completion will render this school one of the best equipped centres for secondary work in the West Highlands."

An annual government grant was made to each school provided that certain conditions were met in the operating of the school and the size of the grant was dependent on the report made by the School Inspector after his annual inspection.

Before 1905 classes in what is now called Primary School, then Elementary School, were called Standards. Infants were called, appropriately enough, "infants" and then each class was numbered Standards I to VI. From 1905 to the 1930s, the classes were arranged, in order, Infants II, Infants I, Juniors II, Juniors I, Seniors III, Seniors II and Senior I, Senior I being the highest class in the Elementary School. Today, when progress through primary school is simply dependent on age, it is difficult to appreciate that formerly a pupil remained at one particular stage until he had thoroughly mastered the work of that stage and this led to occasional complaints from parents that their children were being held back unfairly. An instance of this is given in the School Board minutes of 2nd October, 1893:
"There was read a letter from Mr Robert Newton, grocer, of this date, complaining of a daughter of his having been kept back in the last year's Standard. The board declined to interfere with the exercise of the rector's discretion."
At the meeting of 3rd May, 1897, there was the following case before the Board:
"Complaints by Allan McDonald and Dugald McGill as to children being put back to lower standards."
The retaining of some pupils in a particular standard meant that some classes had pupils of widely differing ages and this, on occasions, led to disciplinary problems; it could also happen that a pupil left school at the age of thirteen having only progressed two or three classes above the infant stage. Sometimes this was caused by late entry into school or by frequent absences; at other times it was the product of lack of parental interest in education and lack of pupil motivation or by simple lack of ability.

After 1872, the main subjects throughout the elementary schools were reading, writing and arithmetic which, in view of the system of payment by the results achieved at the annual inspection, were taught with great intensity with heavy emphasis on rote learning; there was little scope for individuality or imagination. The medium of instruction was English and for many, for whom Gaelic was their native tongue, reading and writing must have presented considerable difficulties. The grant of three shillings for each pass was not to be had for the asking nor was the grant of two shillings for each pass in class subjects. In the later stages of elementary education, in Standards V and VI, the specific subjects were introduced and these were taken by those capable - and perhaps not so capable - of benefiting from them. The specific subjects offered depended on the qualifications of the teachers and would normally include such subjects as Latin, Greek, French, German, Navigation and Domestic Economy, which consisted of cookery and laundry. Following the abolition of payment by results in 1890, changes occurred in the curriculum to enhance interest and a wider range of subjects was introduced. Some of these were designed to exploit individual abilities and to promote observation and self-expression, such as Nature Study, Gardening and Physical Exercises or Drill.

Handwriting, in those days called Penmanship, was given a place of prominence, now long lost, because of its commercial value in the days before typewriters were commonplace and there were frequent references in the Inspectors' reports, normally none too complimentary, on the subject of handwriting. The subject was taught with thoroughness: strokes were followed by curves, clockwise and anti-clockwise, and mastery was sought with ascenders and descenders, the loop, the copying of actual letters, the spacing, the joining and the tails. The task was made more difficult through the use of the slate and slate pencil whose surfaces were much too rough for fine work but, at least on occasion, use was made of paper, ink and the steel pen or quill with the higher classes.

Grammar was another grant-earning subject and in consequence received considerable attention, the emphasis being on parsing, and much time was spent on spelling. In these language skills, the abler students must have been more competent than the majority of their counterparts today but many must have approached their work with no little sense of boredom. Composition as a subject was regarded as a test of writing, spelling and grammar with the additional demand of some intelligence in handling the subject matter. In the lower classes, a few sentences on the slate were normal, but with the higher classes the work had to be retained for the annual inspection. With these, trial efforts were made on slates and the finished composition had to be copied into an exercise book, known as a copy book, which was often of good quality paper. Composition, which had numerous rules, was taught as an exercise requiring strict accuracy in the use of English language. What concerned the teacher and the inspector most was not the content of the composition but the grammar, spelling and penmanship.

In the teaching of arithmetic the learning of tables, often by class chanting, was important and the list of these tables in the senior standards was formidable: it included weights, lengths, capacities, time, square measures and even Scotch weights and measures. The syllabus included prime and composite numbers, vulgar and decimal fractions, simple and compound interest and even metric units, following the sanctioning of the use of the metric system in the United Kingdom by the Weights and Measures Act of 1878.

Both History and Geography were grant-earning class subjects and were given much prominence. Similar teaching methods were used in both and depended much on a retentive memory. To a large extent History consisted of the memorizing of lists of dates and events, although there were some efforts to make the subject more interesting, while in Geography the emphasis was on learning lists of geographical features, countries and capital cities. To judge from the Inspectors' reports, these subjects were consistently well taught in the school in Oban - at least when measured against the aims set for them.

Singing was another subject which attracted a grant, although a more modest one than with other subjects: one shilling in 1872. Often this could be unaccompanied singing but it was not long before the Oban School Board equipped the Rockfield Road building and later the Soroba Road building with a pianoforte at a cost of £21 each. Industrial Work (as needlework was called) was also grant earning subject and was paid at the same rate as singing. Local ladies often took an interest in this subject, which was confined to girls, and would supply materials for the teaching of the subject. Today, when all essential educational materials are supplied by the state, this may seem strange but in those days the pupils had to provide most of their own and for many of the poorer parents this was impossible. Other problems with which the young seamstresses had to contend in those times of gas lighting and coal fires were days of dark classrooms and intense cold when Industrial Work had to be discontinued because the girls either could not see properly or their fingers were too cold work the needles.

If the pupils were expected to provide themselves with the materials necessary for their education, there were times when the teacher had to supply her own equipment as in the case of cookery. At the Board meeting on 10th October, 1890, shortly after the opening of the Soroba Road building, "It was resolved to institute the teaching of cookery in the new school and to employ Mrs Vass, Craigard Road, as teacher. The chairman reported that she had offered to undertake the work at the rate of 12s 6d per week (teaching for two hours on each of two days in the week) and to provide all the necessary materials and dishes, excepting a pot and pans which the meeting agreed to."

Initially, drawing was taught only to boys but it was later made compulsory for girls too. Before 1885, it was taught as model drawing in outline and plane geometry. Then, in 1885, the Scotch Education Department brought in a scheme which lasted ten years and included ruler and scale drawing, solid geometry and light and shade from the cast in addition to freehand, model drawing and plane geometry. In 1895 a new syllabus, called free-arm drawing, introduced drawing large scale on blackboards.

The School Board was especially active in establishing courses in September and early October 1891. The Board minutes of 7th September stated:
"The committee appointed at the last meeting with reference to the proposal to introduce callisthenics were authorised to arrange with drill instructor Elland for giving lessons therein.

"The meeting approved of schemes of instruction in bookkeeping and shorthand as specific subjects which the clerk was directed to submit to the Scotch Education Department for their sanction. The headmaster was requested to submit a scheme of introduction in Gaelic.

"Messrs MacKinnon and Robertson were appointed a committee to arrange for instruction in pianoforte to be given at the rate of ten shillings per quarter."

The Scotch Education Department approved the scheme of introduction in Shorthand and in Bookkeeping with the proviso that double entry bookkeeping was included in Stage Two of the latter subject and the Gaelic scheme of introduction was also approved. However, there were at the time some difficulties in finding a teacher of piano to remain long with the school. On 5th October, it was agreed by the Board that Mrs Vass would be engaged to teach cookery on the same terms as the previous session and Miss Fraser's request to give instruction on the kindergarten system on one day each week was approved by the Board and they authorized the expenditure of £1 10s for the necessary articles.

Other dates of interest from the School Board minutes were: 21st November, 1887, when Mr McLean, member of the Board, submitted a report on the subject of higher education and it was resolved that a class for German be held every alternate day under Mr Faichney, assistant teacher; 3rd September, 1895, when it was agreed to accept the Rector's suggestion that elementary science should be taught to boys only under Article 19 (a) 5 of the Code; and 7th October, 1895, when a request by several of the teachers to have a twice weekly French conversational evening class in Soroba Road School was granted.

Drill, as physical training was then called, was another important part of the curriculum and it was introduced into the Oban school in June 1885 at the same time as drawing. It was often taken by a gentleman of military background. For instance, in October 1892 the School Board decided to separate the posts of Board (or Compulsory) Officer and janitor which, until then, had been undertaken by one man, the Compulsory Officer, part of his remit being responsibility for seeing that the children of school age in the burgh attended school in Oban. In the words of the minutes of 10th October, 1892:
"The meeting had under consideration the expediency of separating the offices of compulsory officer and janitor and appointing to the former a man who should act also as drill instructor and the clerk was directed to advertise for such a man at a salary of £1 10s per week."
The advertisement produced 78 applications. The minutes of 7th November continued the story:
"The committee appointed at the last meeting to consider the applications for the post of compulsory officer and drill instructor having reported that they had sent for Sergeant John Martin, late of the 1st Highland Light Infantry and at present of the Arbroath school board, and Sergeant Martin having visited Oban and met with the members of the board, the meeting unanimously appointed him compulsory officer and drill instructor during the pleasure of the board at a salary of one pound ten shillings per week on condition that the should provide himself with a uniform."
Provide himself he did. He was a veteran of the Crimean War and his uniform was navy blue with a red line on the seams of his trousers, black braid on the tunic on which he wore his service ribbons. No doubt he would have presented something of a fearsome aspect to pupils and their parents and this would have made his tasks rather easier - as, no doubt, was appreciated by the Board when they appointed him. He began his duties on 5th December, 1892 and it was not long before he made another appearance in the minutes of the Board:
"Sergeant Martin, the newly appointed officer and drill instructor, attended and submitted patterns of the Indian clubs and dumb bells which he proposed to use. The meeting authorised 20 pairs of clubs and 60 pairs of bells to be procured."
A month later, further equipment was purchased:
"The meeting [of 9th January, 1893] authorised other 20 pairs of Indian clubs and 3 dozen of bar bells to be procured."
Later, in the minutes of 12th October, 1894:
"It was resolved to provide additional apparatus for physical drill as recommended by the rector, viz. 20 pairs of dumb bells for Rockfield Road and 60 pairs for Soroba Road, 20 barbells and 20 Indian clubs, both for Soroba Road."

Boys and girls received the same instruction in drill, the girls exercising with dumb bells and bar bells while the boys used Indian clubs. In September 1891 drill instructor Elland had introduced callisthenics to the curriculum and on 2nd May, 1892 the Board "resolved to introduce physical drill and musical drill in the infant department and Miss Fraser was authorised to procure the requisite articles and also to hire a piano".

There were other musical accompaniments to school drill. The minutes of 22nd December, 1897 stated:
"It was agreed that Mr McDougall, janitor of Soroba Road School, should supply bagpipe music for drill purposes."
And this arrangement was continued after McDougall ceased his duties as janitor the following June. In April 1899, the Board had before it a request that guns be bought for use in military drill. The decision was delayed and it is not known what their decision was but military drill was certainly offered in the evening school as an entry in the minutes for 25th November, 1895 shows.

When it was wet and muddy, Drill, which was often done in the open until the opening of the gymnasium in the Soroba Road building, must have been rather unpleasant for both pupils and their instructor.

Swimming was regarded as an important activity for the boys in the School and formal arrangements were made on 7th May, 1894 to provide proper swimming lessons; the Board was well aware of the need to consider the safety of the boys:
"The committee appointed at the last meeting to consider as to providing instruction in swimming reported that they had arranged for lessons being given at Ganavan on Saturday forenoons to the boys in Standard VI and the Secondary Department by Mr McLaren, assistant teacher, assisted by Sergeant Martin, and that for this purpose they had engaged a boat for three hours each day with two boatmen provided with lifebelts, at a charge for the boat and men of 2 shillings per hour; and further that the town council had granted the use of the bathing boxes. The board unanimously approved of the proposed arrangements."

In order to facilitate the movement of the boys to the shore immediately opposite Dunollie castle and to the deeper water of the little bay known as Camas Ban a little further to the north, the board arranged with Colonel McDougall that the boys, under supervision, would be allowed to walk through the Dunollie policies on Saturday mornings. This arrangement was continued under Colonel McDougall's successor, Surgeon-General Henry McDougall.

It is evident that some of the boys in the School became strong swimmers as is witnessed by the presentation to Lachlan MacLachlan, Oban, of a testimonial on vellum from the Royal Humane Society commemorating his rescue of three men from a boat which capsized off Aros Point on Mull in 1st September, 1901. There was also following item in *The Oban High School Magazine* of December 1910:

"The great swimmers have been at it again. Three of them swam across the Sound of Kerrera - one of them going towards Kerrera and the others from the island to the Gallanach side. When we consider that one of them had to keep an eye on the movements of the steamer 'Chevalier' and the others had to see that they did not get into too close touch with His Majesty's fleet, we can see that the business is not so simple as one would think. But it is a credit to the school to have boys who can undertake a swim like that without bad effects. When any of them think of undertaking to swim the English Channel, we hope they will let us know!"

Between 1873 and 1892, pupils who had passed Standard VI subjects and who wished to continue their education or were too young to leave transferred to Ex VI. These pupils studied the three Rs at an advanced stage in addition to specific subjects, some with a view to university entrance, others until they reached school leaving age. In 1892 the merit certificate was introduced and it was issued as a leaving certificate to those who had completed their education. To obtain this a pupil had to pass in two class subjects and one specific subject. By 1898 the merit certificate became the test for admission to secondary education but its use in this respect was abandoned in 1903 in favour of the qualifying examination conducted by the Inspector at the time of his annual visit.

In the latter half of the nineteenth century and at the beginning of the twentieth, Gaelic was the language spoken by most of the people of Argyll. English had to be studied in school and this was the medium of instruction in many subjects and this caused difficulties for teachers and pupils. Often it was hard to find a teacher capable of teaching Gaelic but the Board did make efforts to do so and with success. However, in the early days of the Board, Gaelic had a low priority in the teaching of the School, although not in the requirements of the janitor as the following contrasting entries in the Board's minutes showed. The first was dated 2nd November, 1874:
"The clerk [to the Board] read a letter from Mr James Miller, Bookseller, dated 28th ultimo, offering on behalf of Mr Donald Kennedy, Jermyn Street, London, certain sums of money to the children attending the board's schools as prizes for proficiency in Gaelic. After consideration, the meeting, whilst according their thanks to Mr Kennedy for his offer, are of the opinion, after consulting their teachers, that they cannot meantime establish classes for the instruction of Gaelic in their schools without abstracting the attention of the children from other branches and therefore in these circumstances they feel that they cannot accept Mr Kennedy's offer. The clerk is directed to communicate these views to Mr Miller."
From the minutes of 26th August, 1879 comes:
"The clerk read a letter from Sergeant McKechnie of date twentieth instant intimating his resignation of the office of school board officer and caretaker of the school buildings. The meeting accept the resignation as at twentieth September, being one month from the date of intimation. The clerk is directed to advertise for a successor in the Oban newspapers, the salary to be twenty five pounds per annum and a knowledge of the Gaelic language being indispensable."

The post was given to John Carter, the first Board Officer, who was in and out of that job in the early years of the new school. He did not last any longer this time than in any other tenure of his posts: he had resigned again by the end of the following January and was succeeded by Lachlan McLaren, a shoemaker who lived in Shore Street and was presumably also a Gaelic speaker.

On 25th May, 1891 it was agreed by the Board that Gaelic should in future be taught as a specific subject and on 7th September of that year the headmaster was requested to submit a scheme for the teaching of Gaelic in the school, while almost two years later the Board adopted new staffing arrangements for the following session. These included the appointment of a certificated male teacher, capable of teaching Gaelic to Standard V at a salary of £90 per annum. The minutes of the meeting on 23rd August, 1893 revealed that the advertisement for this post had attracted no applications and it was decided to advertise the post again but without the reference to teaching Gaelic. The salary was to be £80. However, by the time of the next meeting on 4th September, 1893, two applications had been received for the Standard V post, both from people who were able to teach the language and one of these - Mr Neil Maclaine, an assistant teacher in West Burgh School, Forfar - was appointed to the position at the annual salary of £90. The meeting of 4th September also received a letter from Mr Duncan McIsaac, 1 Albany Street, accompanying a copy of a new Gaelic school book issued by An Comunn Gaidhealach entitled, *Scottish Gaelic as a Specified Subject* and it was resolved by the members of the Board to adopt the book for instruction in the language.

On 12th October, 1894, the Evening School Committee of the Board submitted a report, which was adopted, containing a scheme for subjects to be offered in the evening school and this included the teaching of Gaelic. Mr Archibald Munn was appointed to teach the language at the rate of 2s 0d per hour, a post he was to retain the following session, 1895-96. However he was disinclined to take the class thereafter and the post was advertised without eliciting a response so that it had to be readvertised. On 27th October, 1896 it was reported to the Board that Munn had offered to act as teacher of the Gaelic class in the evening school and the Board approved of his appointment at a salary of three shillings per hour and this was followed, on 2nd November, with the appointment of Alexander McPherson, Fawn Cottage, as teacher of Gaelic in the day school at a salary of three shillings per hour. It is clear from the hourly form of remuneration that McPherson was engaged solely to teach Gaelic. In a circular dated January 1906, the Scotch Education Department recognized Gaelic as an instrument of higher education by putting it on the list of subjects which could be taken as part of the Higher Leaving Certificate and the board agreed to "proceed without delay on the lines of the circular to make provision for systematic instruction in Gaelic as is done for French and German". On 15th October of that year, Miss Mary Macrae of Dunvegan was appointed teacher of Gaelic at a salary of £100 per annum. Then, on 21st December, 1908, the board resolved "that Miss Macrae be freed from Gaelic teaching in the Rockfield Road building to enable her to devote her whole time to Gaelic teaching in the Soroba Road building, and that the rector be asked to draw out a detailed scheme and timetable for instruction in Gaelic to pupils who desire it in the senior division, the supplementary course and the higher grade department (including junior students)".

In the middle of 1898 medals were given by Gregor T Drummond, jeweller, and the Honourable Miss Elspeth Campbell for excellence in Gaelic - at the same time as Drummond gave one for excellence in Mathematics or in Chemistry, the decision on which to be left to the Board.

Before 1872 most elementary schools provided higher education which consisted of Latin, Greek and Mathematics. In 1873, these subjects as well as Agriculture and Domestic Economy were identified as specific subjects, to be followed soon by others, and a pass in one carried a government grant of four shillings. There were three stages in each specific subject and to earn the grant many schools presented pupils only in the first stage in three or four specifics, the study of which began in Standards V and VI. By the 1880s it was clear that there was insufficient provision for secondary education which was in much the same position that elementary education had been before the Education Act of 1872. In 1888, the standardization of secondary education was fixed by the institution of a leaving certificate examination, the subjects for which were English (which included History and Geography), Mathematics, Latin, Greek, French, German, Conics, Analytical Geometry and Dynamics. There were two levels: higher and lower and a pass certificate was awarded in each subject. In 1908, it became a group certificate of four highers or three highers and two lowers. To make good the fall in School Board income with the abolition of fees, the Education and Local Taxation Relief (Scotland) Act of 1892 granted £265,000 of which £60,000 was to pay for secondary education.

It was not long before the Oban School was able to take advantage of the new leaving certificate examination as was recorded in the Board's minutes of 25th April, 1892:
"There was read a circular from the Scotch Education Department, dated 20th instant, stating that they were prepared to admit to the leaving certificate examination beginning on 13th June candidates from any higher departments of ordinary schools which might appear upon enquiry to be of a character to claim a share in the grant for secondary education under the Education and Local Taxation Relief (Scotland) Bill now before parliament. After consideration and hearing the views of the headmaster and Mr Faichney, who attended for that purpose, the meeting adopted a statement of the character and organisation of the higher department of this board's school, including the names of six candidates for the leaving certificate, of which a draft was submitted, and directed the same to be forwarded to the Department. It was resolved that candidates from this board's school should compete for the bursaries of the Trust for Education in the Highlands and Islands."

The school's achievements in the leaving certificate examinations were sometimes recorded in the Board's minute books. It is of interest to compare the results of 1893, 1894,1896, 1902 and 1910:

	1893	1894	1896	1902	1910
Higher English	5	2	6	4	9
Lower English	11	13	17	20	14
Higher Latin	Nil	Nil	1	2	5
Lower Latin	1	2	7	6	5
Higher French	Nil	4	7	6	3
Lower French	6	9	15	13	11
Higher German	Nil	Nil	2	1	-
Lower German	3	Nil	9	1	-
Higher Mathematics	Nil	Nil	Nil	5	1
Lower Mathematics	4	3	9	14	11
Higher Arithmetic	Nil	Nil	6	2	-
Lower Arithmetic	16	18	10	9	-
Lower Book-keeping etc	Nil	Nil	Nil	3	-
Higher Greek	-	-	-	-	1
Lower Greek	-	-	-	-	1
Lower Science	-	-	-	-	21
Lower Drawing	-	-	-	-	25
Gaelic pass	-	-	-	-	2
Totals	46	51	89	86	109

Thus, there was a generally continuing expansion of the syllabus and improvement in school performance. Higher Mathematics proved rather too demanding for the pupils - and perhaps for the teachers - in the early days of the secondary department but this appears to have been overcome by the beginning of the new century. This improving performance is reflected in the higher grade department report of the School Inspector for session 1904-1905. The report contained the following comments:

"English: The first year pupils in English form a very intelligent and promising class. The work studied in the school is most thoroughly done. ... The same remarks apply to the second year pupils who are an exceedingly bright and pleasing class. ... The united (third and fourth year) class made a highly satisfactory appearance in every branch of the subject. ... the evident care and thoroughness of the teaching are worthy of very high praise.

"Classics: The training given in Classics in this school is exceedingly good and the pupils are successfully carried on to an advanced stage in the subject. ... the pupils know and understand in a most creditable manner the books they have read.

"Modern Languages: Modern Languages are taught with praiseworthy efficiency. The programme of work prescribed for the first year's class in French - reading, elementary phonetics, conversation, grammar, repetition and singing - is thoroughly up-to-date and the teaching is marked by skill and enthusiasm.

"Mathematics: Sound and effective instruction has been given in the different branches of Mathematics during the past session. Arithmetic and algebra have been well taught in all the classes.

"Science: Last summer the managers converted a science lecture room into a laboratory which has been admirably filled for instruction in Experimental Science. In this way it has been possible to make a beginning with this work in all the classes of the Higher Grade Department.

"Drawing: Work of an excellent character has been overtaken in all the classes, showing most careful, intelligent and conscientious teaching on the part of a highly skilled art master."

The first mention in the minutes of the Oban High School dux medal appeared against the date of 9th January, 1893 in the School Board minutes:
"Mr Munro produced a letter from Mr Shairp, factor for Mr Macfie of Airds and Oban, dated 29th ultimo, stating that Mr Macfie was pleased to observe the advanced movement in higher education in Oban and wished the board success in the undertaking and that he offered a subscription of £5 or should the board prefer it a gold medal for competition. Mr Munro stated that Dr McKelvie had also promised a gold medal, Mr Birkinyre, MP, a donation of £15 and Mr Westmacott, Craigmoraig, a donation of £5. It was resolved to accept Mr Macfie's offer of a medal and the clerk was instructed to convey the hearty thanks of the board to each of these gentlemen."

There were, in fact, a number of gifts and donations made to the school not long after the secondary department opened, some being mentioned in the minutes of 14th November, 1892:
"The clerk reported the receipt of a contribution by Mr Macfarlane, MP, of £10 in aid of the Secondary Education Scheme and that he had thanked him on behalf of the board. Mr Munro reported the promise of a donation of £5 for the same purpose by Sir John Bennet Laives, Bart, Ardchattan Priory, to whom the clerk was directed to convey the thanks of the board."

Medals for excellence continued to be offered by school benefactors as is shown in the following minutes, the first dated 2nd July, 1894 and the second 1st July, 1895:
"It reported that Mr Macfie and Dr McKelvie had each again promised to give a gold medal and that another gold medal had been promised by Dr McCalman and three silver medals by Sheriff McKechnie."
"Mr Munro reported that Mr Macfie, Dr McKelvie and Dr McCalman had each again promised to give a gold medal to be awarded as formerly."

As a result of his goodwill towards the school, Macfie was invited to open the extension to the Soroba Road school in April 1897 and the following year Mr and Mrs Macfie were presented with an illuminated address of congratulation on the occasion of the sixtieth anniversary of their marriage. Sadly, before a year had passed after this happy event, Macfie had died.

In the 1880s, there began the practice of ending the session with a public examination of the pupils in the School and prizes would be won by the leading scholars. The minutes of 3rd August, 1885 gave the following information about the prizes that year and the next:

"1 A prize will be given to every scholar who had made 350 attendances up to 31st May 1885 [each day had two attendances, morning and afternoon], provided he or she is qualified by attendances and is presented before Her Majesty's inspector at the annual inspection.

2 A prize will be given to every scholar who, at the next inspection, makes a complete pass in Standards IV, V and VI

3 A prize will be given to every scholar who, at the next inspection, makes a complete pass in Standards I, II and III.

4 A prize will be given to every scholar who passes in two specific subjects.

5 Three prizes in the senior and junior departments for Bible knowledge:

Senior department: Book of Genesis. Junior department: the gospel of Matthew.

Three prizes in the senior department for any 20 questions in the Shorter Catechism.

Three prizes in the junior department for the first 20 questions and the ten commandments.

Three prizes in the infant department for general religious knowledge.

6 Needle work and knitting according to Schedule III of the Code:

Six prizes below Standard I.

Four prizes from Standards I to IV.

Three prizes in Standard V.

Two prizes in Standard VI

7 No prizes will be given to any scholar who does not continue to attend school from the government inspection until the public examination.

The total cost for providing the prizes amounted to £14 1s 4d."

After the prizegiving ceremony the pupils and teachers would take their summer holiday which, in the earlier years, generally extended from the second half of July to the middle of September; later this holiday started at the end of June or in early July and ended in early September. The holidays were set by the Board and were issued sometime during the session.

Occasionally before 1903, the school closed for the midwinter vacation before Christmas Day and resumed early in the new year, but generally it did not close until the week between Christmas and New Year, although pupils did absent themselves on Christmas Day and in some years Christmas Day was given as a single day's holiday. Certainly, when Christmas Day was a school day, the majority of pupils attended as, for example, on 25th December, 1901 when 750 pupils were present, this representing 87.2% of the school roll. From 1903, Christmas Day was always a holiday, initially as a single day and from 1908 as part of the midwinter vacation.

The meeting which set the 1899-1900 holiday dates also approved of the school sports being held on the 5th July, 1899 and it was agreed to give the sum of £5, as formerly, to provide prizes for swimming and gymnastics. The first school sports in the history of Oban High School were held on the afternoon of Thursday, 11th July, 1895 at Mossfield Park and were organized by Mr C H Owen, a member of the teaching staff. As part of his preparations for the sports, he sent a letter to all potential benefactors seeking donations or prizes and, to judge from the numerous prizes which were awarded, his appeal was favoured with a generous response which was repeated in subsequent years. The following is an extract from his letter: "The athletics of the school comprise football, cricket, lawn tennis and swimming, besides daily drill and gymnastics (under Sergeant Martin); and the programme of the sports - which will be thrown open to the whole school - will include the ordinary flat races, obstacle races, jumping, tug of war etc; also a swimming contest and a tennis tournament are to be held and the prizes are to be awarded on the sports day."

Prizes there were galore with the first three in each competition normally receiving a prize, many of which seem to have been of some value. However, it is probable that these were, in the main, second hand items which the donors were content to part with, perhaps rather in the way that people give to jumble sales today. Among the prizes that year were a compass watch pendant, golf clubs, a life buoy, a life belt, a case of teaspoons, handbags, hold-alls, a tennis racquet, a garden swing, hammocks, a travelling bag, a writing desk, a camp stool, knives, fishing rods, a football, a nickel champagne knife, a walking stick, a cricket bat, a tourist spirit stove, a watch and chain and a pot of heather honey - and the prizes of 1895 set the standard for the prizes in the sports in the following years. The winners of the premier competitions - the swimming championship and the quarter mile championship were presented with silver medals. There were all the track and field events usually associated with school sports and an intriguing one called the "Object Gathering Race". The next year other novelties were added to the programme: the hoop trundling race, the apple race, the apple and orange race and the iron hoop race.

The weather for the first sports day was quite inclement as was reported in *The Oban Telegraph* under the headline, "Oban High School Athletic Sports". It began:
"These sports came off on Thursday at Mossfield. Unfortunately the weather was most unpropitious. The rain it rained in torrents, and eventually, when the twenty-fourth event had been finished, a halt was called, and the games were ended for the day. So far everything had gone on in the most satisfactory manner, and great was the success which had attended the meeting - the first of its kind in Oban, but certainly not the last, for all concerned, and everyone more than another, seemed determined to make the High School Sports a success. There is no doubt that they are destined to become an annual fixture, and will probably be looked forward to by and by as one of the events of the Oban Season. Much praise is due to Mr Owen, MA, in whose mind arose the conception of the games, and who wrought like a Titan in carrying them out, and had his reward in the great success that attended everything.

"Two marquees were on the ground, and afternoon tea was served in one of these. The Boys' Brigade Pipe Band was present and played a number of pieces, which added zest to the proceedings. All the events were well contested, and some very creditable results were accomplished. Sergeant Martin's display of Indian club and dumb bell exercises were much admired. The events which were not finished on Thursday were accomplished on Friday forenoon in the playground at Soroba School."

41

There was a school Athletic Club which embraced cricket, football, golf, swimming and harriers, all apparently for boys, and lawn tennis and targette for girls. To judge from the school records, the most active were the cricket club and the football club, although they played few matches against other clubs and often simply had to play among themselves. In 1896, for instance, the cricket club had fourteen matches on their fixture list, only six of which were played and none of these outside the town. They were well beaten by a team from a visiting naval training ship, *HMS Northampton*, and they thrice beat teams from the Oban Pro-Cathedral School. In the other two matches, the players were all members of the club: the Captain's team versus the Vice-Captain's team and the Secretary's team versus the Treasurer's team.

As with the cricket club, the football club practised three times a week but played few games against other teams. The club's report for the 1898-99 season read:
"There were no matches played this season. At the close of the season, a five-a-side competition roused a great deal of interest and evoked some good play on the part of the players engaged, especially amongst those of Standards V and VI."
However, it continued:
"There seems to have been some bad feeling between some of the secondary boys which those in office as captain and vice-captain ought immediately to have reported, unless able of themselves to overcome it. The boys must be impressed with the necessity of obeying those in office and, especially, the captain must see to it that his orders as well as the rules of the club are immediately and fully carried out."

By the beginning of 1892, the Oban School Board, as well as the boards in Dunoon and Campbeltown, were demanding that a higher grade school be established in their respective towns and this was achieved. Apart from the government grant for secondary education, money for the provision of secondary education came from the county council grant for technical education, the town council, endowments and local subscriptions. Technical education embraced subjects such as Mathematics, Physics, Physiography, Agriculture, Mechanics, Domestic Economy (cookery and laundry), Dairy Work, Fishing, Navigation and Wood Carving. The Highlands and Islands Education Trust made grants on certain conditions of which religious instruction in every class was a *sine qua non*.

The elevation of the School to the rank of having a secondary department decided the Board to retire Hugh Skinner and to advertise for a new Headmaster and some additional staff. This was discussed at the meeting of the Board on 20th June, 1892 and the outcome was recorded thus:
"Mr Skinner afterwards attended the meeting and the board having conferred with him as to the proposed reorganisation of the school it was moved by Mr Robertson, seconded by Mr Munro, and unanimously resolved, that the board offer Mr Skinner a superannuation allowance of seventy five pounds per annum in consideration of his resigning the office of headmaster, the resignation to take effect on 1st October next. Mr Skinner accepted the offer and stated that he would send a formal letter of resignation."

This letter of resignation was duly received by the Board and it was produced at the next meeting of the Board on 27th June when the Board attached two conditions to Skinner's retirement allowance. These were: "(1) that Mr Skinner shall not at any future time engage in teaching within the burgh or the parish of Kilmore and Kilbride, and (2) that he shall not at any time become a member of this board or of the school board of Kilmore and Kilbride." Skinner was willing to accept the second of these terms and undertake not to set up a school but he wanted to be left free to assist any students who might wish to avail themselves of his services privately. The Board would not agree to this and Skinner accepted. It is quite evident that the Board was concerned that their school should face no competition from Skinner after his retirement and that his influence in educational matters in the district should be at an end. The meeting went on to propose a rearrangement of the staff after the reorganization of the School. It necessitated advertising for a male assistant and a lady superintendent.

At the meeting of 1st August, 1892, the Clerk produced sixty-four responses to the advertisements for a Headmaster of Oban High School, twenty for that of Assistant Master and seven for that of Lady Superintendent. At the next meeting on 15th August "the meeting, having considered the applications for the headmastership, reduced the same to a leet of four, viz.: James Beattie, St Andrews; Alexander Campbell Robertson, Anstruther; Alexander L Taylor, Ayr; and Robert Young, Paisley. Mr Robertson and Mr Taylor, having already visited Oban and called on the members, it was resolved to ask Mr Beattie and Mr Young each to come here and meet with the board on an early day".

The outcome was revealed in the minutes of 19th August:
"The minutes of meetings held in committee on 15th instant and today were read and adopted and in accordance with the latter the board hereby appoint as headmaster of the school during their pleasure Mr James Beattie, MA, at present English master in Madras College, St Andrews, and that at a salary of two hundred and fifty pounds per annum together with a bonus of five per cent in the capitation grant to be earned annually in the secondary department."

At the following meeting, on 25th August, it was agreed that the headmaster should be designated Rector of the school and he was to be consulted about the appointment of a second assistant at a salary of £100 per annum. On 5th September it was decided to delay the appointment of a Lady Superintendent and to appoint two male assistants, both at a salary of £120 per annum, one of these being William McLaren, MA, an assistant in the Huntly Gordon Public School. The other post proved rather more difficult to fill but, after a short delay, James Paterson, MA, assistant in Lanark Grammar School, was appointed. It was not long before the decision was made to appoint a Lady Superintendent to the School, this being made at the meeting on 10th October with the proviso that it should be done "as soon as sufficient accommodation for her can be provided". At the meeting of 5th September, it was also resolved that no fees should be charged in the secondary department and that a High School committee should be appointed to confer with the Rector from time to time as to the working of the School.

The first Lady Superintendent in the secondary department was Miss Annie D Harris, who came from Wallace Hall Academy, Thornhill, Dumfriesshire, and she commenced her duties on 9th January, 1893. One of the responsibilities of the Lady Superintendent was to provide piano lessons at a charge to the students of fifteen shillings for ten lessons of one hour each or twenty lessons of half an hour each.

The secondary department of Oban High School was opened on 19th September, 1892 and the entry about the occasion in the School Log read:
"School reopened [after the summer holiday] on 19th September. The formal opening of the Secondary Department was made a public function. Among those present were Colonel Edward Malcolm, Sheriff McLachlan, Mr Patten McDougall of Gallanach, Rev M McCallum, Muckairn, Dr MacKelvie, Dr MacNicol, Mr Anderson, Burnbank, Mr D McGregor, solicitor, Mr J M Campbell, solicitor, Mr Archibald Campbell, burgh fiscal, Mr Angus Macintyre, Glasgow, Rev A Ingilby, the Rectory, Rev James Forbes, Provost MacIsaac and the following members of the [school] board: Mr Livingston [Chairman], Mr John Munro, Mr A Robertson, Mr John McDougall.

"Mr Livingston said there had been a general feeling that an important centre like Oban should have its secondary education as well as primary. The [school] board had provided a secondary school which would now be second to none in any provincial town in Scotland. The board had also after due consideration made the education free and it was expected that boys and girls would no longer leave their Highland home for schools abroad but would come to the secondary school in Oban.

"Sheriff McLachlan, chairman of the Science and Art Local Committee, formally opened the Secondary Department. Oban, he said, was now the chief town in the county and he hoped it would now also become the educational centre of the West Highlands.

"Mr Patten McDougall congratulated the board upon the prospect that lay before them of furthering the interests of the youth of Lorne. Oban had been unfortunate in its lack of endowments, but the county council were prepared to give substantial aid to the school under their scheme for the advancement of technical education. He thought Lord Elgin and his committee deserved their gratitude for the interest they had taken in the Highlands and Islands in connection with the proposals for the allocation of the Equivalent Grant. He was gratified to see so many pupils had already joined the Secondary Department. He thought Highland boys should get their school education in the Highlands.

"Colonel E Malcolm expressed himself delighted with the equipment of the school. He would encourage the pupils to look abroad for scope for their talents: the British Empire was theirs as much as Scotland was.

"Mr John Munro was ashamed that Oban had done so little for secondary education. He wished he could rule it into the hearts of every mother that the best legacy she could give her boys was a good education. Some people objected to their making education free. But it could not be free. Somebody had to pay for it. The new scheme would not affect the local rates. With twenty pupils, they would have government grants amounting to £120; endowments or local subscriptions to the amount of £100; a grant from the county council of £75; a grant from the town council of £68; a grant from the Highland Education Trust of £150; a grant of £120 to £200 from the government for aid of burgh or higher schools. He calculated upon having a total of £623 for the Secondary Department. A balance to the good, after deducting the salaries of the teachers, would be left amounting to £133.

"The rector spoke upon the meaning of secondary education and upon its progress throughout Scotland. He asked the cooperation of parents and pupils in making the Oban High School equal to the first school in Scotland. He outlined some of the features that he intended to make characteristic of the school.

"Mr John Anderson, Rev M McCallum and Mr Alex Robertson also gave short addresses.

"The successful candidates in the St Andrews University 'Locals' were then presented with their certificates."

James Beattie worked tirelessly for education in Oban over the eighteen years during which he was at the helm and this, in spite of obstacles placed in his path by the more parochially minded of the people of the burgh. Fortunately, he had, in general, the support of the School Board who were also anxious to see the development of the School as a centre of learning. Eventually he was to leave the School to take up an appointment as rector of Greenock High School in which post he remained for a further eighteen years until his retirement in 1928. He was honoured by the Educational Institute of Scotland by being made a Fellow of the Institute in 1901 and becoming its Vice President in 1899 and 1903 and its President in 1910. Born in Longside, Aberdeenshire, in December 1864 and educated in the University of Aberdeen, he was assistant teacher of Classics in Rothesay Academy, then English master in both Morrison's Academy, Crieff, and Madras College, St Andrews, before his promotion to Rector of Oban High School. Although he devoted himself to the School and its interests, he still found time to distinguish himself in other ways: he contributed articles to educational journals, wrote a book on Germany and became a fellow of the Royal Scottish Geographical Society. He retired from the teaching profession in 1928 and died in Edinburgh in June 1935. His son, Colin, became an academic of distinction, qualifying in Arts and Medicine. He became a Rockefeller fellow, Senior Lecturer in Bacteriology in the University of Edinburgh and Professor of Bacteriology in both the Universities of Baghdad and Sheffield.

James Beattie did not achieve his successes without a great deal of labour. Much of his time was devoted to teaching and examining classes and to administrative and clerical work. There were times when the workload he bore became rather taxing, perhaps especially in the middle months of 1896, when he gave expression to his concern in his School Log Book. After a number of brief references to the amount of his time which had to be devoted to the needs of education, he made the following entry, dated 15th September, perhaps to draw attention to the demands of the job:-

"8.30 am	School correspondence.
8.55 am	Bringing opening drill into line.
9.00 am	Enrolling new pupils.
9.10 am	Finally adjusting pupil teachers' timetables and explaining methods to the teachers.
9.30 am	Drawing up schemes of work.
10.00 am-10.55 am	English class and classifying pupils.
[10.15 am	Enquiring into discrepancy in attendance numbers.]
10.55 am	Seeing about bell rope etc.
11.00 am-12.05 pm	Latin class and examining Standard V 'awkward squad' for classification.
12.05 pm-12.30 pm	Examining and signing orders for free books to pupils.
1.30 pm	Supervising drill.
1.35 pm	Latin class and examining Standard V 'awkward squad'.
2.40 pm	Visit from Mr Wann.
2.50 pm	Examination continued. Admission numbers of pupils etc hunted up. Arranging new science class - Subject I - and selecting suitable pupils etc.
3.45 pm	Dismiss Standard V pupils. Visit from Mr McCallum.
4.15 pm	Correspondence - Kennedy Trust etc.
6.00 pm	Leave for dinner.
7.30 pm	Correspondence - Science and Art Department etc, etc. Examining school catalogues. Adjusting history and geography syllabuses.
10.15 pm	Retire.

The above are the events of today, 15th September, 1896. J B."

On one other occasion during his long rectorship, Beattie provided an itemized list of his daily duties in the School Log. It was dated 21st September, 1904 and reads:-

"Today's work:

8.30 am	Inspected class-rooms.
8.45 am	Made arrangements for the conduct of Miss MacColl's class during the absence of Miss MacColl at the Mod in Greenock.
8.52 am	Attended 'ranking up' of boys in playground.
9.00 am	Prayers in the Higher Grade Department.
9.10 am	Set George Hope, pupil teacher, to work upon copying a timetable for the Highlands and Islands Trust.
9.20 am	Interviewed by Miss E MacLennan, pupil teacher, regarding her university bursary examination.

9.30 am	Interviewed by Miss Agnes MacDougall, pupil teacher, regarding the university preliminary examination and her arrangements for the ensuing week.
9.40 am	Discussed with Mr Winning the English work for the preliminary examinations etc and arrangements for the conduct of the library.
10.00 am	Made out specifications of science apparatus for the school board. Wrote list of articles required from Messrs Baird and Tatlock.
10.30 am	Sent additional order to Mr MacDonald, Bookseller.
10.40 am	Visit from Mr Eadie, Glasgow.
11.00 am	Visited with Mr Eadie the rooms and grounds. Superintended the work of the gardening class.
12.00 am	Discussed with each teacher the work to be undertaken under 'Repetition'.
12.30 pm	Superintended dismissal of scholars.
12.40 pm	Luncheon.
1.00 pm	Saw the country pupils about their luncheon etc.
1.30 pm	Visit from Rev N MacKinnon, Acharacle, regarding the enrolment of his daughters.
2.00 pm	Superintended entrance of pupils.
2.10 pm	Discussed work of housewifery class for the session.
2.20 pm	Examined elementary classes.
3.35 pm	Explained matters in connection with maths classes to interim maths teacher.
3.45 pm	Wrote letters to parents regarding the work of their children.
4.10 pm	Visit from Mrs MacIsaac with reference to her daughter's curriculum
4.30 pm	Wrote further letters to parents.
4.55 pm	Left on bicycle for home (Connel Ferry)."

On 30th September, 1892, shortly after the opening of the secondary department, the Rector recorded the attendance in that department as forty five - sixteen girls and twenty nine boys - while the average daily attendance of the whole school (the Rockfield Road and Soroba Road buildings combined) for the previous fortnight was 576. However, pupils were still enrolling as they were freed from their summer work. A week later the roll had increased, as was shown in the entry in the School Log for 7th October, an entry which also gave information about the impressive list of subjects studied by the secondary pupils and those in the Standards V and VI and an insight into the decorum expected from the schoolchildren:

'Attendance in the secondary department still growing. 54 on the roll - 21 girls and 33 boys. Classes now definitely arranged and all timetables finally adjusted. Subjects taught in the secondary department are: English, Latin, Greek, French, German, mathematics, arithmetic, civil service, writing, bookkeeping, physics, mechanics (theoretical), botany, agriculture, geometrical drawing, model drawing, free-hand ornament, drawing from cast, singing, drill, religious instruction. 'Specifics' taught in Standard VI are Latin, French and mathematics;

in Standard V, Latin. Have given general instructions to the teachers to see that the children come with washed faces and hands; and have told every class to observe such rules of politeness as lifting caps etc."

Later, in March 1899, the Rector
"Instructed all the teachers regarding the standing up of their class on the entrance of visitors into the room. Instructed the drill officer as to instruction of salute drill to the boys."

In an entry dated 22nd March, 1897, James Beattie provided the following statistics about the school:-

Number of scholars in the elementary division of the school: Standard I - 112; Standard II - 118; Standard III - 124; Standard IV - 99; Standard V - 109; Standard VI - 62.

Estimated number of elementary pupils present for annual inspection:

	Boys	Girls
Under Standard III	296	249
In Standard IV	58	40
In Standard V	54	48
In Standard VI	27	30
In Ex VI	35	46

Military drill to 301 boys; cookery to 141 girls.

Number of pupils studying specific subjects at the different levels:

Mathematics	Level 1 - 36; Level 2 - 15; Level 3 - 9.
Greek	Level 1 - 2; Level 2 - 2.
Bookkeeping	Level 1 - 4.
German	Level 1 - 7; Level 2 - 6; Level 3 - 6.
Latin	Level 1 - 54; Level 2 - 29; Level 3 - 19.
French	Level 1 - 60; Level 2 - 30; Level 3 - 20.
Gaelic	Level 1 - 19; Level 2 - 5; Level 3 - 4.

Then, from the first entry for session 1897-98 comes:
"20th September, 1897: School reopened this morning at nine o'clock. The number present today was:

Soroba	341
Rockfield	387
Total	728

There were 80 present in the secondary department."

The figures for 26th October, by which time all those with summer work would have returned to school, were:

Soroba	372
Rockfield	434
Total	806

In secondary department there were 107 present and 112 on the roll.

By mid June 1898, the number of pupils in fairly regular attendance in the School was approaching 900 as is revealed in an interesting entry, dated 9th June, in the School Log Book: "Attendance today 878 - record attendance. Have intimated to the school that one pupil has made perfect attendance for four years running (Annie Waddell, Standard VI); four pupils for three years; twelve pupils for two years; and 49 pupils for the year ended 31st May."
Incidentally under the date 29th June, 1905 Beattie made the following entry:
"Teachers subscribed today 26 shillings towards a memento to Mary Jane MacFarlane, the first pupil to complete 8 years' perfect attendance."
Then, on 30th June, the final day of the session, he noted:
"Mary Jane MacFarlane, Oban, was presented by the teachers with a drawing-room clock as a memento on the occasion of her having completed 8 years' continuous perfect attendance."
A remarkable achievement, even today; it was the more so in the days when illness and epidemic were so much commoner.

The salaries of school staff varied from school board to school board, the boards having absolute power over the salaries of their employees. Some offered a fixed salary to the teachers; others paid them a smaller salary but they were allowed to receive a proportion of the annual government grant if they emerged from the Inspector's report with sufficient credit. The latter was the system adopted by the Oban School Board for the first twenty years but those who also taught in the evening school had the annual government grant for that school divided among them and this was a useful addition to their salary. In these years it was also left to the individual members of the staff, including the Board Officer and janitor, to seek from the Board increases in salary and teachers had to apply to the Board when they felt that an increase in staffing was required. Sometimes these applications were granted; at other times they were not - although it does seem that the Board responded fairly favourably to them. Incidentally, it appears from the minutes that if the janitor had to employ additional help in carrying out his duties, he had to find the money to pay for this help out of his own pocket. The practice of paying teachers quarterly in the early days of education in Oban under the School Board must have placed on the staff the need for careful husbandry of their resources. Later, when this practice was changed to payment monthly, the situation would have eased. In February 1896 a formal salary scale for the teachers was adopted by the Board and this was revised in October, 1899. As was customary in those days, men were paid significantly more than women. The following is an extract from minutes of 9th October, 1899:

"In dealing with the salaries of any teachers in their service, the board consider themselves entirely free to take all the circumstances of the school and the resources of the board into account; and, while for their own guidance they have prepared a scheme for dealing with salaries, they wish it to be understood that as in the past so in the future they make no bargain with any teacher beyond what is contained in his or her letter of appointment or any other letter modifying the terms thereof.

"Scale	Minimum	Maximum	Biennial Increase
MALE TEACHERS	£	£	£
Junior - Untrained with parchment or normal trained	90	100	5
Senior - Normal trained or graduate with certificate	100	120	10
Graduates (uncertificated) in Higher Department	90	90	-
Graduates (certificated) in Higher Department	110	150	10
Second Master - Graduate normal trained or with parchment	130	160	10
Workshop and art master - graduate	110	150	10
FEMALE TEACHERS			
Untrained with parchment or normal trained	55	90	5
Infants' mistress	90	120	10
Mistress of Junior Division	90	120	10
Mistresses of modern languages and lady superintendent in the Higher Department	100	120	10
Mistresses of Housewifery	50	70	5"

The salary scales introduced in early 1907 were given in the minutes of 21st January of that year:

"Scale	Maximum	Minimum	Biennial Increase
MALES:	£	£	£
In the Higher Grade Department	120	150	10
In the Elementary Department	100	120	10
Second and Department Masters	130	160	10
FEMALES:			
In the Higher Grade Department	90	120	5
In the Elementary Department	75	90	5
Infants' Mistress	90	120	10"

The pupil teacher system began in 1842 and lasted until 1905. At the age of thirteen a pupil wishing to become a teacher was indentured as an apprentice teacher. Before and after school and at the lunch-time break pupil teachers received instruction in Latin, Greek, Mathematics, History, Geography and Music from the Headmaster or from the particular teachers under whose supervision they were. Each pupil teacher, who was given charge of a group of pupils for elementary work, was attached to a particular teacher who was responsible for seeing that the pupil teacher was properly trained and was meeting the requirements of the training. It was a form of apprenticeship which lasted five years or so and involved regular examinations conducted by an Inspector in the course of his annual inspection of the school or by an examination centre in either Edinburgh or Glasgow. At the end of their time as pupil teachers they could sit the Queen's Scholarship Examination at a training college where they would undertake further training. The School's most notable pupil teacher achievement in its first thirty years came in 1899 and was recorded in the Board minutes of 3rd April of that year: 'It was remitted to the chairman to send a letter to Miss Skinner, pupil teacher, offering her the congratulations of the board on her success in obtaining the first place for Scotland in the Queen's Scholarship and Studentship Examinations."

This was followed by further successes in 1900 and 1904 as is reported in the School Log Book under the date 20th February, 1905:

"George Hope, pupil teacher, has gained first place for Scotland in the King's Scholarship Examination and has been awarded a bursary of £25. This is the third time this distinction has been won by Oban High School - by Miss M A Skinner in 1898 [sic], by Miss Grace MacDougall in 1900 and now by George Hope in 1904."

Miss Mary Ann Skinner was to return to the School where she established a redoubtable reputation as teacher of Modern Languages, eventually being promoted to the post of Lady Superintendent.[3]

In the early years of the Oban School Board pupil teachers were paid a salary of £10 per annum for the first year and this increased by £2.50 in each of the subsequent four years and it is known that they worked eighteen and a half hours per week in 1896. From the point of view of the School Board, they were cheap labour but it was one method of entry to the teaching profession. Sometimes pupil teachers were found from within the local community or Argyll; sometimes there were advertisements placed by the Board in *The Scotsman* and *The Glasgow Herald* in addition to *The Oban Times*, *The Oban Telegraph* and *The Oban Express*. On other occasions, particularly when the Board wished to make a high calibre appointment or when they were looking for someone with specialist teaching skills, approaches were made to the Rectors of the Free Church and Established Church Normal Schools in Edinburgh and Glasgow, these being institutions with a high reputation which attracted the most promising of the pupil teachers in the country. On 17th November, 1881, for instance, after Mr Skinner's department in the school lost an assistant teacher when he resigned his post to take up another teaching position in Greenock, the Board directed the Clerk to the Board to apply to the

Rectors of the Normal Schools in Glasgow to supply a successor who "must be able to teach singing and ... it will be a recommendation if he can teach shorthand writing, the fees for which will be in addition to his salary".

After 1905, the pupil teacher system was replaced by that of the Junior Student. Schools with a high academic reputation were selected as junior teacher centres by the Scotch Education Department and in 1906 Oban High School, Dunoon Grammar School and Campbeltown Grammar School were recognized as such centres. It was a teacher apprenticeship in which the training lasted three years. The Junior Student had to be over fifteen years of age and have taken the Intermediate Certificate. A teacher in the centre was appointed master of method and coached the students in the Art of Teaching and at the end of the training the Junior Student took the Junior Student Certificate. Most also took the Leaving Certificate and proceeded to training college or university. The Junior Student system was eventually abolished in 1924.

If vandalism is common enough today, it was certainly not unknown in those early days of the School's history as is revealed in the occasional entry in the minute books. One, dating from 1st December, 1890, has already been mentioned but there were others. For example the minutes of the meeting of 5th May, 1890 contained the following entry:
"The clerk was directed to call the attention of the police to the frequent breaking of the school windows by boys, chiefly between Fridays and Mondays, and to ask that steps be taken to prevent this as far as possible."
From the minutes of 7th August, 1893:
"The janitor, having reported that 6 panes of glass in the windows of the Soroba Road building had been broken since Saturday last, it was resolved to offer a reward of £1 for such information as would lead to a conviction of the person or persons who had done the mischief."
And from those of 2nd July, 1894:
"The visiting committee for last month reported verbally as to their visits to the school. A suggestion by them that notice boards be put up in the school grounds threatening prosecution for any malicious destruction of property was adopted."

There are many individual entries in the School Board minute books during the last three decades of nineteenth century to Peter Thomson, glazier, stating that his account had been passed for payment. It is to be wondered how much of his work was the result of vandalism. It is also to be wondered if this Peter Thomson was the same gentleman who appeared before the School Board in early 1875 for failure to have his children properly educated, apparently because he was in financial straits.

Periodically, there was also the problem of bad language among the pupils. It appears that on 5th June, 1893 the Rector made some reference to the use of foul language in his regular monthly report on the attendance statistics because there is the following entry:
"It was remitted to Messrs MacKinnon and Munro to made a representation to the magistrates with a view to the suppression of the foul language referred to by the rector."
At the board meeting on 7th March, 1898,

"Mr Clements having called attention to complaints which had been made as to bad language used by boys coming to Oban by train to attend the Secondary Department, it was remitted to the higher education committee to investigate the matter."

However, in this case for some unexplained reason he withdrew the allegation at the meeting on 4th April, 1898.

The School was not without its internal discipline problems which are illustrated by the following entries in the School Log:

"15th July, 1887: Had three cases of insubordination this week, two in the infant and one in the junior departments. In each case the boys refused to be punished and gave insolence. Two submitted to be punished by the headmaster; the other refused and had to be expelled. The boy's name is Ferguson."

"10th October, 1892: Had general meeting of boys at Soroba to investigate a case of scribbling on walls. Boy confessed during the evening."

"9th January, 1894: Boy, irregular in attendance, unwilling to come to school, is brought to school this morning by his elder sister, refuses on command of teacher to sit down, expresses his wish to get home, is sent home."

"22nd January, 1904: Dealt with case of smoking on the part of one of the boys and warned school of dangers in such a practice."

Not long before, on 19th October, 1903, smoking among pupils had been raised at a meeting of the School Board:

"Mr McDougall, having called attention to the growing practice of cigarette smoking among the boys, it was remitted to the school visitors to bring the matter under the notice of the teachers."

The evening school, which was attended by children rather than adults, became an important part of the Board's school and offered a variety of courses. Some of its teachers also taught in the day school while others were employed solely to teach in the evening school. It started in 1877 under Hugh Skinner and was to show a steady advance during the remainder of the nineteenth century under the direction of Alexander Faichney, who had come to the Oban school from Lerwick in November 1885 and was eventually to be made Headmaster of the evening school as well as a Fellow of the Educational Institute of Scotland. The Board had been rather concerned with the inspectorial report on the day school issued in July 1877 and the members of the Board had decided to make no immediate increase in Skinner's salary at that time but they hoped for a better report on the evening school. They were not to be disappointed. It was inspected in May of the following year and the report was available to the Board at their meeting on 6th June. As the minutes record:

"The clerk laid before the meeting report from Scotch Education Department with reference to the evening school from which it appears that the school passed a very creditable examination. It was stated that a grant had been earned of fourteen pounds one shilling which the clerk mentioned had been paid to Mr Skinner of which the meeting approve."

By 1897 the grant had risen to £138 19s 6d.

Until 1894, it was the practice of the Board to remunerate the teachers in the evening school by allowing them to retain the fees from the pupils in their respective classes and to allow them to share the whole of the government grant received annually for the evening school, its amount being determined by the Inspector's annual report on the evening school. The number of subjects offered and the size of the evening school staff generally increased, although some subjects came and went. Shorthand, which the Board regarded as an important subject owing to its commercial value appeared on the curriculum at the end of 1890 and by session 1893 94 Cookery and Physical Exercises had been added with Military Drill taken by Sergeant Munn and Mr Donald McLucas in the Memorial Hall at the end of 1895. However, sometimes a subject had to be removed as the following entry for 6th December, 1897 in the minute book showed:

"Dr Baily, convener of the evening school committee, reported as to the attendance of pupils at the evening classes and on his recommendation it was resolved that the class in theoretical chemistry be discontinued."

A change in the operation of the evening school came at the Board meeting on 3rd September 1894. The Board now took full control of the evening school and education in it was now to be free. On 12th October it appointed staff. By this time the staff were paid by the Board rather than relying on their fees, as these had been abolished. In addition to Mr Faichney, the Headmaster, who was paid £65 per annum, and two Assistant Teachers, who were paid 1s 6d per hour, teachers of the following subjects were appointed (the hourly pay is in brackets): Cookery (1s 3d), Gaelic (2s) Building Construction (3s), Navigation (3s), Bookkeeping (1s 3d), Vocal Music (1s 6d), Physical Exercises (1s). The £65 earned by Mr Faichney was added to his annual income of £120 for his post in the day school. Unfortunately his Headmaster's remuneration dropped to £50 for session 1899-1900. In the session following the revision, there were two more Assistant Teachers and a class in Dress-cutting replaced the one in Bookkeeping.

It was required by the Scotch Education Department that a regular check be kept of attendance in day schools. The School Board would set a time when the daily register of the School's attendance should be marked for the morning and afternoon sessions and it was required by law that a member of the Board should visit the school at regular unstipulated times to check that attendances marked in the register coincided with the actual number of pupils present. This member of the Board signed the register and entered his findings in the School Log. These entries were checked by the School Inspector on his annual inspection and at other times when he might make an unannounced visit. The staff of Oban High School were efficient in the marking of registers, no discrepancies being noted in the School Log Books or in the Inspectors' reports.

In order to qualify for the annual government grant, each school had to open 400 times a year or 200 days as the morning and afternoon openings were regarded as separate. It was not uncommon for schools to exceed this number to allow for unpredictable closures of the school, such as severe weather and high pupil absenteeism. If the number of pupils present in the morning was below a certain level, perhaps because of the prevalence of illness in the community, the school would be closed in the afternoon. This was at least partly because an excess of low attendances would affect the attendance average for the year and this in turn might affect the size of the government grant for the following session.

In the days when there was less awareness of the need for hygiene and less in the way of medical attention, days also when medical bills had to be paid by the patients or their parents, epidemics were fairly common and schools had to be closed by order of the local medical officer of health, sometimes for lengthy periods. When this happened, a medical certificate had to be sent to the Scotch Education Department so that allowance could be made for the closure of the school in the attendances required for the annual government grant. With rooms that were frequently draughty and inadequately heated and often with ninety and more pupils in a room, infections and diseases spread easily and rapidly and it was of concern to the School that all the children in a home where one of the family was infected should be kept off school, although by the time the infection had manifested itself it was normally too late. Sometimes the rooms were very cold as is witnessed by the following entry in the School Log Book:
"13th January, 1902: At 8.40 this morning the thermometers in the different rooms of Soroba Building indicated a temperature of between 35 and 40 degrees Fahrenheit. No thermometer indicated a degree higher than 40 degrees. At 1.30 pm the thermometers varied between 40 degrees and 42 degrees in the older building and between 40 degrees and 45 degrees in the newer building. Consulted janitor regarding the matter."

The sizes of the classes in Oban High School were given in an entry for 14th August, 1893 in the Board's minute book. The meeting that day had submitted to it a scheme for the arrangement of the school staff for the following session and, after discussion, it was adopted by the Board. The scheme, whose class sizes were presumably rounded up to the nearest ten, shows that from Infants through to Standard V classes within each level ranged in number from 30 to 70, while Mr Faichney's Standard VI was 70. The total envisaged was 820. An idea of the extent of the overcrowding is provided by the following entries in the minute book. The first is from 6th November, 1893 and refers to the report made to the Board by the School Visiting Committee for the previous month.
"Standard V. Overcrowded. Room seated for 70 and average attendance is 90 this week. Every other class room is filled."
The second entry is taken from the minutes of 3rd April, 1899:
"With reference to the rector's suggestion as to the placard required to be exhibited in each classroom in terms of Article 17 (c) of the new Code, Mr Clements moved that the accommodation of the infant rooms be calculated on the 8 foot scale and the other rooms on the 10 foot scale, which motion was seconded by Mr Vallance. Dr Baily moved as an amendment, and Mr Robertson seconded, that the 10 foot scale be adopted throughout the school. The chairman and Mr Campbell supported the amendment which was therefore carried."
At least the Board decided to give the infants a little more room.

The commonest epidemics were measles, mumps, scarlet fever and whooping cough and the headmasters' Logs make frequent reference to illness in the town. There were also numerous references to wild weather, partly because this almost invariably affected the daily attendance since many children did not have sufficient clothing to protect them against poor weather and partly because such weather was always likely to increase infections in the area. When the school was forced to close, information about the reopening of the school was communicated to parents and pupils through the local newspapers and handbills.

A measles epidemic was certified on 7th July, 1883 and the school was closed from the following day until 26th July which must have marked the start of the summer holiday. There was another one in late October/early November 1887 but the medical officer found it unnecessary to close the school. There was another outbreak of the disease in early November 1891 when the school was closed for a fortnight. Then, on 8th December, 1893, the following record was made in the Board's minute book:

"There was read a report by Dr Baily, medical officer of health for the burgh, dated 7th inst, recommending that the school be closed from this date until 8th proximo on account of the epidemic of influenza and whooping cough prevailing in the burgh. It was resolved to close the school accordingly."

And on 4th January, 1895 there was the following entry:

"The clerk produced a certificate from Dr Baily, medical officer for the burgh, to the effect that measles was at present epidemic within the burgh, in view of which he recommended that the public school be not reopened on Monday next but remain closed for at least a fortnight from that date. It was accordingly resolved that the school should remain closed until Monday 21st instant."

The epidemic, however, took rather longer than this to run its course as is shown in the minutes of 17th January, 1895:

"The clerk produced a certificate by Dr Baily, medical officer for the burgh, to the effect that measles was still epidemic within the burgh, in view of which he advised that the public school should be closed for a further period of two weeks. After consideration, it was resolved that the school should remain closed for another week from Monday next, and Dr Baily was requested to report further as to the epidemic on 24th instant."

The school was to reopen after the epidemic on 28th January, 1895.

Under 31st January, 1899, the minutes stated:

"The convener of the Attendance Committee called attention to the large percentage of children absent from school on account of sickness and there was submitted a certificate by the medical officer of health as to mumps being at present epidemic in the burgh. After consideration, it was agreed that the day school and also the evening school be closed, in accordance with the medical officer's recommendations, from today until Tuesday, 14th February."

On 6th February the Board directed the janitors in the Rockfield Road and Soroba Road buildings to carry out the medical officer's requirements that the schoolrooms and other parts of the buildings be thoroughly cleaned before the reopening of the school.

There was smallpox epidemic in Glasgow in the earlier part of 1901 and, as a precaution against its spreading to Oban, the pupils of Oban High School were vaccinated against the disease. This seems to have had the desired effect and the disease was kept at bay for the remainder of 1901. However, in March 1902 it did make an appearance in Oban as the following entries in the School Log Book make clear:

"27th March, 1902: Intimation received from clerk of school board today that the local authority have ordered the exclusion from school of children living in 1 Tweeddale Street, 1-12 Back Combie Street, 14, 17, 21 Airds Crescent and 6-10 Combie Street (Waterhouse) in consequence of outbreak of smallpox in the burgh. Attendance today 717 or 83.9%"

"4th April, 1902: Attendance today 720. No further cases of smallpox. General revaccination and consequent decrease in attendance."

The outbreak was successfully contained to a small number of homes.

In the years of Beattie's reign the final epidemic (this time of measles and whooping cough) closed the school from 23rd November, 1907 to 19th January, 1908 and the attendance was still only 606 or 67.6% of the total on the day of the reopening.

In the days before the National Health Service, many families could ill afford medical bills and it was imperative to try to prevent the spread of infectious diseases by keeping apparently healthy children from infected homes off school to restrict the spread of disease. Parents would take matters into their own hands and keep their children at home if there was a fever scare in the area. This happened towards the end of 1881 and was recorded in School Log, the first entry being for 27th October of that year:

"Attendance very irregular up till Thursday when a fever panic occurred which reduced the attendance to less than a half on Friday. Scarlet fever is very prevalent in the town and it is feared that the school must be closed by the medical authority."

However, owing to a difference of opinion among the doctors, the sanitary inspector refused to close the school. Two months later there was another epidemic fear as the School Log entry for 23rd December showed:

"Dismissed for the Christmas holidays till 3rd January, 1882. Attendance scarcely up to the mark. Bad weather and the fever scare still keep away the children from school. The janitor reports the prevalence of measles and whooping cough in certain parts of the town."

Epidemics could also affect school holidays as is revealed by the minutes of 6th March, 1899:

"Dr Baily and Mr Vallance were appointed school visitors for the month. It was remitted to them to confer with the rector as to the alteration of the scheme of holidays in view of the recent closing of the school owing to the epidemic of mumps."

Minor illnesses were a constant cause of non-attendance at school. Colds, sore throats and toothache were common and there were many cases of absence due to sore feet which resulted from children going barefoot and suffering cuts and abrasions which became septic, this being one reason why it was essential to keep the playgrounds of the schools as free as possible from broken glass and sharp pieces of metal. At a time when all pupils walked to school - along roads which were often muddy and waterlogged - and many were ill-provided with shoes and clothing, a day of storm and heavy rain meant low attendance and on these occasions there was often what was called a double school day: a lunch-time break of only five or ten minutes and then dismissal at 2.00 pm with the register marked twice.

Among the older children, seasonal employment was a source of absenteeism. With the coming of the better weather in the spring, pupils ceased attending school to work on the land - planting, lambing and so on - and in the months of September and early October they were often engaged in harvesting; others were employed in shops in the summer months. It was not until the second half of October that the school roll for the session could be determined with accuracy and it may be that this is the explanation for the opening of the evening school session being delayed until towards the end of October. The Board was prepared to take action against both the parents and employers of pupils who were working when they should have been at school as is revealed by a minute book entry for 23rd May, 1889:
"The officer reported several cases of children who had left school and were employed at herding; and the clerk was instructed to write to the parents and employers threatening prosecution.'

In cold weather, absenteeism among the boys was sometimes attributed to skating as was witnessed by several entries in the Headmaster's School Log. For instance, against the date 5th December, 1879 was the following entry:
"Attendance somewhat irregular: owing to the frosty weather a number of the children are slipping away to the ice."
Another interest was indicated at the Board meeting on 3rd December, 1888:
"Mr Hutton brought before the meeting a complaint of the officer as to boys frequenting the slaughter house during school hours and the clerk was directed to write to the superintendent on the subject."
And from the School Log Book:
"19th December, 1890: The attendance this week has been bad. On Monday there was a football match which drew a large number of the boys. On Wednesday again there was a show of livestock at the auction mart that helped to keep a number away."

Attendance was important in the days of payment by results. In 1872, compulsory attendance at school was a novel concept and parents were often reluctant to send their children to school, the more so as fees had to be paid and books had to be bought for the privilege. School boards normally appointed an officer to round up the absentees and often this was often combined with the task of the school janitor. A great deal would depend on the zeal of the Board Officer in the execution of his responsibilities and on his firmness, diplomacy and persuasion; some were undoubtedly more efficient than others. The Compulsory Officer employed by each school board had as his main duty the gathering-in of pupils absent with no legitimate excuse. There were cases of truancy but absenteeism of this kind usually had the parents' assent. The determination of the School Board to enforce the compulsory clause of the Act also counted. In this regard, the Oban school board seems to have been diligent although every effort was made to avoid having parents and guardians prosecuted.

On the whole, the School was well-served by its School Board Officers and janitors in the first forty years of its existence, although from time to time some criticisms appeared in the pages of the School Log Book, the chief of these coming in June 1901 with the following entries:
"5th June, 1901: Warned janitor of Soroba building today that the school was not being kept clean."
"6th June, 1901: Repeated warning to Soroba janitor today whom I found asleep in country boys' room at 3.35 pm."
"7th June, 1901: Soroba janitor appeared at school at 4.35 pm this afternoon. He informed rector he was working in his garden till within a half hour of that time. Rector informed him he must be at school by 3.00 pm, having interval from 1.30 pm till 3.00 pm."
"10th June, 1901: Could not find Soroba janitor about the school buildings at 8.00 am today nor at 8.30 am. On finding him at 8.45 am, showed him rooms unswept, there being thick layers of sawdust etc under the desks and pipes. Received reports from the teachers on the conditions of their rooms."
"11th June, 1901: Rooms again untidy - some not appearing to have been swept. Searched whole school building for janitor - and could not find him - at 8.20 am. Found janitor at 8.30 am and again warned him as to condition of school buildings. My search yesterday morning included outside buildings; this morning it did not."
Matters seem to have improved after this because no further complaints were entered in the School Log Book.

In addition to the janitor, the Board employed a cleaner or two to assist in keeping the school clean, although it was always hoped that, if the janitor were married, his wife would provide some help. Payment was poor as is shown in the minutes referring to the appointment of the first cleaner under the Board in September 1873:
"It was resolved to offer five pounds per annum of wages to a woman to take charge of the schools, her duties being to light fires in both schools daily during winter, to sweep out the schools once a week and to wash them once a quarter. The clerk is instructed to offer the situation to Mrs McColl, Kirk Street, on these terms."

On 6th August, 1894 - as long as four years after the Soroba Road building was opened - it was resolved to have a janitor for each of the school buildings. Robert Fisher, Corra Linn Cottage, was appointed as the additional janitor and he became caretaker at Rockfield Road with the existing janitor taking responsibility for Soroba Road. They received each 21 shillings per week. At the end of the century, the board built a house for the janitor at the Soroba Road building and he took occupancy of it in 1900. As stated in the Board's minutes of 4th December, 1899, "It was resolved that Mr Anderson, janitor of Soroba Road buildings, should occupy Burnside Cottage after Whitsunday next and that his emoluments after that day should be fifty eight pounds per annum with free house."

For many years a continuing problem for the Board and for the school janitors was the state of the school lavatories, or "offices" as they were also called. There can be little doubt that greater attention could have been paid to providing suitable lavatory facilities for the pupils in both schools but the situation in Oban was no worse than it was in so many other places in the land. The cleaning of the lavatories must have been the least pleasant of the tasks of the janitors and very often it must have been rather neglected to the possible detriment of the health of the pupils. The School Board minute books are punctuated with references to the unsatisfactory conditions of the lavatories. On 28th February, 1876, for instance, it was recorded:

"The clerk [of the board] laid before the meeting a letter from the Clerk to the Police Commissioners of Oban requiring by direction of the Commissioners that the dry earth closets at the public schools in Comby Street and High Street be put into and kept in thorough repair and cleaned out at least once a month and that separate provision be made for each sex. The meeting direct the clerk to do what is necessary in compliance with the requisition."

In April 1886 the board received a letter from the burgh inspector "calling attention to the filthy condition in which the outside water closets, urinals and play sheds are kept and requesting the board within four weeks to erect proper sanitary facilities".

Before the same meeting there was another letter from the burgh inspector stating that there was waste of water in the lavatories and requiring that this be repaired. The Board, however, was aware of the deficiencies and already had the matters in hand.

On 6th April, 1891,
"There was read a letter from the Scotch Education Department, dated 2nd instant, containing a report by Mr Binnie, sub-inspector, to the effect that on a recent visit he had found the offices at the junior school [Rockfield Road] in a very dirty condition. The janitor was instructed to have the offices flushed daily and the clerk to inform the Department that arrangements had been made for having the cleaning regularly attended to in future."

On one occasion, the pupils and the staff found their summer holiday lengthened because of lavatory problems. To quote from the board minutes for 6th September, 1897:
"It was reported that the alterations on the lavatories at Soroba Road School could not be completed before the opening of the school on 13th instant and it was agreed to instruct Mr Crawford, plumber, to have temporary closets erected."
However, difficulties remained at the time of the next meeting on 17th September and "In view of the incomplete state of the lavatories at Soroba Road, it was resolved that the school be not reopened until 20th instant and the clerk was instructed to advertise accordingly."

The annual inspection by Her Majesty's Inspector of Schools was the most important single event in the school year and it came at the end of the school session which in those days was sometime in the month of July. Indeed, so important was it that the attendance of the pupils at the school during the two day inspectorial visit was generally higher than at any other time of the year - only to drop away immediately after the visit was over. Considerable efforts were made to secure as high an attendance as possible and sometimes this involved the Board in expense. For example at the Board meeting on 23rd June, 1890 "the treasurer was authorised to pay the return fares from Taynuilt of Peter and Duncan Anderson, children of Donald Anderson, mason, lately of Oban, to enable them to be present at the inspection of the school this week". Pupils and their parents responded well to the appeals for full attendance.

For much of the first forty years of the life of the School, the Inspector was John Boyd as is witnessed by the large sprawling signature with which he signed the copy his report entered into the School Log; he made his first appearance at the school on 9th and 10th July, 1883 and his last on 21st February, 1902 when he made a brief visit. Soon afterwards he was appointed Senior Chief Inspector of the northern division of Scotland and James Beattie attended a dinner in Glasgow on Friday, 3rd October of that year to mark the occasion. The following morning, Boyd was presented with an illuminated address from the teachers of Argyll and Renfrew. Although it was known that the School would always be inspected towards the end of the session, the Inspector did not give much notice of his impending two day visit to the Clerk to the School Board. The inspectors had a wide-ranging remit and their reports carried great authority. The Inspector was responsible for examining the pupils, assessing the teachers, passing judgement on the school buildings and facilities and recommending the government grant which the School should receive for the coming session. One of the chief tasks of the Inspector was to examine the pupils as to their progress and to this end schedules had to be completed by the teachers in the school and passed on to the headmaster who sent them to the Clerk for use by the Inspector on his arrival. To be eligible for presentation for examination by the Inspector, a pupil had to have a minimum of 250 attendances to his credit during the session, morning and afternoon counting as separate attendances. A member or members of the School Board usually accompanied the Inspector to watch the examination procedure.

Examination was comprehensive: oral work, written work, delivery and intelligence and also attitude towards the teacher and the Inspector. For several weeks prior to the inspection much time and effort was expended in drilling the pupils to produce their optimum performance, an exercise not enjoyed by either pupil or teacher - as was indicated in the following entries in the School Log Book:

"23rd June, 1882: Teachers and scholars seem to be wearying for the inspectors."

"7th July, 1882: Busily at work drilling up for the inspection. Attendance miserable in the senior department. A number of boys have left for work on condition that they would put in an appearance on the day of the inspection."

"14th July, 1882: Attendance in senior department not much improved. Children getting very wearied of the constant drill they are undergoing for the inspector."

The annual inspection was on 17th and 18th July with quite dramatic subsequent consequences on school attendance:

"21st July, 1882: School completely disorganized after the annual inspection. Attendance down to nearly a half the following day. The attendance over the whole school was 158. The best of the scholars are away."

If satisfactory results were achieved by a pupil, he would receive a pass in the standard. All subjects were examined and, for the purposes of the School and the grant to be awarded, progress was measured by the overall class performance and any sign of pupils helping one another with the answers was frowned upon and could affect the size of the grant. Following the visit, his report was issued by the Scotch Education Department and a copy was sent to the Clerk to the School Board, entered in the School Log Book and signed by members of the School Board and by the Inspector. By the mid 1880s the Oban School Board had started the practice of sending a copy of the inspectorial report to the local newspapers.

The annual inspectorial reports show how the school developed into a leading educational institution in the West Highlands, attracting pupils from a wide area. For example, from the Inspector's report for session 1898-99:
"On the secondary department, HM Inspector reports as follows:
The development of this department within a few years and in the face of serious difficulties says much for the enlightened and resolute policy of the school board as well as for the zeal and ability of the rector and his staff of teachers. It is satisfactory to note that a higher level of attainment has been reached than in any former year. In English, portions of the works of Chaucer, Spencer and Shakespeare have been successfully studied and many of the essays written at the examination are most creditable productions as regards both matter and style. Less proficiency, however, is shown in higher arithmetic but, as this subject is improving in the junior classes, a steady advance here may also be expected. Latin is good in the second and third stages, though in the former the irregular verbs might be more fully known. Classes beyond the stages of the Code are reading from Livy, Cicero, Horace and Virgil and show a very creditable acquaintance with what is professed. The classes in Greek, French and German acquit themselves very well. There is a good pass in mathematics and elementary science is admirably taught. Intelligent and successful work has also been done in bookkeeping and shorthand. Physical training, singing and needlework continue to merit cordial approbation."

Many different organizations and individuals requested the use of rooms in the school for their activities, whether these were of a recreational, religious or educational nature. Consideration was given to the nature of the activity and the requests were by no means always granted; when they were terms could be attached to the let as, for example, in November, 1887 when the board granted permission for the Oban Draughts Club to use the school room, rented in Stevenson Street from Robert Macfarlane, for two hours on Tuesdays and Wednesdays of each month for six months on payment of one shilling per night inclusive of coal and on condition that no smoking take place on the premises. Those who used the school for their own purposes normally had to pay at least a contribution towards the cost of the gas for lighting and the coal, coke or wood (which was obtained from the Lorn Combination Poorhouse) for heating; sometimes they also had to pay rent and sometimes remuneration to the janitor for the work involved in opening the school for them. In October 1883, there was a request from the town clerk that the town council be allowed the use of the board room in the school for their own meetings and for the meetings of the police commissioners. As the minutes recorded:

'This communication having been considered, the meeting agreed to the request of the council, they arranging with the janitor to remunerate him for the additional trouble to which he may be put and paying for the coals and gas which may be used at their meetings as may be afterwards arranged."

As it transpired the board room proved to be too small for the meetings of the town council and for the accommodation of the press and, in response to a further request from the town clerk, the town council and the press were given the use of a classroom adjoining the board room for their monthly meetings.

At the end of the nineteenth century, those children who lived in parts of the Highlands and Islands not accessible to daily travel to Oban but whose parents wished to avail themselves of education in Oban had to be accommodated in lodgings in the town. The admission registers show that Oban High School enrolled a significant number of these pupils who came from such places as Coll, Tiree, Mull, Islay, Jura, Skye, North and South Uist, Barra, Lewis, Ullapool, Ardnamurchan, Ballachulish, Fort William, Glen Coe, Glen Etive, Killin, Inveraray and Lochgilphead. In session 1899-1900 the son and daughter of Claud Bald, a resident in Darjeeling, India, were enrolled and soon afterwards - in 1903 - a pupil whose parents were living in Patagonia in South America was enrolled. Unfortunately, there is little information to be gleaned about the lodgings provided for pupils in either the School Board minutes or in the School Log. The sole reference in the minute books appeared under 2nd October, 1893 when it was said:

"It was resolved to keep a list of persons open to receive boarders at £20 for the school session, being the amount of the bursaries offered by the Technical Education Committee of the county council."

Pupils who travelled to Oban High School daily from the outlying parts were transported by train, the Callander and Oban Railway having opened in July 1880. Inconvenience could be suffered by these pupils when the railway company altered its schedules and on these occasions the Board would make representations to the appropriate agency. For instance, from the minutes of 3rd October, 1892 is the following entry which refers to "mixed trains". These appear to have been trains in which passengers of both sexes were permitted to travel, rather than trains consisting of both carriages and freight waggons.

"It was resolved to bring to the notice of the Board of Trade the inconvenience felt in consequence of the reduced train service resulting from the prohibition of mixed trains on the Callander and Oban line whereby children from the country are prevented from attending school in Oban and to petition for a withdrawal of the prohibition."

The meeting of 14th November, 1892 was presented with the reply:
"There was read a letter from the Board of Trade, dated 24th ultimo, stating in reply to this board's communication as to the reduced train service that they were not prepared to alter more than one mixed train daily each way as at present, but that they had every desire to consult the convenience of the inhabitants of the district, and especially to facilitate the access of the children to school, and would be prepared to consider any representation from the railway company as to the particular train to be allowed. It was resolved to communicate with the

Board of Trade again with the view of getting them to allow a local train from Dalmally in addition to the other mixed trains and further to ask the assistance in the matter of the members of parliament for the burgh and county and other Highland constituencies."

The matter was resolved at the beginning of 1893. The minutes for 9th January, 1893 contained the following information:
"There was read a letter from the railway department of the Board of Trade, dated 6th instant, stating that having given the matter their very careful consideration, they would be prepared to allow the railway company to run the morning train from Dalmally to Oban as an additional mixed train. The clerk was directed to thank the Board of Trade for this concession and to communicate with the railway company with the view of getting them to give the desired service."

Five years later the board again acted in the interests of the country pupils in the school. At the meeting on 7th March, 1898,
"On the motion of Mr Robertson, the board unanimously resolved to make a representation to the Secretary for Scotland and the Postmaster General in favour of the continuance throughout the whole year of the early mail train to Oban, hitherto run during the summer months only."

James Beattie ceased his duties in Oban High School on 30th November, 1910 and was succeeded by William Kennedy, who had been Rector of Invergordon Academy, at the start of the following term on 4th January, 1911. The occasion of Beattie's departure was marked with ceremonies which were reported in the December 1910 issue of *The Oban High School Magazine* in an article entitled *The Thirtieth of November*:-
"The last day of November 1910 was a day worthy of more than passing note in the history of Oban High School. It was on that day that Mr Beattie left to become Rector of Greenock Higher Grade School. He had practically made the upper department of the school; he had seen it grow from humble beginnings until it occupied the prominent position which it holds now and he had in it all the pride that a man has in seeing the success of his labours. The high opinion which people in general have formed of the excellence of his work may be seen from the almost unique send-off which he got in the closing days of the month.

"At the Musical Evening on the 11th, he received a fountain pen and a silver-mounted clock from the Junior Students. Then on the 25th, at a social meeting in connection with the Oban Scientific and Literary Association, he was presented with a pair of silver candlesticks and a silver cigarette box by the members, the presentation being made by ex-Provost Dugald MacIsaac. Then on the 28th we had our own particular ceremony - the presentation of a study desk and chair from the teachers and pupils. Mr Gall made the presentation and referred not only to the progress the school had made under Mr Beattie but also to the way in which he had always held before his pupils a high moral ideal - to his emphasis on such qualities as self-respect, self-restraint, a keen sense of duty, moral courage, kindness and consideration for other people - qualities which would stand them in very good stead, no matter where their lot in life might be cast.

"Mr Beattie made a very interesting and impressive reply. He spoke at length of the early days of the school and the humble beginning from which it had grown. As a parting message to his older boys and girls, he advised them to have faith - faith in goodness, faith in themselves and faith in the ultimate triumph of right. Then they were to have hope - the hope that could fight its way through difficulties and which never lost heart. They were also to have charity - not the spurious charity that called a thing good when it was bad, but the charity that could see goodness and greatness in spite of superficial defects. In thanking them for their gifts, he assured them that he valued them very highly and that he would never forget the old school. After the ceremony, Mr Beattie was entertained by the staff to tea in the Art Room.

"Then on the 29th the public presentation took place in the Station Hotel. A large company of influential Oban people gathered together to witness the handing over to Mr Beattie of certain gifts subscribed for by the public. The presentation was made, in the absence of the Provost, by ex-Baillie Robertson who asked Mr Beattie's acceptance of an illuminated address, a bookcase, a filing cabinet and a writing table for Mrs Beattie. Mr Beattie made a suitable and interesting reply, after which short addresses were given by the Dean of Argyll, Mr J Munro, Rev D J Martin, Dr Baily and Mr Duncan MacGregor, all of whom expressed their admiration for Mr Beattie's splendid work in Oban and regret at his departure.

"Then, at the station on the 30th, the final scene took place. A good many of the pupils of the Secondary Department, almost all the staff and a number of personal friends came to see him off. A hearty cheer was raised as the train moved away and Mr Beattie went off to Greenock encouraged by the thought that his work in Oban had been so much appreciated and strengthened for his new duties by the good wishes of the friends he was leaving behind in Oban."

NOTES

1   It is interesting to compare the assessment for education in the years 1873-74 and 1874-75 with the other responsibilities of the parochial board:

	1873-74	1874-75
Poor Assessment	1s 5d	1s 5d
School	4d	5d
Police	10d	8.5d
Water	1s 0d	9.5d
Prisons	1.5d	1.5d
Lunacy	1.5d	1.5d
Road	6d	6d
County	2.3d	2.2d

2   It appears that, at the time when these arrangements were being made, the members of the Board were not aware of a bequest of £300 made in 1873 by a Mr Thomas Kennedy of Kilmarnock, "to assist in the erection of an academy in Oban". However, as the School Board minutes of 23rd October, 1877 said of this bequest, "the scheme for the erection of such could not be carried out for want of sufficient subscriptions otherwise and the money still remains in the bank." Later it was to be converted into a trust fund to be administered by a committee composed jointly of three members of the Board and three members appointed by the Town Council. Initially, it was used to help parents who had difficulty in paying school fees and, when these were abolished, for a short time its income was applied to purchasing books and other educational material for the evening school. From 1896, it provided higher education bursaries to pupils from the secondary school.

3   See further Chapter 4.

CHAPTER 3

From 1910 to World War II

DUGALD MACARTHUR

In September 1910, the Oban School Board noted with pleasure that the Rector, James Beattie, had been elected President of the Educational Institute of Scotland and that the Congress of that institution would be held in Oban at Easter 1911. However, the main item on the October agenda was the resignation of Mr Beattie on his appointment as Rector of Greenock High School, but with commendable speed the Board advertised the post at £350 rising to £400, selected a leet of nine, all Rectors or Headmasters, and appointed W D Kennedy, from Invergordon Academy, all within five weeks. The interesting point is that the nine were sent letters asking for reports on their schools, on attendances, numbers of presentations and passes in Higher and Intermediate Certificate Examinations and lists of successes in University Bursary or other examinations. After these had been assessed, the Rectors of Fraserburgh, Larkhall and Invergordon were invited to interview.

On 4th January, 1911 Mr Kennedy was installed as Rector of Oban High School after nine years at Invergordon and short periods at Stornoway and Inverness. He had over twenty Junior Students, a fact that must have been in his favour because Mr Beattie had already built up a thriving group of these future teachers under training from the inauguration of the scheme in 1906.

While he was still settling into his new post, Mr Kennedy was involved in a unique function in the forenoon of 14th March, 1911, when the Chairman and Vice-Chairman of the School Board, together with the Provost and ex-Provost, visited Rockfield and the High School, "to mark the centenary of the recognition of Oban as a Burgh of Barony". At Rockfield Mr Munro showed some ancient relics, after the speeches, and the Junior School was dismissed at 11.30 am. At Soroba Road, short speeches were repeated and Mr Munro presented an old lamp (possibly a crusie) as a nucleus of a museum and three volumes of Mrs Grant's *Letters from the Mountains* to the High School Library; Mr Faichney presented two copies of his *Guide* and two of *Oban and the District Around*. The School was dismissed at 12.30 pm.

A day or two later, the Rector addressed all the pupils in the Higher Grade Department[1] urging them to work at least two hours per night and to work hard during that time. Absences and changes of teachers meant that he himself had to teach much and frequently all day. He was dedicated to examining and testing each class, after which full reports were drawn up and the relevant sections given to each teacher.

Mr Kennedy vigorously supported the action of the School Board in prosecuting parents of truant children, and on 21st April he felt that the work of the school "is suffering on account of the ceaseless turmoil brought about by changes and absenteeism among members of staff". A few months after his arrival he addressed all the Primary Teachers on Corporal Punishment when he "urged them to make sparing use of the tawse".

In June 1911, the school was closed for a week to mark the Coronation of the King and Queen, prior to which rehearsals took up some time.

On 7th July the school closed to re-open on 28th August. This session nine of eleven candidates passed the Leaving Certificate and twenty-two of the thirty-seven the Intermediate.

When the School re-opened after the summer vacation, the Rector found "too many pupils absent because of the Season". The tourist business reached its peak in mid-September with the Argyllshire Gathering and associated events which meant that many town school children were employed in one way or another; and a year later on 10th September, 1912 he bemoaned the fact that "the school being closed for a whole week for the Games is not helping the attendance or the enrolment". There followed the Autumn Holiday on 25th September and the Fast Day on 31st October, after which he had to record "the very low attendance of 736 out of 871". The comment was "In Oban the Fast Day always spoils the attendance of the whole week". The point about this is that the Fast Day, being on Thursday, tended to encourage too many to add Friday as well.

The Rector was always alive to the importance of the attendance and the statutory number of openings because the figures were taken into consideration when grants were awarded after visits of the various Inspectors. The percentage attendance had real meaning and after school resumed in January 1912 he addressed the Higher Grade pupils on the necessity of returning promptly after a holiday, and he reprimanded severely those who had taken a few extra days after the Christmas holidays. The pupils from the islands inclined to take extra days even when the weather did not impose them.

Epidemics of measles, whooping cough or scarlet fever were frequently experienced, especially as the School took in pupils from many rural areas which had not been badly affected for some years. Coal strikes affected the train services to and from Oban, and so the attendance of pupils. For example in March 1912 "on account of the Coal Strike some of our train pupils have been arriving very late this week". "Very poor attendances on account of the train service and the scare about measles" was the report a week later.

The school closed on 4th to re-open on 17th April. The scare was justified because on 17th the school was closed on medical advice for five weeks "on account of an epidemic of measles". Such a period of closure called for a medical certificate from the Medical Officer of Health, which was forwarded to the keeper of the Register Record in the Department in Edinburgh. In the following year, 1913, an epidemic of scarlet fever brought the loss of a fortnight's school work in April, and another that of three weeks from 15th September till 10th October.

As there were no hostels for the pupils who attended from the islands and other rural areas they lived in lodgings or with relatives in the town, and as coastal communication was by steamer it was more convenient for a pupil to go to Oban from Ullapool than to Inverness. We get an account of the Boys' Club and Girls' Club in the School Magazine for March 1912. These met weekly in the School, under the supervision of a teacher, and joint meetings were held on special occasions. In October 1914, a special "At Home" was organised in the Art Room to which all country and island children in lodgings were invited to discuss ways in which their welfare could be attended to elsewhere than in the Class Room. Mrs Green, who supervised the welfare, was present with the Rector and Mr David Munro Fraser, HCIS for Western Area, who led the discussion. Another meeting was held shortly afterwards to draw up "rules regulating their conduct after school hours".

I have received a first hand report of the activities of Mrs Green from Mrs Cumming who attended OHS from 1913 to 1916, when her name appears in the Prize Lists published in the annual prospectus. She remembers the arrival of Mrs Green "appointed to look after the children from the islands ... We looked forward to the tea parties she arranged [about 5 or 6 girls at a time] in the house where she lived, and of course to the outings." She gives a long account of a trip to Lismore which was made by boys and girls, with some teachers, including Mr Nesbitt who brought the necessary equipment for cricket, in which all participated. It is very similar to a 1920 account of the picnic to Gylen Castle, which refers to the Boys playing cricket against the Girls and Masters' team. A visit to Connel by the old road was followed by a meal in a large house where they were entertained by someone playing a pianola!

Mrs Cumming confirms that Mrs Green had nursing qualification and that she went off to the War. In fact she joined the famous Scottish Womens Hospital Unit, led by Dr Elsie Inglis, which served with great distinction in Serbia, France, Corsica and elsewhere. Among her colleagues from Lorn and Mull were persons like Dr Katherine MacPhail, who returned to Belgrade to found a Children's Hospital after 1918. The School Magazine of 1916 reports "Mrs Green, who proved a good friend to many of the pupils before she left for Serbia, underwent some trying experiences in the great retreat .... When she reached this country she lectured on her experiences, and thereby obtained a good sum of money for the Scottish Nursing Association ... under this same organisation ... Mrs Green is now in Corsica."

Her name appears in the nursing section of the *Roll of Honour*, published in 1916, and another informant, who left in 1922, has happy memories of Mrs Green's help and guidance up to that date.

Soon after the school re-opened in January 1914, the Rector is recorded as being absent to attend the funeral of two boys drowned while skating, and later, on 15th May, the school apparently closed at 3 pm on account of the funeral of the Duke of Argyll. There may have been a parade or service. On 24th June, when Bannockburn Day was celebrated as a holiday by order of the School Board, the Chairman, Mr T Stevenson, arranged a cinema show for all departments of the High School and of St John's and St Columba's Schools, which required morning and afternoon showings to accommodate everyone. The Town Council decided on only a half holiday for shops because of the visitors in the town and the presence of three light cruisers in the Bay, from which many sailors landed daily.

The School was on holiday when the Great War began on 4th August, 1914, an event which is not mentioned in school records until December. Meantime the old questions of space and staff became acute when it was found necessary to divide the First Year Secondary pupils into three classes instead of two. The ingenious solution was to abolish IIIb which was divided between IIIa and IIa, so freeing the equivalent of a teacher and a room.

The first mention of the War is the record, on 18th December, 1914, of Mr W Scrimgeour, Head of Mathematics, departing for military training in the Reserve Battalion of the Argyll Mountain Battery. He was followed by Mr J Wood, Head of Art, who was summoned to Stirling in connection with a temporary commission in "Lord Kitchener's Army". A few months later he is reported as commissioned in the 23rd Manchesters, while Mr J J Clarkson, Assistant in Science, appears in the 13th Argyll and Sutherland Highlanders. The numbers of these Battalions give some indication of the huge growth of the Army in response to Kitchener's call, and by May 1915 the Rector had begun to complete a Roll of Honour of staff and former pupils who were serving in the Forces. This was eventually published in January 1916, but of course the names of those who joined in the following years are not included.

The School took an active part in raising money for various local War charities and those supported in 1915 included "Fund for comforts for Oban soldiers in Flanders and the Dardanelles" and flag days for "Gallant Little Serbia" and for "The Russian Jews". These indicate the campaigns which were much in the public mind. The pupils had early in the War asked that funds spent on school prizes should be diverted to War Charities. The work of the School went on steadily and at the 1915 examination ten Full Leaving Certificates were gained together with twenty-three Intermediate passes.

On 6th September, 1915 the School closed at 12 noon to enable the staff and pupils to attend the funeral of John Munro, who for may years had been a tower of strength to the School as a member of the School Board.

The Rector must have had an anxious time in November 1915, when a detachment of military officers "inspected the school buildings with a view to location of troops in Oban". Very fortunately, nothing more was heard of the plan, so that staff and pupils escaped the experience of Campbeltown Grammar School, which was occupied by a Naval Training Unit for six years in World War II.

In January 1916 it is recorded that the School Roll had fallen below 800, "the lowest for several years", but the work continued as usual. In March an "Egg Week" meant that each day eggs were brought to school to be forwarded to a central depot for distribution to the wounded, who by this time were to be found in auxiliary hospitals all over the country. "Egg Weeks" were common in rural areas, as were the organised collecting and drying of sphagnum moss for use in supplementing cotton wool bandages for dressings.

From now collections were taken and special efforts made for the "Oban High School War Relief Fund", eg a School Concert in the Argyllshire Gathering Hall, which raised £53, and a Flower Day, which brought in £46. There was also a collection at a football match between the School First XI and a team from "HMS Robert Smith", a naval ship based in Oban. This match was part of the activities on the day before the School closed at Easter, when the afternoon was devoted to rambles and games, which was very much in line with Mr Kennedy's ideas. We do not know whether he himself went on a ramble or refereed that match, but in March 1912, the School Magazine certainly indicates that he refereed the game between the First XI and the Masters, which was won 2-0 by the Pupils.

There were quite a number of small vessels based on Oban, mainly minesweepers and small escort vessels, the latter because of the fact that the U-Boats operated quite close in, sinking ships off Islay and even attacking the MacBrayne steamer "Plover" between Tiree and Barra on 29th July, 1918, without success. It was a common sight to see the "NLS Hesperus" escorted to the lighthouses and to the Sound of Iona, where she spent the night between reliefs. Other coastal steamers such as the "Dunard Castle" and the "Hebrides" were escorted in open waters on a less regular basis. When camouflage was introduced, they too were painted "in a coat of many colours", as were the escorts.

In 1917 and 1918, the War Office organised a local volunteer force of men in reserved occupations or over military call-up age, which in the Oban area was the First Battalion Argyllshire Volunteer Regiment. We remember the Second War Local Defence Volunteers, quickly re-named the Home Guard, but their predecessors are largely forgotten and seldom referred to, but they drilled regularly with Lee-Enfields and wore the ordinary khaki uniform on formal occasions, though for drills, usually in a school playground after 4 pm, the ordinary Volunteer appeared in his working clothes with his rifle, belt and bayonet.

Since the Rector is obliged to record the absence and return of each member of the school staff, we get a reference in October 1917 to his own absence in Glasgow in command of the Oban detachement of Volunteers for an inspection by HRH The Duke of Connaught. He was absent for four days attending a Senior Officers' Course in Edinburgh in January 1918. This was followed on 15th February by an inspection in Oban of the School Cadets[2] by Lord Breadalbane, accompanied by the Duke of Argyll, Major MacLachlan of MacLachlan and others. There was a full muster and Captain Kennedy, Rector of the School, was in command. "The Cadets did extraordinarily well, and were highly complimented by the Inspecting Officer." This inspection is logged at 10.15 am followed at 11 am by the entry "Rector left school on military duty", from which he is shown as "returned" three days later. He was almost certainly "attached" to the considerable inspecting party, which would proceed on a round of inspections. About this time, one large inspection party went to Knock in Mull, where the Volunteer units in Mull and adjacent Islands were instructed to assemble, those from the Ross of Mull and Iona being collected at Bunessan and Iona in the morning by a large armed yacht and brought back in the evening.

On 26th April, 1918 the Cadet Corps was inpsected again by Major MacLachlan of MacLachlan and Captain Scott, OC and Adjutant respectively of the First Battalion Argyllshire Volunteer Regiment. The report was "The Cadets are making excellent progress".

There are references in the school reports to the great struggle; teachers being allowed off to comfort parents who had lost a son appear several times, while one entry records a presentation to a Surgeon Probationer who was safely back from Germany where he had been a prisoner of war. As this was in March 1918 he was presumably exchanged through Holland as a non-combatant. In this First War the Navy employed unqualified medical students as Surgeon Probationers at sea in small ships.

The weather continued to hamper education by causing illness and affecting shipping services, and there is an echo of the long autumn struggle in the mud of Flanders where the third Battle of Ypres dragged on at Passchendale. In Oban the Rector summed it up at the end of November 1917, when storm and rain caused the third 1 pm closing in ten days, "For the last twenty weeks the weather has been unspeakable". In 1917 and 1918, two or three male teachers were medically examined but not called up. An unusual request was made by pupils in lodgings who asked for leave from 8th July, 1918 as they were being turned out of their lodgings "on account of the great demand for rooms by holiday seekers". These may well have been munition workers snatching a holiday when the schools closed.

The School closed in July when the total subject passes in the Leaving Certificates was 204 as against 158 in 1917, giving eleven Full Group Leaving Certificates and thirty at Intermediate Level. The new session began with the usual thirty teachers, but by 28th October four teachers and 213 pupils were absent because of the influenza epidemic. The following day the medical authorities closed the school which was to re-open on 12th November, but that did not happen. Though all the staff turned up on the 19th the authorities delayed the opening until the 26th when the attendance was 75%. Some of the lost time was made up by working until 1 pm on the 27th December, though an early closure at 11 am was made on Christmas Day. This was exactly a repeat of the mid-winter break in 1902, 27th December till 4th January.

The War had ended on 11th November when the school was closed because of the influenza which killed many civilians and service personnel in camps throughout Europe. A newspaper stated that there were no fatalities in the Oban area, but this situation may not have continued in the "fresh outbreak" which led to another period of closure from 26th February until the 12th March, 1919. Meantime, staff in the Services were returning, Mr Lindsay, Principal Science Master and Major J Wood MC, Principal Art Master, among them.

The School was closed on 10th April, 1919 "on account of the Election of the new Education Authority", which became responsible for the work carried out since 1872 by the independent School Boards, which in Argyll numbered forty-six. Each of these new Education Authorities required a Director of Education, and within a matter of weeks, the new Argyll organisation at its first meeting on 20th May, 1919 began the search, as presumably did the other Counties, for when the Rector returned to school on 7th July, 1919, it was announced that he had been selected as Director of Education by Banff as from 31st August.

The Education Authority appointed Dr C M MacDonald Director early in August, followed soon afterwards by the choice of Mr Angus MacLeod, MA BSc, as Rector. As he could not take up his duties until 6th October, the Oban School Management Committee invited Mr Kennedy to return to Oban to carry out the enrolment of pupils for the new session, which he completed on 15th September.

Mr Kennedy received presentations from various organisations in the town and neighbour-hood, and after he retired in 1943 following a very successful period of service, extended by three years, he was co-opted on to the Elgin Town Council. Later he became Convener of Housing and finally he was Burgh Treasurer for four years before his second retirement in 1950. He was awarded the OBE for his services to education in 1943, and he maintained cordial relations with the teachers in the County of Banff. G M Bain, a member of his staff in Oban until 31st May, 1912, when he became Headmaster of Taynuilt, appears to have returned each year to give exhibitions of high jump up to 5' 8", which is referred to as three inches below his best. The Rector stated at one prize-giving when the Chairman congratulated him on a substantial increase in the numbers of successes in the Leaving Certificate and Intermediate examinations that one must not make a fetish of certificates as health and character must also develop. He certainly believed in all forms of sport and he saw to it that swimming and rowing for both sexes were encouraged. Swimmers had races at thirty yards for beginners, extending later to fifty and one hundred and fifty yards for others, while both boy and girl rowing crews tackled lengths of $^1/_4$ mile Single, $^1/_2$ mile Double plus coxswain and one mile for Fours with cox.

Mr Kennedy was among the guests when the post War extensions to the High School Buildings were opened in 1933. He saw the four additional classrooms, the new staff-rooms and offices and the fully equipped gymnasium which he had so long advocated. The lack of adequate equipment he found a great handicap in the instruction of the Junior Students.

One project which Mr Kennedy had in mind was the formation of a Former Pupils' Club, which he referred to in his closing day speech in July 1914. A meeting was to be held in Oban in September during Mod Week, which he hoped would be well attended. He added that the proposal had been taken up with enthusiasm in Glasgow. The next issue of the *Oban Times*, on lst August, 1914, carried the news that war had been declared between Austria and Serbia, and much more than the Mod was abandoned within the following weeks. It was 1949 before the seeds of the FP Club were sown, as related in Chapter 9.

In Glasgow in 1930, 1931 and 1932 Former Pupils studying or working in the city arranged reunions on Charities Day. They registered as a collecting party, which meant that they were allocated a district such as part of Ibrox or Giffnock, a restaurant for lunch, and an official lorry to transport them there and back. The area had to be surveyed in mid-week to ensure effective coverage.

In 1933 a minor FP reunion took place at the Inter-University Sports in Glasgow when a party of some six from Edinburgh and a least one from St Andrews met colleagues in a break from degree examination preparations.

After the former Rector departed in September 1919, there was a period during which Mr W Scrimgeour was in charge until 6th October, 1919, when Mr Angus MacLeod took over. He arrived as scheduled despite the fact that the first post-war Railway Strike operated from 4th to 11th October of that year, during which one train a day arrived in Oban.

However the new Rector was not without visitors. On the 8th the School Cadets, under Mr Wood, were inspected by Colonel Brown, accompanied by Major Bennett, Chairman of Argyll Education Authority, and Dr Campbell, Oban. On 10th October Dr C M MacDonald, Director of Education, made his first visit. The second week showed signs of a diphtheria epidemic, with up to ten notifications in one day, but the Rector was able to have his first meeting with all three years of the Junior Students, between 4 pm and 4.30 pm, when he lectured on teaching methods. At the end of the week he deputised for the Art Master, the first of many hundred occasions on which he filled gaps in the timetable. The next two weeks brought the exclusion of three classes from which the great majority of the diphtheria cases came, and the MOH did not permit the school to open fully until 3rd November.

On 11th November the school closed at 1 pm "... the day being a general half holiday on Armistice Anniversary Day. At 11 am, when the church bells rang, the pupils stood in their lines at attention for two minutes." This the first ceremony became the general pattern in the twenties and thirties, except that when the weather was doubtful everyone assembled in the Hall. This was followed nationwide until 1939, the ringing of church bells being the signal which brought traffic to a halt.

Another echo of the War brought an unscheduled half day on 18th November, when seven women teachers were asked to attend an afternoon function at which awards were being made in recognition of extra war work. "With two others off, the depleted staff could not cope, so the school was closed at 1 pm."

One interesting development of an old idea of the first two Rectors was the resolution of the newly formed Argyll Education Authority to provide school hostels for Argyll County Bursars in the three main schools - Campbeltown, Dunoon and Oban. This was reported in the press on 9th August, 1919, and action obviously having been taken (probably by September 1920), the Rector reported on 9th December, 1920, that "of all the Bursars *not* residing in the Hostel whom he interviewed, none desired to leave their present rooms". Oban was therefore quickly off the mark as far as the girls were concerned, and no provision was made for boys who lived in lodgings until over thirty years later. First lodgings were usually recommeded privately to the parents, but thereafter changes were made, usually on the initiative of the pupils themselves. Full board cost 15/- to 21/- per week in 1923 to 1928, which was more than twice the pre-war rate, and that covered all meals, everyday, and no weekends away from Oban in the session. Ninety per cent of island pupils went on holiday only three times a year, the single day holidays, Fast Days etc being useless because of travelling arrangements. A train excursion to Glasgow was possible, but service buses did not exist, though many local buses were available for tourist excursions in the Season.

A considerable number of "train pupils" came daily from as far away as Ballachulish and Dalmally, and many of these were away from home up to eleven hours. They brought their own provisions which they heated in two rooms provided in the Woodwork and Cookery Blocks. There was an experiment introduced by Mr MacLeod on 27th November, 1919, when he interviewed the train pupils regarding "the provision of soup at 1 o'clock in the school". This began on 8th December when twenty took advantage of the offer. It is not known how long this continued or what the charges were.

The Magazine of June 1919 shows that the Girls' Club continued throughout the War. The Boys' Club was functioning in January 1920, when a list was posted of masters charged with evening duty. The Magazine of 1923 contains the important announcement under the Literary and Debating Society report: "The Society involved an amalgamation of the Boys' Club with the Girls' Club, which was dissolved when the School Company of Girl Guides came into being .... Special features ... a paper on 'Norway' with lantern slides by Mr Scrimgeour and an amusing paper on the *Mikado* by the Rector .... The Society owes much to Mr Milne, who was responsible for the new move, and a good one. He attended all the meetings and in every case proved a great help." George Milne arrived in January 1922 and he continued to help the Society by his attendance and his comments on the talks and on the contents produced on "Hat Nights".

The School Cadet Corps was apparently founded in 1917 in time to earn the very complimentary report in February 1918. Regular inspections are reported until June 1922, but no further record has been traced until a diary records on 5th June, 1926 "the first meeting of the

75

resuscitated Cadet Corps". Thereafter regular reports of inspections, together with further details, appear in the School Magazines until at least 1934. No magazine seems to have been issued in 1935; but the customary Cadet Corps report does not appear in those for 1936 and 1937, nor was the Corps listed as parading at the Oban ceremonies at the time of the funeral of King George V in January 1936, when the Scouts and Guides did participate.

The School Log entry for 7th February, 1928 records: "In accordance with the request of the Town Council on the occasion of Earl Haig's funeral, the school was closed at 1 pm today. The School Cadets and Boy Scouts were on parade for the memorial service at 2 pm in Oban Parish Church." In addition to these there were the two detachments of Territorials and a huge contingent of ex-Servicemen (British Legion etc), who by general agreement constituted the smartest unit on parade. Some at least claimed that the School Cadets came second! Curiously enough, neither unit was in uniform as the School Cadets did not acquire their uniforms until after 1928, when a fund was raised for extras. A photograph taken at the Lochgilphead camp of 1929 or 1930 shows 35 cadets in uniform.

In August 1928 the pupils of Oban High School were divided into three Clans - Fingal, Ossian and Somerled - in order to introduce a measure of competition in various fields. The Editorial in the School Magazine of June 1932 reports: "To several of our school activities the Clan System introduced since our last issue has given order and significance, keenness and point, as well as helpful direction. Altogether it is an aid to smoother working that has been appreciated by scholars and staff."

This statement definitely explains the length of the gap in the School Magazine file from 1929 to 1931 inclusive but apart from the knowledge that I myself missed the "System" by the length of the long vacation, an examination of the newspaper reports of the school sports from 1929 onward indicates the presence of the Clans and the claim that Fingal produced all the winners of trophies in that year can be substantiated. In session 1933-34, the Football Club's winter tournament was organised for the first time by Clan instead of A, B, C etc[3].

The School Magazine of March 1912 states that Shinty was introduced in that Spring Term and that the numbers playing now equalled those of the Football Club. The latter played several matches against town teams as well as the usual five-a-side tournaments. In the 1920s there was no School Shinty team though the game flourished in Oban, especially after Oban Celtic was founded to challenge Camanachd. Most of the schoolboys who played at lower levels were local. However there are indications that five- and six-a-side tournaments were organised by the Football and Shinty Clubs after 1945.

In the 1920s and 1930s the boys played football and hockey, and the girls tennis and hockey. Matches were arranged against local teams and against other schools such as Kinlochleven in the early 1920s and Lochgilphead from 1929 onwards. Hockey matches against Former Pupils (usually mixed teams) were evenly contested. These usually took place before or after the Easter holidays when local FPs from Universities and Colleges were on vacation.

The post-war Cricket Club had practices up till 1925, but matches against a dormant Town Club were rained off more than once. The Town Club team came to life when the Navy arrived and when matches were arranged against the ships. Mr Scrimgeour and Mr MacKenzie, the groundsman, were always included and each time the Head of Mathematics took a wicket the cheers from the schoolboys in the stands brought out smiles of appreciation rarely seen in Room 11.

Tennis was one of the sports introduced by Mr Beattie and it continued to be played by the girls. In 1913, a Cake and Candy sale brought in £76 to provide a new tennis court and to extend the school library.

In Athletics, the Annual Sports was quite a social occasion when many people, including those who provided prize items, were invited. Full programmes and lists of entrants were also printed, the audited accounts showing that the printing bills were shared by the three local weekly papers. The meetings began in 1895, and after a few years in Mossfield, the venue was the Argyllshire Gathering Field. The Rector's Cup was competed for by the Senior Boys; there were items for Former Pupils and exhibitions. The Tenga Cup for the under-16 Boys was presented in 1923, and the Rosebowl for the Girl Champion in 1929, when Frances Gardner was the winner. The only person who won the Tenga Cup twice, in the early years at least, was Angus MacIntyre (1925 and 1926) who, unlike most of the other winners, did not go on to the Rector's Cup as the Science Master persuaded him to apply for a bank vacancy before the end of the school year. His successes in the Highland Games over a long period show that he was perhaps the finest athlete of the two inter-war decades, and had coaching been available inter-scholastic and international success would have followed as they did for his sons.

It is interesting to note that the Annual Sports were incorporated in larger events on more than one occasion. In 1935, the Silver Jubilee of King George V involved assembly at Rockfield for the march to the service at Esplanade Park, followed by a march to Mossfield where Junior Sports were held. The School Championships were part of the Oban Jubilee Sports which took place in the afternoon. Much the same routine was followed on Coronation Day, 12th May, 1937, with the addition of the Provost taking the salute in Argyll Square and the distribution of Coronation gifts from various bodies. In between there were Parades to Argyll Square from both buildings to hear the Proclamation of King Edward VIII on 24th January and that of his brother, George VI, on 15th December, 1936. These were read by Provost MacAllister in English and by Ballie MacNaughton in Gaelic. There were no athletic implications after the pupils of both schools were dismissed for the day at 2.45 pm nor was any record made of the Abdication in either language!

In the middle twenties the school population, at least as far as the Higher Grade was concerned, split into four distinct groups outside school hours. Those whose homes were in Oban went home; the train pupils went off about 5 pm and did not normally participate in weekend activities; the girls from rural areas lived in the Hostel; while the boys from rural areas were in lodgings, for the most part from George Street to the South and East. The last group played a great deal of football, on their own or with town bank clerks etc and occasionally some of the local pupils joined them, especially in the higher classes. Many of the country boys were invited to small dances in the Hostel between the two grand parties, held there in the first and second terms. Mr Milne, the English Master, seemed to play piano for three-quarters of the evening in the same type of dark suit which successive generations saw in Room 12 for over thirty years. There was never any difficulty in getting a second round of 'Strip-the-Willow' as he could go on and on, looking at the dancers most of the time.

The early twenties was a period of change after the breakdown of the Coalition and the General Elections in three successive years brought politics very much to the fore. The rural boys attended as many meetings as possible, mainly to listen to the heckling, an art which has now been lost. Questions were always allowed at the end; they and the answers were clearly heard, though there might be applause and derision after each. The braying of slogans had not been invented.

The schoolboys were not normally admitted until just before starting time, just in case we took up seats for voters. We always argued that we would have a vote at the next election. The Hostel girls did not participate: they would probably not have got permission, and in any event women under thirty had no vote until the "Flappers" Act of 1927.

A notable meeting, unconnected with an election, was that of 1st October, 1927, when the Argyll Conservative Association brought the Home Secretary, Sir William Joynson-Hicks to the Argyllshire Gathering Halls. "Jix" enjoyed a reputation as a wit, and he delivered a rousing speech in which he urged everyone to work harder. As a considerable proportion of his audience was drawing unemployment pay at 15/- per week, this was badly received until it was drowned in laughter as Dugald the Horse's loud voice cut in "You are talking to the platform now". (There were at least three rows of officials, wives and friends from all over the county behind the speaker). Later at question time, an experienced heckler asked for views of the speaker on why the people were recently forbidden to collect firewood from the woods in Tiree. Jix began by the usual time wasting expression of two sides to every question before the Chairman stepped forward to whisper in his ear. The next question was called for after the gale of laughter subsided!

The Conservative MP for Argyll from 1924 was F A MacQuisten KC, also a notable wit who often took the opportunity of talking to his constituents in the street, at places such as the 'Fountain' which stood in the triangular space where the flower beds are in Stafford Street. These meetings, like all others, were publicised by the official Bellman, who in the early twenties was accompanied by his daughter as he was blind, but he had a large hand bell and a voice to match.[4]

Mr MacQuisten obviously enjoyed speaking and handling a persistent drunken heckler, but as his Chairman, if any, had gone, the KC had to devise a concluding vote of thanks to all for listening to him; he said that he considered us "all fit and proper persons to vote for him at the next election".

In the 1920s few households had wireless sets, the telegraph being the usual fast means of communication. Chalmers shop displayed summaries of the special news bulletins issued by the BBC during the General Strike in 1926, while the *Oban Times* office posted up the results of the 1924 General Election as the telegrams bringing the results arrived. We heard that Stanley Baldwin had diverted Winston Churchill's energies into editing the official *British Gazette*, specially produced for the occasion, but that was not readily available to the public in Oban.

The School Log shows that Oban High School was connected to the Post Office Telephone Exchange on 18th November, 1935, though there had been a direct line between Soroba and Rockfield for many years. It is interesting to note that the Oban School Board deferred consideration of the offer of a telephone company until the financial situation for the next session was clear in 1893! Sometime after that the direct line to Rockfield was installed, but when is not known. However, the speedy telegram from the Director could arrive at the school in time for temporary teacher, Miss X, to go home to collect her bag and go off by mid-day train or steamer on the first stage of her way to her next temporary post! There was always a reserve of newly qualified teachers awaiting appointment ready to respond. Many firms had their registered telegraphic address, still advertised along with their telephone when that was installed. Telegrams cost one shilling for twelve words, with an extra 6d on Sunday, Christmas Day and Good Friday, when the Post Office was open for telegraphic business for one hour.

NOTES

1   ie pupils in Classes I-VI but not those Primary classes which from the beginning were taught in four rooms round the Hall in the Soroba Road building.

2   The first recorded inspection of the School Cadets was on 15th February, 1918. The School Cadet Corps was apparently founded in 1917. While it is not mentioned in the School Prospectus of 1915-16 (printed in 1915), in the Prospectus of 1919-20 (printed in 1919) Major James Wood MC, Officer Commanding and Principal Art Master, described it as "of very recent formation". Major Wood had been with the army from December 1914 and the Corps was formed in his absence. He was succeeded as OC in 1921 by Captain T S Lindsay, Principal Science Master until 1930.

3   Clan Diarmid was established in 1947. The Clan system was in abeyance during the Second World War and there were no sports championships from 1940 until the Victory Day Sports of 15th June, 1946 (see Chapter 4). In 1948 Diarmid won three of six relay races.

4   The audited accounts for the first Oban High School Athletic meeting in 1895 includes the Bellman's fee of 2/6, which means that he went round the town for a whole week, as a journeyman's wage at that time was about 6d an hour. It was 7d an hour in 1903.

APPENDIX

ANGUS MACLEOD - GAELIC SCHOLAR

Angus MacLeod's qualifications were in Mathematics and he listed himself as an Assistant teacher of that subject. In the 1920s he took the Fourth Year, working the class at such a pace that we had covered about seven eighths of the Higher Syllabus by the time the Highers were sat in March. This was probably a mistake not rectified until space and staff were provided to separate the teaching of those aiming for Higher from those aiming for Lower Mathematics. He also deputised for absentee teachers in every other subject except French and German. In February 1935 it is recorded "For three weeks the Rector has been teaching all day." It was clear that he enjoyed taking the Gaelic class most of all. The pupils gradually became aware of his growing reputation as a Gaelic scholar, though his first major work did not appear until 1933, when *Sàr Òrain* (three long Gaelic poems) was published by An Comunn Gaidhealach. This is No 1998 in the Scottish Gaelic Union Catalogue compiled by M Ferguson and A Matheson for the National Library of Scotland in 1984.

In 1934 Angus MacLeod, became one of the founders of the Scottish Gaelic Text Society, and, as he had already published one of Duncan Ban Macintyre's poems in *Sàr Òrain*, he was chosen to edit all this poet's work. He had this task on his hands throughout the war when there were not many opportunities to pursue a hobby. The Society was revived in 1947, and the editor had continued his work for he stated on 30th January, 1948 in the first of ten letters he wrote to me "The task of editing with translation and notes has been largely accomplished, but much revision is necessary. What puzzled me I found as a rule was equally puzzling to others. In Mathematics you know if you have got a solution. In Gaelic there seems to be no finality now that the poet cannot be questioned about his wodks and meaning."

I had written to him with some details of the early editions of Gaelic books in St Andrews University Library, largely in the McGillivray Collection, and I was able to lend him some material he required. The letters range from 1948 until 1957, and they give some insight into his devotion to Gaelic and to other work of editing and revising which he carried out without any indication on the title page of his part. A good example of this is the third edition of W J Watson's *Bàrdachd*, published in 1959. On 24th November, 1956 he wrote "I spent many months revising the Bàrdachd for An Comunn. It proved to be a tedious and very exacting task, involving reading the sources of a large number of poems. Some doubtful matter in the Notes has been omitted, and the introduction - metrical section - has been rewritten by Angus Matheson. A measure of uniformity in orthography has been achieved, and the vocabulary has been extended, but we could do only a limited amount in that direction as the estimate was

.. for a simple reprint." However the un-named editors managed to add a net ten pages to his revised edition. D J MacLeod's *Twentieth Century Publications in Scottish Gaelic* (1980) indicates that the preface was signed by "Angus MacLeod Convener of the Publications Committee of An Comunn Gaidhealach". At a later date he complained that "the correcting of proofs for Mod songs has taken up a lot of my time", which shows him as a working Convener.

The Gaelic Text Society received a tender for printing Duncan Bàn Macintyre's Poems in December 1949 and in January 1950 the editor was hopeful that it would be published later in the year, but as he said "Donnchadh Bàn has been kept in cold storage for a long time". *The Songs of Duncan Ban Macintyre* finally appeared as Volume IV of the Scottish Gaelic Texts in 1952 (reprinted 1978). This massive volume, the longest produced for the Society, contains all 63 poems in 6003 lines, with Gaelic text and English translations occupying 419 of the 629 pages. The introduction and notes give very clearly the result of the scrutiny of every line of each poem in the six main editions which had variants. Work in such detail had not been attempted, or condensed into such orderly tables and notes. *The Songs of Duncan Bàn MacIntyre* will remain as the chief monument to Angus MacLeod's scholarship, but it is interesting to find that he had undertaken an even greater task before he had received the proofs of Duncan Bàn.

Sometime in 1950, the original editor of Alexander MacDonald's poems found that he could not continue, and the Publications Committee passed the task to Angus MacLeod, who had earlier edited the poet's "Birlinn" in *Sàr Òrain*. In a letter of 22nd December, 1950, in which he requested the retention of certain volumes, he wrote, "I would like these books for reference at the proof reading. Well I am to continue this work ... I have been asked to take up the work on AMD - first of interpreting some 3,000 'hard words', and of preparing text and translation. This is a tough job that the Publications Committee has passed on to me, but the Donnchadh Bàn experience will be helpful in some ways. In any case it is a worthwhile occupation and I shall do what I can with it."

It was clear from the page of titles and queries which followed and from the fact that he had already ordered a photostat that the "tough job" had been begun. It was even clearer in a long letter of 30th December, acknowledging several volumes, when a foolscap page on the scope of the new task finished with the comment "One trouble with the AMD vol or vols will be the vocabulary. He will require a small dictionary!"

The work continued intermittently, but by 24th November, 1956 the editor was able to say, 'I am now at the stage of noting variant readings in A MacD's poems." By 6th March, 1957, when A MD's Third edition was acknowledged the news was "Next week I shall be switching on to L C Maths papers; and the marking takes me about three weeks' continuous work, so Gaelic will have to be pushed aside till April. The correction of proofs for Mod songs has taken up a lot of my time, but I think we have come within sight of the end of that darg."

His work on Alexander MacDonald was not published but some of his poems are to be issued shortly, when no doubt the editor will be able to acknowledge the work done in the 1950s by Angus MacLeod before failing health brought it to a close. He was President of the Scottish Gaelic Text Society for some years before his death.

As an editor Angus MacLeod took endless trouble to establish the facts, and those who heard him lecture to the Literary and Debating Society in 1927 will remember the scepticism with which he viewed the treatment of Highland history by Lowland and English historians. He set out the various versions very clearly. Twenty-five years later he told how he had written scores of pages to possible sources at home and in Canada, until he finally got the answer he needed from Corpach. He could be amusing on the results of his searches, as for example the Highlander whose reported date of birth was 1709, but who was stated elsewhere to have been "out" in 1715 and 1745 - "a good lad he must have been if dates are correct".

He always wore a frock coat, but the later tradition that a top hat was part of his outfit was certainly not true in the mid 1920s. I saw the top hat only once in the school in five years. There is no doubt that his activities as a Gaelic scholar helped him considerably as a relaxation from the heavy demands made on his time by the ever-increasing burden of school administration. Some of this comes out in his correspondence, as for example when he acknowledged receipt of books, he would complain that he could not begin on them until later, as happened as late as January 1950, when he had to deal with the Ministry of Labour demands for very full reports on every pupil who had left at Christmas. His comment was "The only detail not required appears to be the mother's maiden name".

He could also relax: when he and Mrs MacLeod visited our home in St Andrews in September 1950, my wife and I, both former pupils, were astounded to find that he and our shy two year old daughter played hide and seek round the settee on their hands and knees, while we talked to Mrs MacLeod.

His devotion to the well-being of the School was not in doubt as his letter of 22nd December 1950 concludes: "I felt leaving OHS more keenly than I could have believed, but a spell at the Edinburgh Festival and a very busy life helped to ease the situation, and I am now thankful that the burden rests on the sturdy shoulders of my friend John Maclean!"

CHAPTER 4

World War II to 1950

LAKE FALCONER

The decade of the forties was the third and final one of the long reign of Angus MacLeod as Rector, and in many ways it must have been the most difficult, coping as he had to with the austerities and shortages of the war years, which seemed to increase in the post-war period. In spite of it all he remained seemingly unruffled, never allowing slackness to creep in, and retaining his immense dignity as he continued to stride the corridors of the school clad majestically in black frock coat and winged collar. The very sight of his approach was enough to strike fear into the hearts of malingerers, and even innocent hard working pupils experienced a vague feeling of guilt on seeing him stride towards them. Nevertheless, the frock coat was not constantly in use: each summer he would lead a party of senior pupils on an ascent of Cruachan, clad in immaculate plus fours.

His work load must have been immense, for, as well as keeping up with the regular work of administration, he readily filled the gap in almost any department, teaching with equal ease English, Maths, Gaelic, Latin and Science. He did not, so far as one recollects, try his hand at Modern Languages, which he probably regarded as frivolous, and of course the minor subjects of Commercial, Music, Domestic Science and Technical were devoid of any academic content and did not merit his attention.

In 1939 the School re-opened after the summer break on Wednesday 30th August without incident, although the School Log notes that Mr Milne was not on duty "owing to a misunderstanding about the date of opening". One wonders if the unfortunate "Nick" was treated with as much severity as a forgetful pupil might have been!

But already the coming war was casting a shadow. Some of the pupils had devoted part of their summer holiday to the work of assembling and packing civilian gas masks, and on Friday 1st September the School was dismissed before 10 am "in accordance with instruction received in connection with the Government Scheme for evacuation of School children from Glasgow. The staff are engaged on duties connected with billetting these children in the town and rural areas".

So, too, were some of the pupils. The Scouts were involved in helping with the actual arrival of the evacuees, meeting the special train when it arrived and marshalling the long crocodile of children marching from the railway station to Rockfield School, where they were fed, documented and distributed amongst the somewhat unwilling householders of Oban.

Everything was then ready for the blow to fall, and it did. The School Log solemnly records on Monday 4th September, "A state of war between Great Britain and Germany having been declared as from 11 am Sunday 3rd September, schools are to remain closed for the present. The staff is still engaged on duties connected with the evacuation of children from Glasgow. Many children who have been sent from populous areas to reside with friends and relatives in Oban and district are being provisionally enrolled."

Although it was hoped that schools might re-open on Friday 8th September, further instructions from the Government postponed this until the following Wednesday. Before it re-opened, however, the first gap appeared in the ranks of the staff. "Mr A H Davidson, Science Master, who was in the reserve of officers, has left to join his unit in England." Thus the Log records the first of what was to become a steady flow of men from the School staff to the armed forces and to industry.

It was not until 13th September that the school eventually opened, and its first task was to absorb the large number of evacuated pupils who had arrived to live in the comparative safety of Oban. The greater part of the train-load of government evacuees were of primary school age, and enrolled at St Columba's, St John's and Rockfield, which at that time was, administratively at any rate, part of Oban High School and under the command of Angus MacLeod. Eighty-seven evacuees were admitted to Rockfield and forty-one to the High School, which had to cope, in addition, with fifty-two privately evacuated children. The addition of these ninety-three pupils to a roll already standing at 391 must have imposed a real strain on the Rector and staff. The School Log rather plaintively records "classes are now very large". They certainly were.

The government evacuees were all from the Glasgow area, coming from homes in Springburn, Govan and Maryhill, while the private pupils emanated mostly from Glasgow and Edinburgh, with a handful from addresses in Dundee and London. There were some well-known names listed as their former schools, Alan Glen's, Glasgow High, Trinity Academy, Boroughmuir, George Watson's, James Gillespie's, Dollar Academy and Edinburgh Ladies' College among them.

The strain of coping with the swollen roll started to ease fairly quickly, however, when many of the evacuees, finding that the war was not affecting their home towns and that life in a country school was not to their taste, returned to their homes. The trickle back started in early October, and quickly became a flood, with almost all of the government evacuees having gone by the end of the year. The private pupils stayed the course a little better although their number suffered some leakage too, but it swelled again a year later when the war had taken a turn for the worse and a further thirty-three private evacuees arrived, many of whom came from Luftwaffe target areas in England, such as London and the industrial Midlands.

By early October the Rector was able to record in the Log that work was proceeding normally and attendance was good. To some extent the work was hindered by the lack of text books - "evacuated pupils have been slow in procuring books". At that time, of course, pupils had to purchase their own text books and stationery, and one remembers well the huge and ill-disciplined queue which would form at Hugh MacDonald's book shop in Columba Buildings, alas now gone, where the books were stocked.

Although the evacuees came to Oban for safety, the School had to take account of the possibility of the town becoming a target area itself. This was a real possibility, for Oban quickly became a busy Naval base and merchant ships of all sizes assembled in the waters of Lorn to form convoys. Indeed, there was an air raid in December of 1940, when shipping was attacked by a solitary Heinkel, with some casualties. The town became an RAF station as well and throughout the war squadrons of Sunderland and Catalina flying boats operated a convoy escort and anti-submarine campaign from Oban Bay. They too attracted the attention of the Luftwaffe. At school there were practices in "taking up stations for air raid precautionary measures". It proved to be impossible to curtain all the school windows to comply with the blackout regulations - quite apart from the cost involved, the art room windows and the rooflights in the Central Hall presented an almost insoluble problem. As a consequence, the school hours had to be shortened during the winter months. It was more than a year before a partial blackout could be achieved, and not until May of 1942 that the Central Hall rooflights were covered over, with the Rector expressing anxiety that no wire netting had been placed on the inside. Heavy glass falling from this height might, he thought, cause serious damage.

Another precaution against bomb attack was the pasting on to the inside of windows of anti-splinter netting and the older boys were diverted from class work to carry out this task. At first they thought this would be a great wheeze, but they were quickly disillusioned. The netting was impregnated with glue and had to be soaked in water, after cutting to size, to make it stick and the adhesive was a fish glue. The boys soon realised that it was an odious and odorous task and were relieved to complete it and return to classes. It was a long time before the unpleasant smell disappeared.

In October Mr E T F Spence, Physical Education master, was the next staff member to leave for military service. For some unknown reason, he was known as "Wee Magoo", but he bore no resemblance to that myopic cartoon character. Later in life, he was to become the second staff member to become Provost of Oban, following the example of Mr Donald Thomson of the Gaelic department, and he went on to be Chairman of Argyll and Bute District Council. His place in the gym was taken by the return of Mrs C MacLachlan who, as Miss Morrison, had been a PE teacher for many years. Her husband was a prisoner of war, having been taken with the 51st (Highland) Division at St Valéry.

The winter of 1939-40 was very severe, and the combination of weather and illness affected attendance very badly; it fell to 73% in January. In spite of this the work went on and the Leaving Certificate exams were held as usual in March. No centrally set exam took place this year because of staffing difficulties at the Scottish Education Department and the papers were set and marked by the teachers, after which they were sent to the Department for scrutiny. A diversion for the younger pupils during the Leaving Certificate exams was a performance of Miss Waddell's Childrens' Theatre, sent to the school by Glasgow Education Department for the benefit of the evacuated pupils, few of whom remained. One remembers a peculiarity of Miss Waddell - each "turn" was preceded by the sudden parting of the curtains to reveal an apparently disembodied head which announced in dulcet tones "Item number so-and-so ..." followed by details of the item, and which then as suddenly vanished.

April saw the departure to the forces of Mr Allan MacDonald of the English department, whilst in May two senior figures in the school left. Mr A E Hope went off to become principal teacher of Maths at Grove Academy, Dundee (he was later to become Rector of Harris Academy there which was confusing for a school whose motto was "In hope we labour"!) and Mr D McCorquodale, the Attendance Officer, left to become Governor of the West Highland Rest. Mr McCorquodale, as "whipper in", was a well-known figure in the town and would appear quite early in the day at the home of an absent pupil to seek the reason. He knew the favourite haunts of truants, quickly smoked them out and herded them back to school - and the wrath of the Rector.

And so the first session of the war years came to a close. There was no prizegiving "because of the war conditions", although the usual closing ceremony took place and was addressed, no doubt to the intense boredom of the pupils, by a local dignitary. Amongst those awarded the Leaving Certificate was one George K B Henderson, who was to become one of the School's more distinguished alumni, going on to become Episcopal Bishop of the Diocese of Argyll and the Isles and Primus of the Scottish Episcopal Church.

The list of names of the staff who had served through the year triggers many memories. Mr George Milne headed the English department, and presided in Room 16 with immense dignity. He is remembered as an outstanding teacher, who treated the girls with an old-fashioned courtesy and deference which the boys thought both inappropriate and undeserved, and he had a talent for bringing the subjects he taught to life. One wonders what he did to warrant his sobriquet of "Nick". He was ably assisted by Donald Macfarlane, who was inevitably nicknamed "Spanky", after a well known strip cartoon character of the same surname in the *Dandy*, by Miss Jessie Rose, Miss Davina Speed, Miss M A Dow and latterly by Miss May MacLaine, all well liked and able teachers. Miss MacLaine, happily still with us, was responsible for this writer's grounding in English and will no doubt read this with a highly critical eye. The only remark on his report card which he can remember was by Miss MacLaine, who commented in 1940, as she will no doubt say today, "could do better if he tried ...."

The Mathematics department was led by Mr James W Troup, on whom no-one would have dared to confer a nickname. He was simply known as Jimmy, and it is interesting that this habit of familiarity seemed to arise only with teachers for whom pupils had respect tinged with a degree of fear. He was an interesting and charming man outside the school, but inside it he brooked no indiscipline, no distraction, no inattention and no incompetence. Stories of his forays from Room 3 to chastise a passing pupil who failed to tiptoe past his door are legion. He was wont to throw any handy missile at an inattentive pupil, but one bold spirit picked up a piece of chalk which had landed on his desk and threw it out of the open window. "Oh, sir," e replied, "I thought you had finished with it." Jimmy, for once, was speechless. He was ssisted in the department by Miss Agnes Coats, later to become Mrs Hardie, wife of the Head f the Technical Department.

Modern Languages were under the command of Miss M A Skinner, universally known as Mary Ann, a formidable teacher, but a kindly soul. She took a keen interest in all her pupils, ollowing all their careers after they left, and was always anxious about former pupils serving n the forces. One remembers the day when the news came through of the simultaneous inking of the *Prince of Wales* and the *Repulse* off Singapore: Mary Ann was reduced to tears nd had to dismiss her class. One of her less attractive traits was her habit of growing pot plants n the class room: as these included tiger lilies which were highly odorous, Room 12 was not opular on a hot day. She was assisted at this time by Dr R Wilson.

Latin and Greek were the province of Mr George Galt, as Head teacher, and Mr John Thornton. Mr Galt was an excellent, if hard teacher who paid little heed to period bells - he taught on until e realised that the next class was queuing at his door, and to find oneself timetabled for Latin last period on a Friday was agony. The bell to indicate the end of the day, and indeed of the week, rang and was ignored to the discomfiture of all, until eventually a country pupil begged eave to depart for his train.[1] Mr Thornton was a complete contrast. A man with a brilliant mind, who taught Maths with equal facility, he had no idea how to control a class, and baiting Big Mo" in Room 21 became a favourite if cruel pastime. Occasionally, a teacher from nother class had to enter his room to quieten the noise. He was later to become Principal Teacher of Classics at Grantown-on-Spey where, to the complete astonishment of his Oban pupils, he was known as a strict disciplinarian. Oban had taught him something, the hard way.

n the Science department Mr Thomas Marshall, who had come from Glasgow with the vacuated pupils, was in charge in the absence of A H Davidson, assisted by Dr Alex Wood nd Mr Fred Seddon. Mr Seddon was a Liverpudlian by origin and sometimes a little ncomprehensible. He carried, for some reason lost in the mists of time, the nickname of "Wee Bran", which some innocent pupils thought was his real name.

Miss Morgan ran the Art classes single-handed, Miss Whyte was in charge of Domestic Science with Miss Flora MacKinnon, and Technical was under the capable charge of Mr Norman T Hardie, whose initials were alleged to be an acronym for None Too Handsome. Mr William Lees operated the Commercial department from the commanding heights of Room 5, whence he turned out a steady stream of budding accountants and highly competent shorthand typists. Mr Donald Thomson (Donald Beag) with the assistance of Miss Catriona Lowe taught the Gaelic classes. Head Janitor was Colin Campbell, a caring man always ready with a plaster for a broken knee, and (until the practice was stopped during the war) diligent n the ringing of the school bell, sometimes a little early to the consternation of those of us still auntering along Combie Street or queuing for sweets in Katie Watt's Tearoom in Soroba Road. He had Kenneth Graham as his number two.

Romance had blossomed amongst the staff during the session, for March saw the wedding of two members of the English department, Spanky Macfarlane and "Beaky" Dow.

The opening of the 1940-41 session brought a second wave of evacuees, and two new classes had to be formed, one in Fifth year and another in Second year. The problem was compounded by a wave of departures of male teachers on military duties or war work. At the end of August Dr Wood was called up for war service with Imperial Chemical Industries, with no replacement available, Mr Hardie was called up to the RAF in September and Mr Macfarlane departed for the Royal Navy in December, to be replaced by his wife, the former Miss Dow who had only been away from the staff for a matter of months. In those days, married ladies on the staff were unusual and were only engaged on a temporary basis.

The summer holiday in 1940 had been shortened to allow for the release of pupils in the autumn to help with the ingathering of the harvest and lifting of the potato crop. In a hill-farming area like Argyll, this was rather pointless, but the Autumn break was always known as the potato holiday and greatly enjoyed by the pupils. It was even more pointless for those pupils who did have farming connections, for it occurred well before the main crop was ready for lifting, and in a later year the Log laments (on 29th October) that attendance was low, partly due to work on potato lifting, with or without permission. The school itself had a go at raising potatoes, plots having been opened in the playground, most likely where the HORSA huts now stand. The Log records, in September 1942, that "one of the potato plots ... was cleared this week. The yield is poor, due to lack of manure, and wet weather probably".

The spring of 1941 saw the formation of a branch of the Air Training Corps, which became 729 Flight, ATC, and flourished for several years. Curiously, it was the only pre-service organisation in the School, although there was a branch of the Sea Cadet Corps in the town and on the demise of 729 Flight after the war, a branch of the Army Cadet Force was formed under the command of Captain Bill "Nobby" Clark.[2]

The ATC Flight was welcomed enthusiastically by the boys, although their initial ardour was somewhat cooled when it was discovered that the first lecture, taken in after school hours, was entitled "Calculations" which turned out to be Maths in disguise and was given by the Rector. They recovered from this setback however and went on to study exciting subjects like Aircraft Recognition, Navigation (boyish imagination took the boys on long flights over Germany, fighting off attacks by ME109s and FW190s, but they unwittingly picked up some geographical knowledge in the process), Signalling and Engine Maintenance. The Flight was commanded by George Milne as Flying Officer and Jimmy Troup as Pilot Officer, while the Flight Sergeant was Donnie Graham, one of the senior pupils, son of Kenny the Jannie, later in life to become a successful dentist in the town and the respected Session Clerk and Precentor of the Free Church.

There was great excitement as the time for summer camp drew near, to be completely dissipated when it was announced that the camp would be at North Connel airfield. The main ambition of every cadet was to get up in an aeroplane and it was known that there were none at Connel, which was simply an emergency landing strip. There was near mutiny in the ranks, and something of the discontent must have reached higher authority for there was a last minute change in location, this time to RAF Grangemouth.

The Corps set off by train with high hopes. In those days the up train crossed the down train at Balquhidder, and when both were alongside one another another ATC Flight was discovered, going west. "Where bound?" we cried, and how we laughed and commiserated with them when we were told they were going to Connel. They had the last laugh though. RAF Grangemouth turned out to be a fighter station with nothing but single-seater aircraft and 729 Flight was grounded. The lads who went to North Connel had a great time, as the RAF flew up a transport plane for the express purpose of giving the visiting ATC a flip. Our turn came, however, as later on the RAF stationed a de Havilland Dominie, a twin engined biplane with ten or twelve seats, at North Connel and the Oban boys were at last able to get off the ground. Later on the cadets were able to get occasional flights in Oban's Sunderland flying-boats, not on patrols of course, but while they were on routine exercise or test flights.

The mundane work of the school went on, relieved only by such excitements as the discovery of girls playing truant from French and Science by hiding in the third year cloakroom, by the ceiling of Room 7 collapsing (no-one hurt) and by another staff romance in the marriage of Mr Hardie and Miss Coats. Among those awarded their Leaving Certificate at the end of the session was another destined to become a distinguished alumnus - Iain A MacMillan went on to become President of the Law Society of Scotland and a Sheriff and was awarded the CBE.

The re-opening of the school after the summer holiday of 1941 found more gaps in the ranks. Mr Marshall, the Science master on loan from Glasgow, had gone off to war work and Colin Campbell (Collie the Jannie) was on war service. Kenneth Graham was now head janitor with John MacCallum (Big John) as his assistant. Following what was now an established pattern, Mrs Hardie (nee Coats) was back as a temporary teacher, as was Miss Lowe of the Gaelic department, who was now Mrs McClements, while to the astonishment of the boys Mr Hardie's classes in woodwork and metalwork were taken by a lady, Miss Minnie MacKinnon. The next two months saw quite a few staff changes with teachers coming and going so rapidly that they are scarcely remembered.

The health of the pupils was always a matter of concern and August brought the doctors to the school to inoculate the pupils against diphtheria. A few days later the Log laments "Attendance low today owing to the effect of injections"!

At this time, and indeed throughout the war, the School enthusiastically supported the National Savings Movement. Each week the pupils brought along their modest shillings or florins (or in the case of the very rich, their half crowns!) which were recorded in a contributions book, and when the total reached 15 shillings (75p) the money was invested in the purchase of a National Savings Certificate. Special efforts were made from time to time to coincide with national campaigns, and in October "Warship Week" produced a total of £930 3s, a creditable effort.

January of 1942 saw the introduction of the Milk Scheme, under which each child was entitled to a daily $\frac{1}{3}$ of a pint at a cost of $\frac{1}{2}$d. The administration imposed yet another burden on the hard pressed staff. The School had visits at this time from recruiting officers from the various armed forces, although given that conscription was now in force this seemed rather pointless.

The Leaving Certificate results that year must have caused some unease, for the Log notes that the Director of Education and a Committee member visited the school to discuss the results with the Rector and Mr Milne. It was agreed that an appeal for reconsideration should be made to the Education Department in four cases. In the event eighteen Certificates were awarded.

The next session seems to have been a quieter one, there was the usual drain of male teachers to the services, this time from the Gaelic Department - Mr Donald Thomson went off to the RAF Educational Service. There was the usual epidemic of matrimony amongst the staff, with Miss Davidson (the Rector's secretary), Miss Helen MacArthur (PE) and Miss Morgan (Art) all leaving to be married. All three returned, as Mrs MacDougall, Mrs Ross and Mrs de Gaye, on temporary engagements. There was some concern in the spring when a girl was removed from the Hostel suffering from sore throat and suspected diphtheria, as a result of which all the Hostel pupils were excluded from the school. Most returned a week later. Another worry was the onset of accidents in the gymnasium. A special visit was paid to the school by the Director of Education and four members of the Committee to see for themselves the performance of an exercise in which a girl had fallen from the beam. The deputation decided that the exercise was not of a dangerous nature and that on this occasion every care and precaution had been taken by the teacher. One can almost detect the feeling of relief which this finding must have engendered. There are those of us who remember the torture of the beam and the bars with less than enthusiasm! Another special savings campaign resulted in an even better performance: "Wings for Victory Week" produced a result of £1,261 16s while a collection taken for the "Aid to China Fund" resulted in £29 8s 6d being sent to Lady Cripps.

Dux of the school was the Rector's own son, Alasdair M MacLeod, and twenty-six Leaving Certificates were awarded.

When the school re-assembled after the summer holiday of 1943, the number of pupils had grown yet again. New classes IVa and IIIc had to be formed, and at general service the numbers were too large for comfortable seating. First year pupils were instructed to go to their usual RI rooms with their teachers instead of attending the usual weekly service. In the course of this session a scheme for supplying mid-day meals, initially for travelling pupils was introduced, a forerunner of the modern school meals system. A dining facility was arranged in Stevenson Street, rather disparagingly known as the Soup Kitchen, and meals were prepared in Craigard Hostel and carried down. The organisation of this and other extra-mural schemes again made inroads into staff teaching time. Time had to be spent, for example, in measuring pupils to assess their eligibility for supplementary clothing coupons (getting an extra allowance was some consolation for being known as "Fatty"), in checking respirators, and in the continuing work of National Savings. A special effort for "Salute the Soldier Week" brought in the very creditable total of £1,505 and a collection was made for the relief of Greek children.

The Rector's problems were compounded when Mrs McClements left at Christmas, leaving the Gaelic department without staff. An arrival, however, to the Science department was Mr John MacKinnon from Campbeltown. He had the misfortune to arrive at the time when the film "Kipps" was showing at the Playhouse and, as he bore a remarkable resemblance to the eponymous hero, he was instantly so christened by the pupils. This seemed to be standard practice in the Science department, as Mr A H Davidson also attracted the name of a film star, long forgotten, to whom he bore some resemblance. It was about this time, when Kipps had left some senior pupils on their own in the lab, that some wag devised the great wheeze of attaching the footpump to the gas tap and pumping air back down the main until gas cookers in Soroba Road started to go out. One shudders to think of the possible consequences of that prank.

Twenty Leaving Certificates were won.

September of 1944 saw the School re-open with an increased roll yet again. Evacuees were no longer the problem, as only eleven remained: the cause seems to have been an unusually large intake at Fourth year level, from the Junior Secondary schools at Tobermory, Lochgilphead and Tarbert. The strain was eased a little by the return to the Science department of Dr Alex Wood, released from his work in industry by the Ministry of Labour.

The mid-day meals scheme must have been a success, because the autumn of 1944 saw an expansion: as the Log says, "Contractors have begun operations in the playground for the building of a kitchen and dining room in connection with the scheme for school meals." Bearing in mind the grave shortage of building materials at this time *propter bellum*, it must have been regarded as an important measure as well as an act of faith in the future.

These were stirring times, of course. The war was going well, with Allied troops driving eastwards through Europe and the Government being able to take time off from the conduct of the war to debate and pass the Education Act of 1944. The demise of the old playground would be regretted by few - it was a dreadful stony area, optimistically referred to as a football pitch, and was the cause of many a skinned knee. Prior to the war, and for some years after it, the School had the use of the adjoining stadium of the Argyllshire Gathering, and it was a matter of intense annoyance to the Rector when it was requisitioned by the RAF and denied to the School. One remembers football on the old stone playground as being more than somewhat chaotic: we played fifteen or sixteen a side without any distinguishing colours and totally dependent on the one ball. If it burst, as it frequently did, that was full time and the result at that point stood. These were the days when footballs were of leather with an inner bladder of rubber. When that leaked, it was necessary to find a puncture repair outfit, itself a scarce commodity. For all that one remembers these days with nostalgia.

Mumps hit the school in December and winter weather in January. For almost the whole of that month there were no country pupils at school because of ice-bound and snow-bound roads. Even town pupils were affected and by the end of the month the attendance had dropped to the astonishingly low figure of 37.5%. The easing of the sever freeze brought more problems when the school was infested by burst pipes, and several classrooms were flooded and had to be closed. Poor Angus MacLeod - and yet he coped. The annual report of the inspection at this time concluded "War conditions have imposed considerable strains on the school, particularly in the Secondary Division, but standards have been substantially maintained. High commendation is due to the staff as a whole, and a special tribute must be paid to the headmaster for his unperturbed efficiency in dealing with the problems which have confronted him, as well as for his sympathetic and able guidance of his less experienced colleagues." This was truly a fitting and well deserved compliment to an able man. Unperturbed and imperturbable he certainly was, amongst his many other qualities.

Spring brought the excited anticipation of the approaching end of the European war, and the hope of better and easier times to come. Mr Loynd and Miss C A MacDougall were granted leave for one day to play at a concert in the Playhouse in aid of the "Welcome Home Fund" and on the 8th and 9th May the school was closed "on the occasion of the cessation of hostilities in the European war, the Germans having surrendered unconditionally to the Allies", as the Rector rather formally recorded in the School Log. One remembers the great feeling of euphoria which pervaded the school at this time and it was sensible to declare a holiday - nobody would have turned up, so great were the jollifications everywhere.

An important visitor at this time was the Moderator of the General Assembly of the Church of Scotland, Rt Rev J A Campbell DD, who addressed the pupils at the weekly service, and four days later saw the end of the last of the war time sessions. The number of Leaving Certificates dropped to twelve. Dux of the school was Archie Lamont, later to become a distinguished minister of the Church of Scotland, (was he inspired by the Moderator's visit, one wonders?) "Kipps" moved on to Dunoon, and Dr Wood left to return to ICI. Presumably teaching was no longer to his liking.

The first session of peace time opened with the commissioning of the new canteen, with over 100 pupils making use of its facilities, and the staff included Harry Davidson at the head of Science again, back from the forces. He had had a distinguished career serving in the Royal Engineers and returned as a Major, with an MBE. It was his proud boast to have fought in two world wars, for he was an infantryman in World War I, and could tell some entrancing tales. He sometimes did, to the detriment of Science!

Fourth and Fifth years again had to be divided into two sections. Very soon, another two warriors returned in the persons of Donald Thomson and Colin Campbell. For all that, the Rector still had his staff difficulties, and was probably most affected by the departure of his secretary Mrs MacDougall (Annie Davidson). He plaintively records in his Log "Rector has no clerical assistance this week, and has been unable to overtake this work in addition to teaching and supervision." After a month she returned on a temporary basis but only for some three or four weeks, prompting, after her second departure, the comment "Without clerical assistance the rector has found it awkward to supervise his classes." It must have been bad for an uncomplaining man like Angus MacLeod to record such remarks. The problem was soon solved by the arrival of Miss Isa MacInnes, initially for afternoons only, but full time after she was released from her "essential" post with the County Medical Officer. Isa quickly became one of the characters of the school, much loved by all.

October saw attendance affected by an outbreak of scarlet fever "and by cattle sales", which seem an extraordinary combination of causes. Were the streets blocked by droves of cattle, one wonders, or was it just an excuse to play hookey? Perhaps agriculture should have been on the curriculum.

Kenneth Graham, the Janitor, was appointed Attendance Officer. Mr Spence returned from the forces in December, Mr MacFarlane in January and Mr Hardie shortly thereafter.

In June there took place the (somewhat belated) Victory Day Sports arranged by the school Athletic Association, in which Harry Davidson was a leading light, and sponsored by Oban Town Council. The event was held at Mossfield Park and was a huge success. The Rector's Cup for boys' champion was won by Norman K Wilson, who went on in life to become a PE teacher, and the Rosebowl for girls went to Florence Gardiner, with Samuel Mactaggart taking the Junior Championship. It was about this time that Norman Wilson with Bill Gabriel, represented the school flight of the ATC in the Victory Parade in Edinburgh.

As an end of term treat, the entire school was taken to the Playhouse to see a showing of the film *Henry V*. One wonders if there was as much trysting in the back row of the 2s 3d seats as normally happened on a Saturday evening.

The end of the school year in June 1946 also saw the end of an era, when Miss Mary Ann Skinner finally retired as Principal Teacher of Modern Languages. The Log speaks of a teaching career extending over forty-four years, but it was longer than that, for Mary Ann had done her first teaching in Oban High School in about 1895. She had been an entrant under the old Pupil Teacher Scheme (abolished in 1905) under which a pupil wishing to become a teacher was indentured as an apprentice at the age of thirteen. On finishing the apprenticeship the pupil could sit the Queen's Scholarship Competition at a Training College. Miss Skinner did this in 1899, and gained first place in Scotland, the first of three Oban High School pupils to gain this award. She was the daughter of Hugh Skinner who, after a time as a teacher of the Free Church school, went to the newly opened Rockfield School in 1877.[3] Thus arose a splendid family tradition of education in Oban, which went through to a third generation.

The nineteen pupils who gained the Leaving Certificate that year included Anne I MacPhail, who was soon to return to the school as an assistant in the Commercial department, remaining there until her retirement and setting a record almost, but not quite, as long as Mary Ann Skinner.

August 1946 brought at start of term some new faces to the staff. Miss Skinner's niche was filled by Mr Henry (Harry) Dobbins, remembered by one pupil as devastatingly skilful at controlling trouble makers by ridicule. John Cook took over the PE department in place of Mr Spence, who had gone to Dunfermline. Miss Helen Dent also joined the PE staff and the Maths section was enlarged by the arrival of Mr William J Clark, inevitably to be known as Nobby, who went on to establish and command the School section of the Army Cadet Force. The work of the School was at first handicapped by the lack of textbooks and stationery, which had not been received. This was the first year in which the textbooks were supplied by the Education Authority instead of having to be purchased by the pupils.

The School was still being targeted by the forces for recruits and was visited by a military lecturer from the Ministry of Information who gave a "lantern lecture" and in November the school conducted an examination for entrants to the Royal Naval College, Dartmouth. There was one candidate, but history does not show if he was successful.

Bill Gordon took over the Art department and Donald Morrison joined the Gaelic section, two men who subsequently gave the school many years of diligent service. In February the Macfarlanes (Spanky and his wife) left, he to become Principal Teacher at Invergordon.

These staff movements apart, nothing of great note seems to have happened at the school, or perhaps the Rector had lost his enthusiasm for recording events in the Log. In some ways this is surprising, for the winter of 1947 was one of the worst for weather for many years. Snow lay deep on the ground for many weeks, the frost never relaxed its grip and the situation was compounded by a very serious national fuel shortage. The School must have had its problems, from low attendance to burst pipes, but these are not recorded. Nevertheless, the work went on, and went on successfully, for twenty-six pupils were successful in gaining the Leaving Certificate that year. The School entered four choirs in the local Mod, as well as a number of individual competitors. The Rector is too modest to record how many of them returned triumphant.

The Mod - this time the national one - figured early in the Log for the next year, with both Senior and Junior choirs participating at Perth. Again the Rector refrains from boasting about their successes. It may be that he was distracted by the posse of painters who descended on him to paint the 1933 extension and thus conceal the graffiti of the first fifteen years. Classes had to be decanted to the Central Hall.

Mr George G Galt (pupils were convinced that his middle name was Gaius) left the Classics department to move to Dunoon, thus depriving the school of the chance of claiming to have wholly educated another successful FP. His son Eric, who had noticably received no favours while a pupil under his father, went on to study law and became a Sheriff in Glasgow. In his place came Cunningham B Irving, a keen yachtsman who became Commodore of Oban Sailing Club and was later tragically lost at sea with his wife. They had set off on their annual summer cruise and after leaving Coll were never seen again. The yacht drifted in to the Ardnamurchan shore with all sail set and no-one aboard.

The School was beginning to indulge in extra-mural activities which required funds not allowed for in the Education Committee budget, and a sale of cakes, vegetables and jumble in the Central Hall in October raised £205, a handsome sum in those days. The 1947-48 session produced two unexpected holidays: days off were allowed for the wedding of Princess Elizabeth in November and for the celebration of the Silver Wedding of the King and Queen in April.

In the spring a strike of bus drivers prevented many country pupils from attending, although some brave souls walked in from Dunstaffnage, but it was quickly resolved. Most unusually the School suddenly indulged in an orgy of boxing: it was closed one afternoon for an exhibition in the Central Hall of the manly sport by primary and younger secondary boys, with another bout for the senior boys next day. The experiment was never repeated. Later in the spring there was a challenge Hockey match between staff and pupils which resulted in one casualty - Miss Munsie of the Modern Languages department was off for days afterwards with a sprained ankle. After the Leaving Certificate exams, still held in March in those days, there was the usual visit by inspectors: among them, examining for Latin and Gaelic, was one John Maclean, later to become the school's next Rector. In June the recently organised County Youth Sports took place in Oban with Harry Davidson heavily involved along with many other staff members. The Rector laments that the work of the School was considerably disorganised by the vast amount of preparation involved, and the school had to be adapted to provide living accommodation for pupils from Tiree and Islay.

The start of the 1948-49 session saw many changes. The roll had risen to 531, partly due to the raising of the school leaving age in the previous year to fifteen, and classroom accommodation was stretched beyond feasible limits, with classes having to be taken in the Central Hall. The problem was relieved by the transfer to Rockfield of the top primary classes which had always previously met in the High School building, occupying rooms on the ground floor off the Central Hall. The strain was thus thrown on to Rockfield, which had to resort to taking overflow accommodation in the Free Church hall. Eventually the problem was met by the building of the HORSA huts in the playground, the horrible acronym standing for Hutting Operation for Raised School Age. Although intended to be only temporary, they are still in use over forty years later.

Culture was again on the menu, with a party of senior pupils having an organised outing to the newly established Edinburgh Festival, where they saw the film *The Red Shoes* in the afternoon and the ballet *Coppelia* in the evening, and with the entry of two choirs in the national Mod in Glasgow. This time Donald Thomson was also there, as an adjudicator. With his absence along with Mr Loynd and two other teachers functioning as chaperones, chaos reigned in the class organisation, but this was an annual problem. The building was beginning to show its age - a ceiling came down in Room 8, just to compound the Rector's difficulties.

It was about this time that signs were emerging of a strong FP movement, and the Log records that the Director of Education attended the school in December to attend the annual reunion of IV, V and VI pupils with FPs. A school concert was held in June, with a matinee for senior pupils as a dress rehearsal, followed by two public performances.

Sadly, the Rector was unable to complete the term. He fell badly while walking to school and broke a leg, having to spend several weeks in the Cottage Hospital; Mr Milne as Depute Head saw the term to its conclusion.

The last year of the decade started with chaos at the school. Workmen were engaged in the reconstruction of the Technical and Domestic Science building and these classes had to be fitted in elsewhere. It was not until the end of October that the building was ready (complete with the new-fangled AC electricity!), but simultaneously with the opening of the new building the boiler serving Rooms 1, 2, 3, 12, 13 and 14 gave up the ghost, and room had to be found elsewhere for the classes normally occupying them. Three weeks were to pass before these rooms were habitable again.

A little excitement encouraged the School's esprit de corps when an Oban High School team was entered for the BBC's schools' quiz, *Top of the Form*. In the first round, held in the gym, a team of four boys defeated four girls from Madras College, St Andrews by 29 points to 21, but alas, they fell at the next hurdle a month later, going down to Elgin Academy in an away match 35 to 30. The cult of anit-elitism brought an end to such frolics.

Fire drill was always a regular feature, with the building usually being evacuated in one minute. A drill in December was followed a week later by an outbreak of fire, but it occurred after school hours. The fire was in the Science store off the balcony and was discovered between 5 and 6 pm by Janitor Campbell. He telephoned the fire brigade but managed to deal with the blaze himself with an extinguisher and little damage was done although a potentially disastrous situation existed because of the proximity of chemicals. Mr Seddon had apparently left some batteries to charge unattended and the Rector had some hard things to say to him the following morning!

There was a sad record in the Log in February, where it was recorded that a fourth year boy from Mull had died from bronchial pneumonia. He had been at school two days previously. The Rector and four staff members attended the funeral and the Rector followed the cortège to Tobermory.

On a happier note, one learns that four teachers, Miss Kay, Miss Munsie, Mr Shepherd and Mr Troup, were absent to take part in the national final in Glasgow of the Scottish Community Drama Association festival. Sadly, the Log is more concerned with recording their absence than the result. As it happens they did not win, but it is much to their credit to have got that far.

The senior pupils were treated in June (that demob-happy time of year) to a lecture by Professor William Ewart of Glasgow University on "The Moon and Planets," and once again the School participated in the County Youth Sports, this time in Campbeltown. The team was led once again by the indefatigable and enthusiastic Harry Davidson.

The era really came to an end in June, with the retiral of Angus MacLeod. The whole school assembled in Oban Playhouse where George Milne, as second master, presided over what must have been an emotional and happy affair. Rev William MacDonald spoke on behalf of the former pupils and presented volumes of *Carmina Gadoelica* and a wallet of notes to the Rector on their behalf. Spokesman for the present pupils was Miss Elizabeth MacDougall, who handed over books and another wallet of notes. Master Martin Whyte handed a gold wristwatch to Mrs MacLeod and Maureen MacCulloch presented a bouquet of roses. The Director of Education spoke, the School Choir sang and afterwards the FPs and friends were entertained to tea at Rockfield. A memorable day.

Four days later the School again assembled for the prizegiving. Amongst those leaving school at this time was another pupil destined for greater things: Iain Davidson, son of A H, rose to become Professor of Chemistry at Leicester University and is now Pro-Vice Chancellor there.

Angus MacLeod did make one nostalgic visit to the School after the summer break, on 31st August, when he met the classes and staff, and bade them farewell. Next week his successor took office - the same John Maclean who had visited the school as an Inspector.

Throughout the decade Oban High drew its pupils from the three Primary schools in town and from a host of country and island feeder schools. Many of them travelled long distances, and were away from home for long hours, some from 6 am to 7 pm. These pupils were, of course, transported free of charge, mostly by bus, but quite a number by train. There were two trains involved, the Glasgow train, which picked up pupils from as far away as Dalmally, and the Ballachulish one, and in both there were compartments reserved for pupils, quaintly labelled "Scholars". There was intense rivalry between the two trains, amounting almost to gang warfare, and missiles would fly between the two trains, to the discomfiture of the ordinary passengers. Railway staff did what they could to control the situation, but sometimes had to invoke the aid of the Rector. One knew that trouble was brewing for somebody when it was announced at morning assembly "Ballachulish train pupils will report to the Rector's study at 12.30 pm". Who had broken the luggage rack by swinging by the heels from it, or who carved "A B loves C D" on the panelling? The Rector would find out and retribution would ensue.

The Glasgow train, being made up of corridor coaches, could be and was patrolled by the railway staff, but it was otherwise on the Ballachulish line, where tales of pranks were legion and mostly unprintable. As an example, one daring soul would leave the compartment when the train was running and edge his way along the running board clinging on to the handles and hinges until he reached a "civilian" compartment, where he would make a face at the window. Many a crofter's wife travelling home in the dark after a day's shopping in Oban was frightened out of her wits by the appearance of a ghostly face pressed against the window. On another famous occasion a railway employee decided to enforce discipline and at Benderloch entered a compartment full of girls who were misbehaving. He was forcibly ejected from the train at Barcaldine minus his trousers, which were never returned. In spite of all the high jinks there was usually a reasonable rapport between the train staff and the pupils. The driver (known as Baldy or The Red Indian) knew those whom he picked up at each station and would delay his departure for a few minutes to allow a tardy pupil to catch the train.

There were, of course, pupils who could not possibly travel daily, mostly from the islands or the peninsula west of Loch Linnhe, and these had to stay in Oban. For the boys this meant digs, but for the girls there was Craigard Hostel, opened in 1920. Not everone was happy there, but there was an element of compulsion and a girl who declined to stay at Craigard and elected to go into digs would find her bursary cut. There had to be discipline of course and a curfew, but on Saturday evenings the girls were allowed a late pass, and on those nights, as curfew hour approached, every dark corner of Craigard Road and the Hostel grounds would be occupied by a resident with her consort for the night, and they weren't discussing Tolstoy. Miss Mackintosh was Matron initially in these years and later Miss Jackson. Catering at the Hostel could be difficult, of course, in the years of rationing and was a cause of great concern at a meeting of the Education Committee in February 1940. *The Oban Times* reported that considerable discussion took place - a Mr MacPhail spoke of the supply of meals: he had heard of complaints. Mr Skinner retorted that an enquiry had been made at the Hostel "but not a single girl would open her mouth" and emphasised that Miss Mackintosh was an excellent Matron and disciplinarian.

Rather cruelly, *The Oban Times* juxtaposed this item with a report that Miss Mackintosh was resigning to take over the Central Hotel. A subsequent issue of the paper carried a letter signed "Class Six" refuting the criticisms. "As residents of the hostel for a number of years," they wrote, "we are well able to say that not one of us has ever found cause for complaint concerning the food or the manner in which it is served ..." Miss Mackintosh is in fact usually remembered with affection by former residents.

There was always a social life at the School as well as an educational one, and at Christmas the annual dance was always a highlight. It was never called a dance, but was referred to as "the School Musical". The gymnasium was gaily decorated by the Art Department and the catering looked after by the Domestic Science staff and pupils. When the budget would not rise to an orchestra, Mr Milne would perform at the piano. The sexes kept apart, the boys lining one side of the gym and the girls the other, and at the conclusion of a dance the boys just abandoned their partners and returned to the male side of the hall. There was no gallantry in those days.

Oban High, then, had its problems in the 1940s, but was a happy and hard working School remembered with affection by those who passed through it. It produced good results and, as we have seen, some distinguished FPs. Great credit is due to Angus MacLeod for his success. Lesser men would have failed to cope with the strain. But then he was a Lewisach.

1   On Mr Galt's teaching at a time when the evacuees attended the School, Dugald MacArthur relates the following: "I was once asked by an Edinburgh colleague which school I had attended. The name of Oban High School brought the immediate response 'That is a good school. When my two sons returned to George Watson's after being in Oban, they found that they were ahead of their classmates in Latin.' I am sorry that I never had the chance of passing on this tribute to the work of Mr Galt."

2   See Chapter 5.

3   See Chapter 2.

CHAPTER 5

The Fifties: a Campaign for Academic Success and Technical Innovation

COLL MACDOUGALL

Just as Angus MacLeod made his last entry in the School on 31st August, 1950, with that brevity which left out so many details, "The Rector met classes and staff to bid them farewell and this afternoon classes and staff assembled in the Central Hall to be addressed by the Rector who demits office today. His successor: John Maclean MA will enter duty on Monday 4th September", so John Maclean announces his arrival equally succinctly: "Mr John Maclean, the newly appointed Rector, was introduced to the staff and pupils today. The school was given a half holiday in honour of the occasion".

While his entry may have been brief the ceremonies consequent on his arrival were not. The great and good of the community appeared in the Central Hall to be addressed at length by those who felt their importance to be such that the shortest speech which they could decently make was at least twenty minutes in length. John MacNaughton, Chairman of the Education Committee, presided and informed all of Mr Maclean's undoubted talents, "... one of the foremost scholars produced by Scotland in recent times". He was not new to Oban and the School as he had visited there on many occasions before when he had been one of HM Inspectors of Schools. Donald MacDougall Skinner, a former Provost of the burgh and a member of the Education Committee since 1919, extended good wishes to the new Rector as did John Munro, whose family connections stretched back in the annals of the history of the School almost as long as those of ex-Provost Skinner[1]. Finally, and much to the relief of the pupils (the youngest of whom were seated on benches and the middle ranks on chairs with standing room only for the seniors on the balcony) came T G Henderson, Director of Education, who extended a welcome - as George Milne had done before him for the staff - and offered all possible assistance from the administration. But, best of all, he declared a half holiday to mark the occasion.

The following day John Maclean writes: "Mr Maclean took up duty as Rector". But, who was John Maclean? He was one of a remarkable family of seven from the Island of Raasay where his father, Calum, was a crofter/tailor and Curstaidh, his mother, a lady of great charm and determination. All seven of them went on to distinguish themselves academically with John, Calum and Sorley being particularly outstanding figures.

After attending Portree High School John graduated with First Class Honours in Classics at Edinburgh University and went on to further study in Classics and Celtic at Cambridge, Vienna and Uppsala. He started his teaching career at Inverness Royal Academy and became an Inspector of Schools, paying frequent visits to Oban High to inspect in Classics and Gaelic. From a list of distinguished applicants and a short leet of five, all of whom would have made outstanding Rectors, John Maclean was chosen to succeed Angus MacLeod.

The contrast, sartorially and otherwise, was obvious even to the smallest, youngest first-year pupil. Gone was the stiff formal dark-suited figure with black homburg hat; instead there was a relaxed, smiling man in a suit of contemporary fashion and colour. Soon he had learned the names not only of all his staff but of his pupils as well, and in many cases could trace their ancestry if they were native to the West Highlands.

But all was not sweetness and light. Although the Logs record little of what went on behind the closed doors of the study or at staff meetings, it soon became clear to the pupils that John Maclean had plans to formalise many of the facets of school life, to bring a new approach to others and to create for the brighter pupils an era of academic excellence even beyond that which his predecessor had achieved.

Colleagues and pupils learned quickly that he did not like any disturbance to the timetable, over which he had spent most of his summer. If there must be distractions - such as mid-term holidays and a day off for the Argyllshire Gathering - then steps must be taken to see that classes missed were rescheduled. He does not seem to have been too happy about three days being given to cover the Teachers Conference - a feature unique to education in Argyll - and the visit of H C Dent, the Editor of the *The Times Educational Supplement*, was more of a distraction than an honour.

While there had been rumours about conflict between the new Rector and the staff over alterations to existing rules and practice, the first indication that John Maclean intended to formalise a school hierarchy of Captains and Prefects came with their installation eight weeks after his own. Cynthia Gray and Lamont MacKay were the Captains and the first Prefect were: Bella Munro and Hugh MacLean, Helen Graham and Donald Smith, Fay Thomson and Kenneth MacRae, Sheila McSporran and Iain Clark - the clan Captains. In addition, he introduced an election system for a further eight Prefects, who were on the surface elected by the pupils of the senior classes, but were in reality vetted by both himself and the staff.

While no-one objected to the appointment of Captains and Prefects the manner of their selection and the vetting procedures paid scant respect to the principles of democracy which they were supposed to illustrate. Indeed throughout the decade there were incidents which must have haunted John Maclean and caused him to wonder if he had not set too high a store by the system which he had promoted. While he was quick to point out that the duties and privileges which those so set apart enjoyed were to give them leadership experience and that the holding of such office would be useful on applications for admission to university or other forms of further education, many of the staff and of the senior pupils believed that it would have been better to have devised a system which gave all sixth year pupils some such status while ensuring that there also were a number of fifth year pupils who had that experience as well to enable them to lead their contemporaries the following session.

Concern about forms of government and the performance of pupils in the "terminal examinations" - as he always referred to them - gave way in the early days of 1951 to a severe bout of influenza which hit both Oban High and Rockfield, where, of course, the Rector was also Headmaster. Forty -two percent of the pupils succumbed as well as many of the staff. In addition, he had a rash of burst pipes which put six classrooms out of commission.

As he completed his first term and had time to take stock at his new home in Polvinister Road, what did he see? A world which was still recovering from the effects of the second Great War, a Labour Government struggling with severe economic problems as they strove to develop the welfare state, war in Korea, conflict in Malaya, continuing strife on the Indian continent and, closer to home, a crofting society which was in many cases struggling to survive and missed their children as they came to Oban and digs, very few of whom would return to their villages or islands to bring the benefits which their education could give. Many years later Sir Robert Cowan, the Chairman of the Highlands and Islands Development Board, was to stress that one of his urgent tasks was to try to encourage the growth of "age-balanced" communities in so many of the more remote areas of the Highlands.

On his doorstep, John Maclean was conscious of the fact that Oban High lacked enough classrooms to accommodate its growing roll - in Ia in 1950 there were forty-six pupils. It lacked playing fields and proper sporting facilities and it lacked a shinty team - something which he had enjoyed in his days at Portree.

There can be no doubt that he took full advantage of T G Henderson's offer of administrative assistance to stress over and over again the need for more staff. It is noticable in his Log that he records the departure of young teachers who had not been with the school for very long, but who were able to gain rapid promotion as a result of the teacher shortage. Bill Shepherd, who taught modern languages well and made some real effort to provide religious education which was interesting and relevant, was one of those who moved on quickly. Undoubtedly he took advantage of gaining a promoted post, but he also indicated that he found the Rector's obvious bias towards the Classics and Gaelic difficult to come to terms with, as did his Principal, Harry Dobbins.

While John Maclean imposed a strict discipline on the pupils, introducing detention for lateness and for a number of misdemeanours, and was not loath to use the tawse if he thought it necessary, he carried this rigidity over to his control of the staff, who found it irksome. Throughout his career there is just one incident where he records his great displeasure at the conduct of a teacher and records it in no uncertain fashion. When investigated the matter is trivial in today's terms, but was obviously a matter of great importance to him. Being free last period on a Friday afternoon the teacher in question decided to slip away from school ten minutes early. The miscreant was spotted and summoned to the study on the following Monday, where, if the Log is an accurate reflection, a most terrible dressing down was delivered and remarks were passed about a poor standard of teaching. It is somewhat ironic that some months later the Log also records that the same teacher had demitted office on appointment to a promoted post elsewhere. It is also interesting that this is the only mention of teaching ability in the Log for the whole of the decade although all who were at school in that era could name several teachers who were unable to control a class or impart knowledge because of that flaw.

With a great Gaelic scholar as a Rector it was highly appropriate that the Gaelic department of Oban High School should be a distinguished and forward thinking one. The influence of Donald Thomson and Dan Morrison on Gaelic education was enormous. The introduction of the Leaving Certificate for Gaelic learners is just one of their achievements in a time when there was considerable apathy, if not downright antipathy, to the language. Donald Thomson's service to *An Comunn Gaidhealach* as teacher, adviser, adjudicator, administrator and ultimately President was justly recognised by Her Majesty the Queen with an OBE. It is to the discredit of some members of the Argyll Education Committee that they questioned the amount of time off which he had to fulfil these important duties. Fortunately they were in a minority; but they were also Gaelic speakers!

In February 1952 the nation was in mourning for the sudden death of His Majesty King George VI. The Celts' ambivalent attitude to death became obvious to many pupils for the first time. While Christian doctrine stresses to all that death is no more than passing to life eternal and freedom from all paid and travail, the Highlander seems to place more emphasis on a public display of mourning, long, dreary prayers and eulogies. So it was for the late King. It was expected that boys should wear black ties and girls sober clothes during the official period of mourning. This was relieved only by the proclamation of the new Queen at a ceremony redolent with military panoply in Argyll Square.

There was no holiday on the day of the funeral. Instead the Rev Donald MacKenzie of the Free Church, as School Chaplain, conducted an appropriately solemn service of remembrance in the Central Hall. Mr MacKenzie, a man of grave disposition, was affectionately - if somewhat cruelly - nicknamed "Happy" by many pupils who found his monotonous delivery somewhat wearisome. For many years he was to preside over the Leaving Certificate examinations as invigilator and could be guaranteed to do two things: to make the profound statement, "Since we have been x minutes late in starting we will be x minutes late in finishing", and, as soon as he had got the examination session underway, to open his leather case, open a bag of sweets and proceed to unwrap a sweet very slowly, disturbing the concentration of all but the most avid examinee. In later life he turned out to be a good friend, an interesting and knowledgeable companion who was expert at explaining the intricacies of the stock market - something which the Mathematics department had tried, but, in my case, it had not succeeded, to elucidating the meaning of "bulls and bears" or "stock options and breakfasting".

Strange as it may seem, during the Second World War the school does not appear to have had a military connection in the form of a branch of the Army Cadet Force. There had been a branch of the Air Training Corps but no connection with the county regiment, the Argyll and Sutherland Highlanders. This was remedied by the visit in June 1952 of Colonel Biddulph and Major Gordon and the creation of a branch of the Army Cadet Force in the School, linked to the Argylls, under the command of Captain William J Clark, Lieutenant David Ramsey and Lieutenant James Page. As Bill Clark was known affectionately to all as "Nobby", the Cadet Force quickly acquired the title of "Nobby's Army".

For the boys who did join - the age of equal opportunities for girls was decades away - there was the benefit of freedom from classes on Friday afternoons and splendid camps which took many to England for the first time. For them there was also the drawback of having to wear the kilt and suffer the taunts and ridicule of their fellows. For them too was the chore which every recruit to any of the services has experienced, the performance of bull - the endless hours of polishing equipment and blanco-ing webbing and puttees. Although many of the families in the area had suffered grievous losses in the war, which had ended just seven years previously, there does not appear to have been any opposition to the setting up of the platoon. Indeed, many saw it as good training for National Service, which was still compulsory and was to remain so for a number of years. The cadets' prowess at shooting and, in particular, that of Iain Cleaver - now a highly successful hotelier - won the County Commandant's prize over and over again, much to the delight of the Rector who records their achievements in the Log in much more detail than most other successes achieved by the school.

Bill Clark was a man of many parts. All who came in contact with Nobby found him a capable teacher of Maths and of English (when he was allowed to teach it). Despite his public school accent he was very much a Scot and a staunch supporter of Scottish Nationalism although he never tried to inculcuate his beliefs in his pupils. At the time of the removal of the Stone of Destiny from Westminister Abbey he endured with great good humour the drawings which appeared on his blackboard of a stick-figure pushing a barrow with a large stone in it away from a large church. His interest in crofting led him to acquire a holding at Benderloch and to bring his practical knowledge of agriculture and horticulture to the benefit of numerous pupils who were given basic lessons in gardening.

Pupils remember Nobby for his sailing exploits in *The Elk*, an eight metre racing yacht which had come to the Cadet Force under the aegis of the MacDonald family who were to be condsiderable benefactors of the school in this era. While no one ever suffered anything more dangerous than a thorough soaking from falling overboard, the skippering of such a large and fast craft did present Nobby with new challenges and its leaky state presented his crew with arm-aching tasks in manning the pump and bailing buckets.

Bill Clark died very suddenly on a summer evening in 1967 on his croft after a day's racing in *The Elk* during a West Highland Yachting Week. He was buried with full military honours on a dark, damp August day at Achnaba churchyard with an enormous concourse of mourners in attendance. By the time he died he had been promoted to the rank of Major, but he never needed to require respect for that rank: he got it from his cadets and pupils as a man whose actions fully merited it.

If Bill Clark was breaking new ground for a school in an area where connections with the Territorial Army were and are strong, the arrival of Miss Anne Duncan to give the girls a course in Health Education at the request of the Education Committee was greeted with ribald comments and smutty jokes behind held-up hands. In a school in a predominantly rural area few pupils of either sex believed that they needed to be lectured on "the birds and the bees". Unfortunately from what the boys could glean from the girls who attended it appeared that Miss Duncan was a great believer in avoiding the direct approach and the direct question, preferring to hide behind some vague illustration from plant or animal life. But, as the girls were quick to point out, it did get them away from normal classes for two or three periods a week while the boys were denied such a luxury. The boys were also allowed, as far as the Education Committee was concerned, to remain officially in blissful ignorance of matters sexual although there were plenty of unauthorised sources from which they acquired half-truths and downright falsehoods, as they found out from experience in later life. Fortunately, sex education for both boys and girls has come a long way since these prurient days.

If Miss Duncan was not the most effective communicator Dr Katie Anne Brown and her nurse colleagues were very efficient school doctors. Each year they appeared to check on the basic health of a third of the pupils and to report on their discoveries to the pupil's own doctor or to send a note to the pupil's parents recommending dental or medical treatment. Dr Brown, herself a former pupil of the school, with strong Tiree connections, was everyone's favourite aunt. No one ever complained about having to visit her, but some did find the rare visits of her colleague Dr Robert Hardie, with his military manner, unlikely to earn him the title of uncle.

Just as Dr Brown was an on-going presence in the life of the school, so were the heads of a number of the major departments but few were regarded with the same degree of warmth as she was.

In considering how to cover the last few years of the long career of George Milne, Head of the English, History and Geography Departments, a major conflict of conscience arises. From those who had benefitted from his teaching in the two decades prior to the fifties one was inculcated with the belief that here was someone who was just a degree lower than God. His understanding of Shakespeare, Spenser, Milton, Pope and all the classical poets was reckoned to be superb. There would be no difficulty, the young fraternity was told, in acquiring such a wide and dynamic knowledge of English literature and language that a high pass mark in the Leaving Certificate was almost guaranteed.

For those of us who encountered "Nick" in the fifties such was far from the truth. In an age when the visual image of television was beginning to make itself evident and radio was well established the old-fashioned formalism of his approach to the teaching of English turned most students off Shakespeare and many other writers. In two hours at home, listening to the radio, one could hear *Hamlet, Macbeth, Julius Caesar and King Lear* declaimed by many of the actors who were later to become the knights and dames of the theatre. Such wonderful writing was then reduced to Nick's cold, analytical, line-by line annotation of the tragedy or comedy which left its sense and beauty unrevealed and undesired. To take two terms to read one of the plays was enough to put off the most ardent student. Indeed, it took most of us a number of years even to contemplate again opening one of the books which we were required to study for the English Higher under George Milne. When he retired in 1955 a breath of fresh air swept through the English Department with the arrival of Ewan MacDonald and Iain Crichton Smith.

Lest it be thought that I should be so prejudiced that I would not recognise that others found qualities in the man which I did not, let me quote from what John Maclean said of him at his retirement ceremony in 1955 " ... a philosopher, guide and friend. Not only a teacher, a soldier and a well-known footballer - a jack of all trades who could do almost everything. In working for the school he has worked far harder than most people for the community and for this part of Argyll. As Rector I am very sad at losing him and I shall miss his advice and help."

If George Milne did not inspire his latter-day pupils his successor, Ewan MacDonald, certainly did. His modern approach to English literature and language as a living, vibrant means of communication brought a new understanding to many facets of the subject. His constant illustration of points and situations by reference to contemporary events, contemporary writing and contemporary media was as much a "wind of change" for Oban High School as was Harold MacMillan's speech on the future of Africa which has embedded that phrase in English usage. Suddenly the writers, the journalists and the poets who were communicating currently were recognised as valid - no need to be three hundred years dead to be important. Included in this group was a young poet from Lewis whose work was just beginning to become known: the same Iain Crichton Smith who had joined the staff at the same time as Ewan MacDonald. I am happy to say that Iain has given me hours of great pleasure in reading his poetry and has opened my eyes to new situations in life in his prose.

While George Milne was duly listed at the beginning of each session as the principal teacher of History he never taught it in my time at Oban High. In his stead there was the inspired teaching of Andrew J Murray, whose modern methods of making the student search for answers in the prepared text ensured that thought processes were exercised and thought was necessary to understand what the sequence of events was. Apart from that, Murray drew up a list of important dates with a succinct summary of the events which they represented. These were the bare bones of the most significant happenings in history and provided every one of his pupils with handy reference points to which they might relate all other events.

Each five years a whole body of Her Majesty's Inspectors of Schools descended over a period of several months to examine pupils in all years and at all levels of intelligence. Months later they sent a copy of their report to the Rector and this is entered in the Log. Of Andrew J Murray's new approach to the teaching of history it is recorded in 1953: "A new syllabus, involving certain unusual and interesting teaching methods, has been experimentally introduced. Judged from the response of classes, particularly in the first three years, the innovations are meeting with considerable success, and the oral answering of Classes S IB, S IIA, and S IIIA gave evidence of enthusiastic and effective teaching. The experiment is an interesting one provided the burden of fact does not press too heavily on pupils in the first and second years, and is discreetly lightened for those of mediocre ability. European parallels tend to be emphasised too soon, to the total exclusion of Scottish affairs. Faulty English in written examinations should be more severely punished. Praise is due for what has already been achieved, and particularly for the fostering of deductive reasoning in which many of the older pupils, for example, in Class IVB, showed to advantage."

The comment about the total exclusion of Scottish history was rather unfair as both Andrew Murray and Donald Brown, who joined the staff in August 1953, did utilise local historical research to illustrate much wider points. If they had not informed the pupils about the Distillery Caves and MacArthur's Cave and of the significance of Dunstaffnage Castle and Ardchattan Priory no one else would, for most primary school teachers believed that the events of 1066 and 1314 were of earth shattering importance while real, local, immediate history was of no consequence.

If the Inspectors' report came down firmly on the side of Andrew Murray, there were those teachers who were not so favourably treated. To most of the pupils who took French and German the Modern Languages Department was well and popularly staffed. All its members, with the exception of one, could control and motivate classes, yet the report is particularly critical: "State of the Department not more than moderately satisfactory. Not enough being done to give those who leave at fifteen a knowledge of spoken language, customs and life of France . . . better vocabulary needed and greater ability in translating from French into English." To those of us who benefitted from Harry Dobbins' teaching this report is astonishing. Moreover he was a very popular teacher, not only because he could teach without reducing the level to an abject fear of being belted. His dry, sardonic wit was certainly appreciated by his senior pupils and his streak of inherent rebellion endeared him to all teenagers. Likewise, Margaret Munsie and Elma Robertson were highly thought of and went on to gain promoted places elsewhere with the greatest of ease.

Jimmy Troup's innate contention that all pupils were thick and that most were incapable of understanding the easiest of deductions made for a difficult and fraught basis for the teaching of mathematics. His stentorian attitude to the pupils contributed to him being feared at the most tolerant level and loathed by those for whom the theory behind quadratic equations and the Pythagoras theorem would forever remain a mystery. It was Harry Dobbins' theory that teachers who were outstandingly good at their subject were not really good at teaching it as they could not really comprehend the problems which many less able pupils found in it.

Jimmy Troup was testimony to such a belief. He could not understand why everyone who sat in Room 3 could not grasp instantly the intricacies of algebra, geometry and trigonometry. His insistance on all pupils copying down his examples, worked out on the board, was no answer to a lack of understanding, but almost no one had the courage to ask him to explain away their difficulty for fear that such would initiate a ferocious bellow, a thrown piece of chalk or board duster. When he had weeded out all whom he believed to be incapable of anything other than simple addition and reduced his class to those who might be able to cope with at least First Ordinary Maths at university he became a much more civilised creature who did discuss and explain what the Euclidean theory was all about. Yet, for all his fearsome reputation he had a kinder, lighter side. No pupil who was ill in hospital was ever unasked for - or not visited.

As a sportsman, choral singer and amateur actor he dropped the fierce mask and became a great companion with a delightful sense of humour. Long after I had left school he told me that when he first came to Oban he did treat his pupils gently and they took the mickey out of him. Thereafter, he vowed that if the only thing which most pupils would understand was a "reign of terror" then that was the way it would be, and that was the way it was. No wonder shoals of the non-mathematically minded made as early as possible an escape to the classes taken by Margaret MacNaughton, Bill Clark and Bella MacClure - although her tongue could have a distinctly acid taste if she was riled.

If Jimmy Troup was so feared that he did not even acquire a nickname the same could not be said of Cunningham Irving, the head of the Classics Department to whose tragic death reference is made in the last chapter. He was known as "Wee Duffy" to pupils who would never darken the door of Room 14 for the study of either Latin or Greek and to all of those to whom he tried with varying degrees of success to impart the mysteries of such. Small of stature, a fair disciplinarian and a kindly man, he was popular with his pupils and could even be encouraged to show that there were lighter sides to the Romans and Greeks. With a withered right hand he still made a formidable adversary on the tennis court and he was a sailor who could control a boat and race it successfully.

Although he was the Head of the Classics Department he was often robbed of its brightest pupils for John Maclean was a Rector in the mould of his predecessor, Angus MacLeod, and believed that he should be a teacher as well as an administrator. He was fortunate that the mountain of paper which every senior teacher has to cope with today was still kept to reasonable proportions and there was not the constant demand of the educational hierarchy that he should attend this seminar and that "in-service" course. This enabled him to syphon off from the senior classes studying Classics pupils of outstanding ability and, on occasion, those whom he believed needed stronger, individual teaching if they were to get through their Higher. These study sessions were held in his room and were fortunately interrupted from time to time by the pressures of administration as he had a nasty habit of issuing homework at the beginning of a period as well as at the end of it. If the hard-pressed pupils protested he pointed out firmly that his Headmaster in Portree frequently did exactly the same and that he expected both sets of preparation to be done for the next day.

f Cunningham Irving ever felt aggrieved at being deprived almost totally of the bright stars f his department he never made any comment to any pupil about it until long after they had eft school and university.

f John Maclean revelled in the pursuit of teaching Classics he never, as far as I can remember, ried his hand at Science. I think it was a closed book to him and he left it firmly in the hands f A H Davidson (better known to all as "Charlie Chase"), Fred Seddon ("Wee Bran") and Garth Kay ("GAK"). Despite spending a considerable amount of time telling bored pupils ow he won the war, Charlie Chase could point to a continuing stream of notable university uccesses. Today there are a number of professors in the scientific field who owe their basic nowledge to Major A H Davidson MBE.

t would be impossible to ignore Major Davidson's two distinguished colleagues, Fred Seddon and Garth Kay, for both made a distinctive and significant contribution to the life of he School and to their department in particular. Both had the difficult task of implanting the pasics of Chemistry, Physics and Botany into the entire gamut of first year pupils from the very pright to the allegedly dull. Wee Bran's contribution to the teaching of the basics of Science, and several other subjects, to a generation and a half of West Highland pupils cannot be underestimated. It is a great pity that just one sentence in the Log pays tribute to him and no eport appears in *The Oban Times* of his retirement and presentations to him. Anyone who came in contact with him knew him as a character, a sort of typically absent-minded scientist who, in fact, did have all his wits about him and who was never fooled by any pupil who hought they could "take the mickey". Throughout the community he was known for the house which he appeared to be building in Glenmore Road, but which never seemed to get beyond he window stage. The fact that he was making the bricks to go into the houses did lengthen he process somewhat and he never did finish it. After his retirement he sold the site and partially completed building to one of his former pupils who completed a substantial pungalow there.

Garth Kay was known for two things: his ability to teach Physics gently but firmly and his great ove of music. He instituted recorder classes and founded a group which played with great acceptance to pupils and local audiences alike. Indeed, he made a very significant contribution to the expansion of the musical life of the School, which up to then had been limited to one or two periods a week with George Melbourne Loynd, the Gaelic choir and the occasional school concert. Many pupils gained their first insight into making music with Garth Kay and have acknowledged that he brought a new dimension to their understanding of it. GAK - his nickname was simply his initials - was also the music critic for *The Oban Times* and from his reviews one quickly grasped what an enormous knowledge he had of classical music.

It would be unfair even to imply that George Melbourne Loynd, the Head of Music not only at Oban High and Rockfield but in rural primary schools as well, did not also make a significant contribution to the School's musical life, but it was in a different way. In coping with the sheer diversity of the workload placed on him he did an outstanding job. While music plays a major part in the life of every youngster today from a very early age, thanks to radio television and the personal stereo, it was not considered to be important in the life of the West Highland pupil in the fifties. It was a fringe subject to be acknowledged and largely ignored - except for the necessity of the Gaelic choir to do well at the Mod. This Loynd certainly attended to during his quarter of a century at the school. The choir did very well year after year.

As with all musicians G M was expected to entertain the community, play the church organ organise concerts and try to instruct those unwilling souls who were sent to him for piano lessons. All these things he did cheerfully and much more. It was only in the senior years of a pupil's life at the School that one understood just how talented he was, how he could relate the influences of music to art and literature and how he longed for some assistance in the department so that he could offer pupils the opportunity to study music in depth and go on to university to take a degree in it. Unfortunately, Argyll County Council did not see it that way and it was many years later before a proper Music Department was created and the breadth of musical activity which we have today was initiated.

If George Melbourne Loynd ploughed a lone furrow in Room 10 the Art Department immediately above it was well staffed and very progressive when one looks back on it. Although Bill Gordon - fortunately still with us, hale and hearty - did not suggest that every pupil could become a Picasso or a Van Gogh he, David Ramsey and Mrs Stewart - no one ever seemed to refer to her by her Christian name, just "Ma Stewart" - did encourage whatever talent there was against a background where academic excellence was everything and subjects such as Art, Music, Technical Subjects and Physical Education were definitely second class If the academic classes were to be denied access to art - unless it was thought possible that a Leaving Certificate could be obtained - in their last three years they were at least programmed into Art Appreciation, a fact for which everyone who attended these classes has remained eternally grateful. No matter where you are in the world, if you have been through Bill Gordon's lectures and slides on architecture, you are still able to appreciate Doric, Corinthian and Ionic columns, fan vaulting, Gothic, Tudor and Georgian design and the differences between the Baroque and Rococo styles. Likewise, there was an excellent series of lectures on great painters through the ages which informed us of the numerous artists who concentrated on religious scenes, those of the Flemish and Dutch schools who produced disturbing landscapes and detailed interiors with photographic realism, leading to the great English painters such as Constable and Reynolds and finally on to the Scottish scene with Raeburn portraits, the work of the Glasgow Boys and even on to the then contemporary Anne Redpath and William Gillies.

While the Education Committee might have been sceptical about the importance of music in education they were very much in the forefront of the progressives who bought the works of up-and-coming painters, such as Ben Nicolson. For the members of a rural educational body in the heart of the Highlands to be so perspicacious was and is one of the surprising facts one turns up in delving into the history of the school.

While modern ideas and encouragement of freedom of expression were developing in the Art Department the modern approach to Physical Education was brought to the school by the return of Edward Thomas Ford Spence who had taught there prior to his war service. He came back to us from Northern Ireland, whither his predecessor, John Cook, had gone. The latter had one what he could with the limited resources at his disposal as had his assistants, Helen Dent, who later became Helen Davidson, and Chris Morrison, who married Captain Dougie MacLachlan and who died, full of age, as this chapter was being written.

Ford Spence was a dynamic power-driver who argued his case for more money and more equipment with a ferocity which did not brook resistance. He brought a discipline to PE which had been slack during John Cook's reign. His Festivals of Sport brought top class gymnasts to Mossfield Park, where a whole range of sports were demonstrated and where Jean MacDonald's country dancers performed what most of the school had heard her teach in the Central Hall whether they wished to or not. Certainly this dynamic duo made those townspeople of Oban who did not have children at school fully aware of what was going on in the promotion of gymnastics, football, shinty and athletics. Looking back it amazes me that Ford (or "Wee Magoo" as he continued to be known) found time to teach, to coach talented athletes (such as the MacIntyre brothers, Angus, Lorn, Kenny and Eric), develop his home into Kings Knoll Hotel, look after his wife and family, successfully seek election to Oban Town Council (where he joined his colleague, Donald Thomson) and still turn out with the Scottish Country Dance team which entertained the visitors - as they were then called. Immediately on his arrival he campaigned for showers, which he eventually acquired, one of the units being located where the gents' staffroom had once been. Many jokes went round about pupils finding their way through the residual fug of so many pipes which were then the fashionable smoking instrument of many of the male staff.

If there needs to be any proof of the efficiency of Ford's athletics coaching one only needs to look at the report of the school sports of 1957 - it seems to me to be a great pity that there are no longer such events - where no less than thirteen records were broken and two equalled. Angus MacIntyre, son of the famous bank manager-poet, became the senior champion at fifteen while in the fourth year, creating a new high jump record of 5 ft 4 in as well as putting the weight 35 ft 7 in - five feet more than the previous record. Angus, now an Oxford professor, went on to distinguish himself in national contests and built up a considerable reputation in a number of athletic disciplines; in these he was in due course followed by his three younger brothers.

John Maclean longed to give his brighter pupils the best opportunities which they merited to lead them to a high-flying academic career, and in this he succeeded to a large extent. As for those who were not so bright, he would certainly fight for them as individuals were they to be neglected in any way. There was remedial education for those deemed to need it.

As the Head of Technical Subjects, Norman T Hardie (or "Pop Hardie" as he was affectionately known) was innovative, sensitive to the changing needs of his pupils in the pos-war era, which required numerous apprentices for the burgeoning building industry, and in all very much larger than life. This forceful personality did much for his charges who very often admitted that Pop Hardie gave them a very much needed boost to their flagging confidence. To-day, they will tell you that they did feel inferior to those in the academic streams; but are happy to accept that those of us in the hot-house society envied their ability to make things in wood and iron. We might be able to conjugate an irregular French verb, but such was of little use if we had to put up a shelf and couldnot use a saw or a screwdriver. John Maclean saw the sense of this argument and initially decreed that all pupils in the academic stream should have Woodwork in their first year. Perhaps, he saw too many of our pathetic efforts at the end of that sojourn in the Technical Department and decided to end the experiment.

This left Norman Hardie free to concentrate on those who needed his tuition in Woodwork, Technical Drawing and Metalwork. For several years he had a number of staff who stayed a relatively short time. This should not be taken to be a criticism of him and his teaching methods for he was widely respected within his profession for his innovations and leadership. For this and his service to the Educational Institute of Scotland he was honoured with an MBE. Eventually he was joined by John Alexander and George MacKay who stayed with him for many years and made the Technical Department at Oban High School well known for the standard of its workmanship and its good performance in examination subjects which were first presented in the mid-fifties.

The Inspectors' Report in 1953 recognises such achievements under difficult circumstances, making mention of a project which attracted the attention of the whole school: the erection of a Nissan Hut: "Since the last report further progress has been made in metalwork. Under the competent and energetic direction of the principal teacher the boys had erected a Nissen Hut and had also undertaken the installation of the bench and machine tool equipment. This project which now allows a full course in metalwork to be followed, deserves commendation. Although forging is an outstanding feature, techniques of bench and machine tools had received adequate attention."

While the boys were being well educated in the mysteries of dovetail joints, soldering and applied mechanics the girls were, in the other part of the technical building (now demolished), bent to Cookery, Needlework and Home Economics. Janet Whyte, who came into her own, along with her assistants, each Christmas when they conjured up mouth-watering spreads at the Musicals, laboured hard, diligently and successfully to see that what West Highland mothers might not have taught their daughters was imparted thoroughly. While she was not the most popular of teachers - having a biting wit - most of her charges now talk about her with a degree of gratitude for the order she brought to subjects domestic. As they go about their homes they recollect little tips and words of caution which she administered.

Amid the energies of Pop Hardie and Janet Whyte the Commercial Department proceeded as a very efficient secretary should: doing everything so efficiently that she goes almost unnoticed. Bill Lees reigned supreme with Anne MacPhail as his dynamic assistant. The

Inspectors certainly found nothing to criticise: "Programme of instruction, planned on a sound basis, is carried through with imagination and skill. Book keeping and shorthand are very good and typing is excellent."

While these last pages have made mention of the managers of the major departments of the school they were not always the major characters within them. George Milne in his declining years made little impact on the department for those in the first three years of secondary education. The inculcation of the rules of grammar, analysis, parsing and conjugation he left to such stalwarts as Helen MacColl, Jessie Rose and Patricia Stuart. Helen MacColl, who ruled in Room 1 of the pre-1956 building, also taught Latin to first year pupils and was known as 'Minniehaha' - why no one ever knew. Like the Rector she was an expert on the genealogy of Argyll families and soon worked out who were your cousins, aunts, uncles and grandparents. She could hardly be described as an inspired teacher, but she did enough to give her pupils a thorough grounding in English and revelled in the formal disciplines of Latin.

Miss Rose, "Rosie", very rarely referred to as Jessie, could have been the model for Alastair Sim's portrayal of the headmistress in *The Belles of St Trinians*. A well proportioned woman of ample bosoms, dressed inevitably in coarse, light brown tweeds, she swept through the corridors of the school as Assistant Principal of the English Department and Lady Adviser, succeeding the formidable Mary Ann Skinner in that post. When gowns were introduced - much to the disgust of George Milne who refused to wear one - Rosie became an even more voluminous figure. Indeed, voluminous is an ideal epithet to describe her; she declaimed poetry loudly and with dramatic effect, an unfortunate fact for those closeted in Room 3 with Jimmy Troup and prone to giggle at the Joyce Grenfell performance emanating from next door. On occasion even Jimmy Troup was moved to urge Walter De La Mare's 'Highwayman' "to get right up to the old inn door" and to get a bloody move on. However, Rosie was a generous soul who took a very great deal of care over the numerous country pupils who lived in lodgings. The kindly landladies - and, I can never remember any of my contemporaries ever running down any of them - were a bit nonplussed as to how to handle a visit from Rosie. It was rather like taking tea with the minister, one of them told me.

If her teaching of English was very dramatic, it did make her pupils remember what she was trying to impart to them. Unfortunately, despite her faithful and diligent attendance at St Columba's-Argyll Square Church she obviously found it difficult to teach religion, retreating into the obvious shelter of prescribing her classes many verses of the gospels to learn. This was a difficult and boring task to perform in Room 2 and diversionary tactics were required to leaven the half hours of supposedly silent concentration. One of our favourites, and one which we got away with several times, was to place a tin containing ballbearings on the edge of a sloping desk and to encourage a classmate in close proximity to that desk to find an excuse to go out to Rosie's desk. As he, or she, passed the well-positioned can, gentle brushing with the hem of the blazer or jacket sent the contents all over the floor with a deafening racket. While Rosie remonstrated about the noise and such carelessness the majority of the class were down on their hands and knees searching allegedly for the roving silver balls but in reality sending them further and ensuring that as much noise as possible was made and as much time as possible spent in returning the offending miniature marbles to their tin.

When all else failed and some demonstration of the ability to recite St Mark's gospel was required James Burnett could always be relied upon to placate her with copious verses. Little did she seem to realise that James had learned them for recitation in Gaelic at Mods and was translating from the language of the Garden of Eden as he went along. For thirty-five years she taught a generation of Argyll kids who held her in their affections, if only because she never carried out an unfair action against them.

While Rosie was a good teacher she was not an inspired one as was Patricia Stuart who stayed a relatively short time before going off to teach the Turks. "Spider Lady", as she was called behind her back, was in the Ewan MacDonald mould and would probably have stayed longer if she had had him as her Principal. Just as she adopted his modern, relevant approach to the subject, so she was able to draw out her pupils in prose and verse. Her ready acceptance of the suggestion of her third year class to produce a magazine gave Robert Reid, the editor of this book, his first experience of the task of editing and the author of this chapter his introduction to journalism. Some years later, Colin Vincent, who now has a personal Chair in Chemistry at the University of St Andrews, wrote in the school magazine, "... since everyone in the class was involved, a powerful uniting force was felt and as a result of this, most of us agree that IIIA was the happiest class we attended."

When the school magazine was re-introduced after a seventeen year gap in 1956 a remarkable number of those who had been involved in the third year magazine were also involved in its production. Not least of these was Jean Clark (now Mrs Ferguson) who designed the cover and at the same time produced a new badge for the school. She retained the Galley of Lorne, which had long been the badge, but added the torch of learning surmounting the Galley[2]. At the same time Jean revitalised the badge John Maclean introduced a school motto: "Dia Ar N-Iùl" - "God is our Guide."

Glancing through the magazines which are relevant to this decade, I am constantly reminded of facts which I had long forgotten. What a pity that these worthwhile records of school life have ceased to be published.

In his foreword to the 1956 magazine John Maclean summarises succinctly his thoughts on and the actions of the powers-that-be: "Amid the turmoil of changes we have much to be thankful for. We have, for instance, been comparatively unaffected by the growing dearth of teachers, and, despite a continuing increase in enrolment particularly at the infant stage, the problems of accommodation so perplexing in other places are beginning to trouble us only now, when a substantial addition to our main building is in progress of construction. Moreover, the new system of promotion to secondary division, which tends to be rigid and exclusive elsewhere, is administered in Argyll with a humanity and flexibility which cannot ut be most advantageous to our pupils. The hostel for boys, too, and the new playing fields which are soon to be open to us at Lochavullin will contribute greatly to the welfare of the school.

" ... The pupils, if not perhaps the cleverest in Scotland, must be among the healthiest, the most attractive and the best behaved, while the staff are, I venture to say, inferior to none in their desire and efforts to promote the welfare of their young charges morally and educationally. For the continued well-being of our school community I commend to both our newly formed motto, couched in the ancient language of Argyll, and appearing in print for the first time on these pages - *Dia Ar N-iùl.*"

As one would expect these magazines contained a strong and powerful Gaelic section. One writer, using a pseudonym, "Gur-leGug", chose the new motto to pen these lines:

"Tha Fionn an àigh,
Diarmad gun sgàth,
Is Oisean an bàrd air éirigh.

Fingal the fortunate,
Dermid without fear,
and Ossian, the poet, have risen.

Is Somhairl' an saoi
Gun fhiamh is gun fhoill
Fhuair buaidh air Goill is eucoir.

And Somhairle, the hero,
without trepidation or deceit,
who conquered the foreigners and injustice.

Bha neart agus lùths
Maise is mùirn
Seirc agus cliù 's an treubh ud.

Strength and vigour,
beauty and hospitality,
knowledge and fame were in that clan.

Aonghas Mac Leòid
Ceannard nan seòd
Cunbhalach còmhnard reusant.

Angus MacLeod,
chief of the heroes,
steady, level headed, reasonable.

Na h-òrain is dàin
Rinn Donnchadh Bàn
Chuir e 's a' chànain Bheurla.

The songs and poems
that Duncan Ban made
he transalted into the English language.

Le oilean is brigh
Eigse gun chlì.
Gun chearb air ni fo'n ghréin ann.

With scholarship and vigour
knowledge without prejudice
without any defect under the sun in it.

Tha dùrachdean blàth
'Ga leantainn an dràsd
'S e gabhail a thàimh an Dun Eideann.

Warm good wishes
follow him now
as he takes his retirement in Edinburgh.

An Leathanach còir	The virtuous Maclean
Choisinn onair is glòir	who won honour and glory
An cainnt na Ròimh 's na Gréige.	in the languages of Rome and Greece.

Iain Ruadh nan dual,	Brown haired John of the curls
Carthannach cruaidh,	charitable, firm,
B'e ceist nan truagh 'nan éiginn.	he was the darling of the wretched in
	their distress.

Ro dhéidheil air ceòl	Very fond of music,
B' fhileanta mheòir	his fingers were fluent,
Amaiseach òirdhearc eutrom.	accurate, excellent, light.

Reachdairean suairc	Affable rectors,
Geanail 'nan gluas'd	mild in their conduct,
Urramach uasal eudmhor.	honourable, noble, zealous.

Leanamaid dlùth	Let us closely follow
An cleachdadh bu dùth	the custon that was fitting
Do'n dream a stiùr gun bheud sinn.	in the company who steered without fault.

Biodh fineachan òg'	Let the young clans
A' sireadh nan còrn	be seeking the drinking horn
'S a' togail an lòchrain leusaich.	and raising the lustrous torches.

'S Bidh "Dia ar n-Iul",	And let "GOD OUR GUIDE"
An Suaicheantas ùr,	be the new motto
Mar bhàta-siùil 'na reul duinn."	like a guiding star to a sailing ship.

("GUR-LE-GUG")   Translated by Iain Crichton Smith

The following year Jan Houston writes about an event which drew national publicity for the school which was totally favourable: the visit of an number of the staff and pupils to the war-ravaged city of Dresden in East Germany and therefore behind the Iron Curtain. The visit had come about as the result of a long, on-going correspondence between Andrew J Murray, who had by that time been appointed Head of the newly created History Department, and his opposite number at the Martin-Anderson Nexo Oberschule in Dresden. Not only had he corresponded with his colleague, he had encouraged his pupils to write to their counterparts there. After all the visa and diplomatic problems had been overcome, 26 pupils along with teachers, Andrew Murray, Harry Dobbins, Margaret MacNaughton and May MacLaine set off on the long train and ferry journey to the city of Dresden, which was then celebrating its 750th anniversary. The national press interest was, of course, over these intrepid explorers who were coming from the Highlands to be the first British school children to visit a country behind the Iron Curtain.

Staying with those to whom they had been writing, the party had a wonderful time, were most hospitably received and were showered with gifts, including a Canaletto painting of Dresden - probably the School's most valuable asset today. In the early days of its residence in the school it used to hang on display in the Hall, but, due to its increasing value and the chances of it being stolen, it is now safely tucked away. Unfortunately, the worsening Cold War situation prevented the expected return visit ever taking place. These young East Germans have had to wait almost forty years before they could travel with the freedom which the Oban party enjoyed on their visit to them in 1956.

Some of that party, when they returned to school after the summer holidays, found themselves accommodated in the rather splendid surroundings of Kilbowie House, two miles from Oban, along the Gallanach Road. Many years after the girls had been 'incarcerated' in the former Craigard Hotel "thirty-four rough, bustling hustlers - including one or two Rock 'n' Roll jivers", as Gordon Pacey, the first Head Boy wrote, took up residence under the benevolent supervision of Mary MacBride - a remarkable woman who is still with us and who is venerated by all the boys who stayed in the baronial surroundings of the former sheriff's residence.

Mary was an extra-orindary person who used the benefitsof her Irish charm to its full extent while keeping a firm check on her rebellious charges. Her counterpart, Miss MacLean at Craigard, did the same duty but in a vastly different style. She was, and still is, a gentlewoman in the true sense of that word. When boys were admitted officially into the precincts of Craigard she kept a wary eye for any who strayed from the large downstairs room in which dances were held. Upstairs was definitely out of bounds. Her problems in repelling these lotharios were to be compounded in later years when the new fire regulations required an external escape ladder to be erected up the gable of the building.

One of the residents wrote in the 1957 magazine: "We got into many scrapes in our joyous fourth year and I think this little poem will bring back happy memories to many ex-hostelites:

'Irene, Mavis, Nance and the rest,
    Were doing the can-can or trying their best,
    Miss Martin was angry and we heard her say -
    "You'll stay in, me hearties, all next Saturday."

'The can-can's so lively, the clatter it makes,
    Indeed 'tis so gay, the Billiard Room shakes,
    Miss Martin's so angry at us she did glare -
    If we break the floor, the expense will be shared." [3]

When those who had been in the first year when John Maclean became Rector had gone through their six years and left to go to university or teacher training college, do their National Service or enter on an apprenticeship they were invited back to the Musical at Christmas. At the interval of that happy event the Rector invited these former pupils present to join him in

Room 16 to discuss the formation of a Former Pupils' Association. There had been such a body, previously, but it had lapsed. He hoped that, with the formal structure of captains and prefects, those who had been appointed to lead would take a major part in the formation of such an association. This they did and a branch was set up in Oban and another later in Glasgow. While the Glasgow branch has continued to flourish with a number of those who were at that meeting in December 1956 still prominent in its activities, the Oban branch is defunct and seems content to remain so.

In the Log on 4th June 1956 John Maclean recorded, "At the recent Bursary Competition at Edinburgh University Robert Reid, captain of the school, took 3rd place equal. His subjects were English, French, Latin and Greek. In view of this unprecedented honour to the school the Rector dismissed all pupils at 3.00 pm to mark the occasion." Later, Robert Reid went on to win the Duval Major Scholarship at Gonville and Caius College, Cambridge, which had been the college of his teacher of Greek, John Maclean. Thereafter he lectured in Greek at St Andrews University for 24 years. In the meantime, the MacIntyre brothers were carving their distinctive paths through the school, and they were being emulated by a brother and sister who have become as famous as they are and an Appin Minister's son who now reigns at what should be called the High Kirk of St Giles, but is better known as St Giles Cathedral. The trio, William and Anne Gillies - known professionally as Anne Lorne Gillies - and Gilleasbuig MacMillan were contemporaries. The Gillies have both made a distinctive contribution to Gaelic culture, with William now the Professor of Celtic at Edinburgh University and Anne Lorne a singing star and author of a book on her childhood experiences at school in Oban - a book which has not endeared her to many of her contemporaries or the citizens of the burgh.

No one who was at school with Gilleasbuig MacMillan was in any doubt that he wold become a distinguished divine, but few expected that he would arrive at the most famous Church of Scotland in the world before he was thirty and be its youngest ever minister. But so it turned out; the young MacMillan, having caught the ear of St Giles session clerk on holiday in Portree, was translated to that charge and to all the pomp, pageantry and status that the minister enjoys there. Anyone who has been to hear him preach cannot but be impressed with his ability to be stimulating, controversial and dignified. As Dean of The Thistle and Chaplain to Her Majesty he enjoys the title of Very Reverend and is almost certain to become the Right Reverend on his appointment as Moderator of the General Assembly of the Church of Scotland at some future time.

Perhaps what sets the MacIntyre brother apart from almost all other pupils of this decade is their fortunate endowment of academic ability and sporting talent. Throughout their era at the School they collected sports trophies with the greatest of ease and Kenny, now one of the best known broadcasters on BBC Radio Scotland, still plays a mean game of football - or, so his media colleagues claim.

But it was not just in individual sporting achievements that the school was beginning to take its place in the hall of fame. For the first time a boy reached the final trials stage for the national football side. Alasdair D Campbell, a natural all-round athlete, was to be followed by Alastair

MacArthur, who also reached the same stage. The latter is fortunately still with us on the staff of the School and playing a major part in the organisation of the photographic exhibition which forms part of the centenary celebrations. The former, unfortunately, died some years ago on a squash court in the Middle East.

While the boys were enjoying success both individually as footballers and as a team under the inspired guidance of Ford Spence, the girls were wielding hockey sticks equally successfully under the aegis of Jean MacDonald. An increasing number of pupils were drawn to sailing on what are still regarded as the best cruising grounds in Europe and, thanks to the generosity of James MacDonald and his sons, John, Calum and Donald Alastair, a new aquatic sport was introduced, rowing. The Tweed Mill owners presented the funds necessary to build two rowing skiffs and these were launched and kept at Kilbowie, having been built by staff and pupils.

Shinty also came into its own: in 1956 the boys won the MacKay Cup for the first time. It is interesting to note that several of the players in that side went on to distinguish themselves subsequently at the sport: "Dunny" Niven, now managing Oban Camanachd, Iain MacIntyre, Chairman of the Finance Committee of the Camanachd Association and a top-flight banker, Ivor Clark and Fraser Duffy. Two years later many of these boys formed the twelve who won the MacPherson Cup, beating the mighty Newtonmore 3-1 with Alan Hoey scoring twice and Donald Scott once. Joining those in the team photograph is Duncan MacIntyre, now President of Oban Camanachd. Once again the ubiquitous Ford Spence was the driving force behind the increased influence of the School in *camanachd*; both he and ex-provost Donald Thomson were elected as honorary members of the sport's governing body, the Camanachd Association.

One of the major problems which affected many of the pupils was that they lived outside Oban, travelling to school by various means of transport, from train to taxi, from boat to bus. Their necessity to catch such conveyances prevented them from playing their full part in School activities, particularly in sports. While transport by sea was beginning to be modernised and more attuned to the needs of the islanders, the Ballachulish train was still leaving the station there at the same ungodly hour at which it had transported my mother, among others, to Oban forty years previously. The same pranks took place in the non-corridor train and homework was done, cribbed or copied. Sex was discussed at length and stories, mostly apocryphal, of illicit liaisons abounded much to the annoyance of the Rector, who chose to deny them publicly on one occasion and could not understand why he was hounded by the tabloid press. By the end of the decade buses were replacing trains and making life slightly better for the pupils. An élite few were transported by taxi from places such as Gallanach and Glenlonan. One or two came by boat from Kerrera to join the Gallanach taxi, but on the advent of Kilbowie Hostel the boys from the islands were accommodated there, literally a five minute boat trip from their homes.

The Rector's agitation for more classrooms to provide space for the ever growing roll was finally answered in November 1957 when the three storey building costing £95,000, was officially opened by ex-Provost James Marshall, Chairman of the Education Committee. These provided rooms for a new Commerce Department, a new Technical Department, a music suite and one for homecraft, in all eleven classrooms. These were in complete contrast to their predecessors - lots of glass, one level and in the specialist departments the most modern and up-to-date equipment available. In his address, the Chairman of the Education Committee made specific reference to technical education as being one of the requirements of the modern age to justify the vastly improved range of machinery which Norman T Hardie, John Alexander and George S MacKay had at their disposal.

J G Mathieson CBE, the Convener of Argyll County Council for many years and one of the School's most popular speakers at all such ceremonies - his brevity and wit made him so - fired a shot across the Rector's bows in his comment: "For every hundred scientists and academic scholars there were a thousand who went into other modes of life: into shops, offices, services and these boys and girls must not be forgotten. To my mind a sound general education is more important today than it has ever been."

While John Maclean probably agreed with such a view in theory, by his very academic nature he found it difficult to be equally enthusiastic about it in practice. At successive prize-giving ceremonies in the Oban Playhouse, where numerous clergymen were assembled on the platform with Councillors and benefactors (in particular Peter and Bessie Milne, who were very generous patrons of the school), he made plain his distaste for this move away nationally from the formal Classical education, which had dominated the Oban High School scene since its inception, to the promotion of science and technology. In 1958 we find him roundly condemning educational theorists, "many of whom are cranks". He went on to say that the government and various other bodies seemed anxious to promote the material welfare of the pupils, that they did much to encourage young students to go in for science and technological subjects and that it was proposed to change the Scottish Leaving Certificate, probably with the idea that more people would go in for that side of education. He confirmed, "What is forgotten is this: we have advanced so far scientifically and technically that our moral and spiritual development is lagging behind a tremendous amount and the government is failing to pay attention to this fact. To me it is the most important side of education. I'm always pleased if pupils do well, but if we don't try to do our best for them morally and spiritually, I should feel we are not doing our duty properly."

John Maclean might have found it difficult to comprehend that the figment of the imagination of a group of pupils became so real that his personality almost totally dominated them. This "Dutch gentleman" was known as Albert Autumnbottom. Albert was the creation of three fifth year boys who found themselves arguing over what type of pears Albert would like. Soon half of the pupils fell for the reality of Albert and strove to prove sightings of him in various locations in the school, the sports field and the town. He was even claimed to be outside a school dance totally intoxicated by Dutch schnapps. He appeared in the pen pals column of one of the moronic national dailies and drew replies not only from those of the level of ntelligence expected to read such rags but from serious academics who were interested in the derivation of his unusual Dutch surname. In the end he had to be "put down" painlessly before he found his way onto the absentee sheet, whene Mr Graham, the Attendance Officer, would have attempted faithfully to discover the reason for his absence. He might even have recorded, in all innocence, as he did for a young lady of considerable beauty, "In bed with the doctor!"

In the last year of the decade as John Maclean pondered the growth of what the Rt Hon Rab Butler was later to refer to as the age of "red-hot technology", he was provided with more time to devote to his Soroba Road Building and its pupils. No longer would he have to make his way to Rockfield Primary School. On 13th February John Maclean ceased to be the headmaster of Rockfield School and four days later Peter Robertson (usually known to all as Pat) became its first headmaster in residence. As usual there were ceremonies in the Playhouse cinema with the great and the good of town and gown present. All enjoyed hospitality in the Playhouse café thereafter.

Almost ten years after he took up his appointment as Rector, he records on the 10th February, 1960 " ... the sudden death in Edinburgh today of my distinguished predecessor, Angus MacLeod, who had a heart attack a few months ago but seemed to be progressing. ... he was appointed Rector of this school about the age of thirty-four. Here he worked with singular devotion and success for thirty-one years. The school and the community owe Mr MacLeod an enormous debt of gratitude, and it was a proud thing for this district and the Highlands to have had so distinguished a man as head of the school for so many years. ... by his death a blow has been struck not only to this school but also to Gaelic scholarship".

Regrettably John Maclean's own Rectorship was not to last as long as that of Angus MacLeod, but the words he wrote that day serve equally well as a suitable tribute to himself. Two verses of a poem by John MacLeod[4] in tribute to the Rector's brother, Calum, are equally appropriate to him:

"Gun robh foghlum nach gann
'nad cheann agus t'aois glé òg
's thug thu dearbhadh gach àm
le d'chainnt an ionadan mór,
fhuair thu tàlent bho Dhia
's thug thu riarachadh seachad is còrr,
's cha do dh' àicheidh thu riamh
do dhleasndas do d' Dhia 's do chòir

"A wealth of learning
filled your mind from your earliest years,
you proved it time upon time
in the great places in which you spoke:
you got a talent from God
and you have good measure and more
and you never denied
your duties to your God and to your
own standards

Do'n ghinealach òg	To the young generation
gun tug thusa eolas ùr	you gave new knowledge
air cleachdach's air dòigh	of manners and a way of life
's air ceòl a bh'againn o thùs	and music, our own ancient heritage
bha thuar dhol air chall	which would soon have been lost
mur b'e gun do chuir thu ann ùidh -	if you had not cherished them so -
co eile san àm	who else in our time
d'ar cainnt thug urad de rùn?"	loved our language so well?"

Translated by Donald A MacDonald

NOTES

1   Both families are still connected with the school: Mrs Jean Murray, John Munro'
granddaughter, is a very active member of the Glasgow Branch of the Former Pupils
Association and Donald MacD Skinner, ex-Provost Skinner's grandson, is Chairmar
of the Branch.

2   When research was being carried out for the production of this book and for the
centenary logo, which appears on all the memorabilia, it was discovered that at some
time in the last thirty-six years a fish had appeared below the Galley. As no authority
can be found for such it has been dropped from all centenary material.

3   Miss Janet Martin was Assistant Matron/Cook at Craigard.

4   Calum I Maclean, *The Highlands* (Mainstream Publishing Company, 1990), p 38.

(above) **The Duke's School (the"ragged school") (left) at Glenshellach Terrace.**

(below) **Glenshellach Terrace and High Street. The Duke's school is at bottom left and the Free Church Girls' School is on the right in the middle ground.**

(above) **The Secession School (left) and Church in Tweedale Street.**

(below) **Oban High School, 1890 - 1896.**

(above) ***Oban High School, 1896 - 1909.***

(below) ***Oban High School with Burnside Cottage.***

(above) **left: Hugh Skinner;   right: James Beattie.**

(below) **Oban High School in its setting, c. 1904**

(above) **Oban High School, 1910.**

(below) **William Kennedy with pupils who were leaving School after the Higher Leaving Certificate, June 1919.**

(above) *left: William Kennedy;   right: Angus MacLeod.*

(below) **Class IV, 1922/23.**

Back Row: D. Hutton, D. MacAlpine, D. Jackson, T. Dargie, H. Robertson, H. McColl, J. Paterson, A. Cattanach, D. Skinner.
Second Row: F. McGillivray, A. McCorquodale, L. Chalmers, M. McNeill, J. MacVicar, C. McGillivray, I. McNeill, I. McCallum, K. Jackson, A. Mitchell.
Third Row: M. Campbell, M. Skinner, F. Ferla, N. Mair, E. McKinnon, M. Stewart, G. Stewart, M. McNiven, M. McLean, A. McGregor, E. Fletcher, M. Campbell.
Front Row: Mr. Milne, C. Gardner, I. Gillies, M. Skinner, M. MacFarlane, J. MacVicar, Mr. A. MacLeod, C. McTaggart, M. Forbes, M. Coats, C. McKechnie, Mr. Constable.

(above) *School Sports, 1923.*

(below) *Class IIB, 1923/24.*
Back Row: J. McDougall, C. MacInnes, J. Clark, D. McDougall, A. McDonald, J. McNicol, C. McLeod.
Middle Row: M. McIntyre, ?, M.B. White, C. McCallum, J. Dickson.
Front Row: P. McInnes, A. Rennie, M. McKinnon, B. Thomson, J. McLeod, E. Gibson, N. McDonald, J. McNaughton, Miss Rose.

(above) **Staff of c. 1927.**
Back Row: Miss Stark, Mrs. Ford, Mr. Simpson, Miss MacDonald, Miss Micklejohn, Miss MacKinnon, Miss Graham, Mr. Livingstone, Miss Rose, Miss Hope.
Second Row: Miss MacIntyre, ?, ?, Mr. Penman, Miss Ritchie, Mr. Lindsay, Miss Blacklock, ?, Miss Stewart, Mr. Milne, Miss Watson.
Third Row: Miss MacQueen, Mr. Scrimgeour, Miss Rankin, Mr MacLeod, Miss Skinner, Mr. Constable, Mrs. Brown.
Front Row: Miss Flemington, Miss Harper, Miss Thomson, Miss Morrison, ?, Mlle. Umbert.

(below) **Class of c. 1928.**
Back Row: J. Mair, P. MacMillan, A. MacLean, S. MacAskill, H. Ross, ? MacKay?, H. Gillies.
Second Row: C. Menzies, H. MacInnes, N. MacLeod, K. Murray, W. Brownlie, A. MacInnes, J. Knox, I. Hay.
Third Row: M. MacNeil, D. MacPhee, J. Munro, M. Campbell, M. Mair, M. Kilgour, E. Graham, M. Graham, C. Skinner.
Fourth Row: T. Carson, J. Gillies, ?, I. White, J. Scott, J. Colthart, F. Gardner, R. MacTavish, A. Davidson, ?.
Front Row: I. Gibson, ? Carmichael, B. McSwan, J. Campbell, M. Cameron, K. McCorquodale, L. MacDonald, A. Abercromby.

(above) **Class IB, 1931/32.**

Back Row: D. Watt, J. Carmichael, J. Finlay, S. Campbell, A. McColl, H. Ballard, J. Innes, E. Mowatt.
Second Row: H. Saddington, I. Stewart, D. MacKechnie, A. Munro, A. MacDonald, K. Caterer, J. Black.
Third Row: M. MacLeod, C. MacNaughton, M. MacKinnon, A. MacArthur, C. MacPhail, J. Fergusson, E. MacArthur, C. McLachlan.
Front Row: J. Munro, H. MacIntyre, C. Kemp.

(below) **Class IIA, 1931/32.**

Back Row: A. Macintyre, W. Beaton, C. Cameron, I. Cameron, I. MacDonald, R. Walkden, W. Wood.
Second Row: A. Cameron, P. MacQueen, H. MacInnes, J. MacInnes, D. Carmichael, H. MacQuarrie, W. Young.
Third Row: B. MacDougall, C. MacSween, M. Darroch, M. MacCormick, L. Lamb, M. Cameron, B. MacInnes.
Front Row: K. Dunlop, I. MacPhail, J. Yeoman, M. MacKenzie, P. Brown.

(above) **Class V, 1931/32.**
Back Row: C. Palmer, D. Cameron, A. Lindsay, M. Black, P. Stewart, J. Maitland, A. Duncan, K. Cameron.
Second Row: M. Kilgour, H. Myles, D. Rankin, C. Campbell, S. MacInnes, M. Munro.
Third Row: E. Gillies, A. Donald, A. MacNeill, J. MacKenzie, J. MacDougall, J. MacInnes, J.C. MacLean.
Front Row: J.M. McLean, H.M. Bruce, B. Seddon.

(below) **Football Team, 1932/33.**
Back Row: Mr. Lees, T. Doyle, J. Kilcullen, J. MacDonald, K. Galloway, C. Campbell, A. Duncan.
Front Row: A. Ogilvie, J.A. MacInnes, J. Munro, D. Dunn, K. Cameron.

(above) *Football Team, 1943/44.*
Back Row: J. MacPhee, I. MacArthur, I. Slater, F. Cook, J. McInnes, A. Watt.
Front Row: A. Lawrie, H. Campbell, G. Anderson, J. MacLean, J. Dunsmuir.

(below) *Staff of 1948.*
Back Row: W. Lees, W. Clark, H. MacKay, H. Dobbins, W. Gordon, N.T. Hardie, D. Morrison, J. Troup, Mr. Stalibrass.
Second Row: F. Seddon, A.H. Daavidson, D. Thomson, H. Dent, Miss Kay, M. MacLaine, J. Walker, G.M. Loynd, Mr. Evans, C.B. Irving,
Third Row: M. Ferguson, S. Skinner, S. Munsie, K. Brown, M. MacTaggart, J. MacDowell, W. Speed, M. MacNaughton, Mrs. Innes, Mlle. Jacqueline ?, J. Whyte, A. Hope.
Front Row: B. MacClure, R. Keene, Mr. Penman, J. Rose, Angus MacLeod, Miss Rankin, G. Milne, H. Fairley, I. MacInnes.

(above) **Class IIIA, 1947/48.**
Back Row: A. Campbell, I. Phillips, L. MacKay, J. Gray, J. MacCallum, G. Scott, P. MacLeod, K. MacRae.
Middle Row: M. Kidd, M. MacIntyre, C. Gray, K. Gillies, M. MacDonald, J. MacCallum, C. Hoey, B. MacRae, J. MacLellan, Mr. Troup.
Front Row: I. Clark, A. Boyd, I. McGill, J. Balfour, A. MacLarty, P. Hollingsworth, M. Colthart, J.V. Silverton, A. Campbell.

(below) **Staff of 1951.**
Back Row: H. MacKinnon, W. Clark, D. Ramsay, A.J. Murray, W. Gordon, D. Morrison, W. Lees, J. Troup, H. Dobbins, Mr. Smith.
Second Row: C. Campbell, G.A. Kay, J. Page, P. Stuart, I. Marshall, H. MacColl, J. Whyte, A. Hope, M. MacNaughton, M. MacLaine, J. Walker, K. Graham.
Third Row: F. Seddon, S. Munsie, I. MacInnes, A. MacPhail, C. MacClure, Mademsoille, K. MacDonald, Mrs. Stewart, G.S. MacKay.
Front Row: C.B. Irving, D. Thomson, A.H. Davidson, J. Rose, John Maclean, G. Milne, Mrs. Clunie, H. MacKay, N.T. Hardie.

(above) **Class IIA, 1950/51**
Back Row: C. Vincent, R.A. Reid, A. Buchanan, S. McIvor, D. McInnes, A. Gordon, C. MacDougall, D. Davidson, D. Campbell, S. McAdie.
Middle Row: I. Calderwood, R. Dougal, M. MacKenzie.
Front Row: J. Kosinska, A. MacKenzie, M. Fraser, E. MacLean, J. Clark, M. Pacey, M. Cameron, I. Smith.

(below) **Class IIIB, 1951/52.**
Back Row: A. Graham, A. Hall, H. Ross, A. Kennedy, A. Calder, A. McDonald, N. Lockhart, A. Lamont.
Middle Row: I. Turnbull, T. MacKillop, I. McAllister, I. Weir, M. Kitching, A. McGregor, K. Smith, N. MacLeod, H. Ballantyne.
Front Row: E. Crighton, B. Smart, A. Jamieson, M. McIver, E. Thompson, N. Lamont, B. McGregor.

(above) *The Gaelic Choir, 1953, with G.M. Loynd, John Maclean and Donald Morrison.*

(below) *Class IIA, 1953/54*
Back Row: F. Prosser, A. MacNicol, Alan MacIntyre, I. Thomson, F. Walton, A. Begbie, M. MacDonald, J. Henderson, D. Clark.
Middle Row: H. Tait, R. Hendry, Angus MacIntyre, A. Maxwell, M. MacColl, F. Black, W. Carter, A. Taylor, R. Blair.
Front Row: P. Watters, R. MacFadyen, B. McLellan, C. Thomson, D. Paxton, J. Houston, B. Comrie.

(above) **Captains and Prefects, 1954/55.**

Back Row: R.A. Reid, I. Calderwood, S. McAdie, L. Cooper, C. McIver, M. Pacey, D. McColl, M. MacDonald, S. Gilfillan.
Front Row: I. MacLeod, M. Black, John Maclean, D. Walton, J. Munro.

(below) **Oban High School: the 1956 Clock nearing completion.**

(above) **Under-15 Shinty Team, 1959/60.**
Back Row: E. Spence, G. Graham, M. McInnes, G. McLuckie, T. Donn.
Front Row: W. Barnett, D. Buchanan, D. McCann, A. McArthur, N. Evans, D. Scott, A. Hoey.

(below) **Captains and Prefects, 1959/60.**
Back Row: R. Elder, L. McAdie, E. MacKenzie, A. MacLeod, D. MacDonald.
Middle Row: B. Jensen, U. Barbour, R. Gibson, A. Edwards, S. McArthur, E. McLarty.
Front Row: A.D. Campbell, C. McArthur, G. MacMillan, John Maclean, M. Hoey, D. Thomson, M. Robertson.

(above) **County Sports, 1964.**

Standing: R. McCulloch, K. Scott, A. MacDougall, ?, H. Silkowski, L. MacPherson, C. Kirkpatrick, D. Hill, I. Reid, P. Kilshaw, H. MacLean, N. Angus, L. MacLeod, J. Paxton, A. MacArthur, D. Collier, S. Tait.
Kneeling: N. Kilpatrick, M. Gordon, J. Maxwell, I. MacArthur, M. MacInnes, S. Thomson, M. MacKay, C. Dalziel, G. Milton, J. MacIntyre, A. Cameron, K. Robertson, C. Wilson, H. Dawson, M. MacKay, ?.
Sitting: E. MacPherson, A. Irving, T. Heath, S. Watters, G. Smith, J. MacKay, E. Spence, ?.

(below) **Captains and Prefects, 1964/65.**

Back Row: D. Hill, A. Watters, R. McCulloch, A. Gordon, J. Carmichael, I. Quigley, C. Lockhart, T. Lennox.
Second Row: H. Galbraith, A. Adams, J. Paxton, N. MacDonald, A. MacLelland, G. Smith, D. Dairon, T. Heath.
Third Row: M. MacDougall, F. MacInnes, A. MacDonald, S. Walker, M. MacCallum, M. Morrison, J. Sutherland, J. MacAulay, A. Black, C. Chalmers.
Front Row: H. Dawson, A. Naismith, C. McGarva, I. Reid, M. Beaton, John Maclean, A. Irving, C. Dalziel, E. Thomson, E. MacDonald, S. Robertson.

(above) **left: John Maclean;   right: Farquhar Macintosh.**

(below) **Oban High School, October, 1970. Preparations for the 1972 Block.**

(above) *left: Terence Twatt; right: Brian Mitchell.*

(below) *The Rugby "Grand Slam" Teams of 1979/80 with Ian Thomson and Brian Mitchell.*

(above) **Staff of 1990.**

(below) **Oban High School, 1992.**

CHAPTER 6

The years 1960-1972

ANN MCCULLOCH

The years 1960-1972 saw many changes in Oban High School. These included a change of Rector, the departure of many long-serving members of staff and changes in the system of education itself.

A report in an educational magazine by a correspondent who visited the school in 1965 said, "Oban High School fulfils a dual role; as a junior secondary for the children of Oban and environs and as a highly selective secondary school for two-thirds of Argyll". This was indeed the case. Pupils came to Oban from Coll, Tiree, Mull, Morvern, Lismore, Islay, Jura, Gigha, Colonsay, Mid-Argyll and as far north as Kinlochleven. From some places pupils came in first year, from others in third year and, after the introduction of the "O" grade exam in 1962, some came in fifth year. This meant that academically Oban High was "top-heavy".

At the present time the school has quite a different composition: Islay, Lochgilphead, Tobermory and Tiree have their own six-year schools and, since the reorganisation of local government, pupils from Morvern, Kinlochleven, Glencoe, Ballachulish and Duror fall within Highland Region and now attend Lochaber High School. Oban High now serves a much smaller area and no longer "creams off" the most academic pupils from a large part of the county. It would be unfair therefore to compare the School of today academically with the School of the sixties and early seventies.

Oban High did have an excellent academic record then. John Maclean was especially proud of the School's record in the Edinburgh University Bursary Competition. Between 1961 and 1965 the School had four first places, three in Classics (William Gillies 1961, Kenneth MacLeod 1963 and Ann Naismith 1965) and one in English (Anne Gillies 1962). The other universities did not have their Bursary Competition split into different subjects as early as this period. The school had some excellent results in these too. In the Aberdeen Bursary Competition, for example, Mairi Morrison was seventh.

In 1964 Alasdair Renfrew won a major Railway Scholarship, while in 1971 Stuart Ross took first place in the University Entrance Bursary of the Highlands and Islands Educational Trust. Many other pupils enjoyed academic success. The school had consistently good SCE examination results. In 1971 David Page, that year's dux, set a record by obtaining seven "A" passes in his Highers.

In 1962 there was a major change in the SCE examinations with the introduction of the "O" grade examination which was taken at the end of fourth year. Many pupils who previously might have left at the end of third year now stayed on until fourth year to gain some qualifications. This change was not to Mr Maclean's liking. He felt that many businesses, by insisting that new employees had "O" grade qualifications, were setting such high standards that they were missing those pupils who, although they were not so good academically, would make excellent employees. The "O" grade, although easier than the Lower grade which it superseded, was aimed at only the top 30% of the school population. Today it has been superseded by Standard grades, which have three levels and can be taken by all pupils in fourth year. Even its future is in doubt, however, until a decision is made on the Howie Report which, among other things, recommends abolishing the Higher grade and moving Standard grade to third year.

With the Primary Memorandum of 1965 there was a major reorganisation of primary education. One of the results of this was that the Qualifying Examination, or "Quali" as it was called, was abandoned. Shortly after this the School was reorganised on Comprehensive lines. John Maclean had always maintained that Oban High was a comprehensive school, in that anyone in the lower classes who did particularly well could be moved up. Moreover, pupils tended to be given the benefit of the doubt: many were given the chance to be in the A class at first, but if, usually after the first term exams, it was felt that the work was too difficult for them, they were moved down into another class.

However in August 1967 pupils were put into mixed ability classes in first year. These classes followed a "common course" with the exception of a small group of pupils who required remedial help. The "common course" comprised the full range of subjects, with one language, either French or Gaelic. At the beginning of the second year pupils were regrouped on the basis of their performance in first year and their primary reports. Latin was offered to those thought suitable for it, while those with no flair for language were allowed to drop French or Gaelic. Over the next few years there were some changes made in the light of experience but basically the arrangement remained the same. To facilitate the "common course" the School day was divided into ten periods instead of eight.

By this time John Maclean had retired after a year's absence from October 1965, caused by ill health, and the Farquhar Macintosh had taken up office as Rector in January 1967. Some people in the town probably thought that these changes came about because of the change of Rector but, in fact, they were inevitable, the result of Government policy. This was the era of Harold Wilson's Labour Governments of 1964-70.

Another change which took place at this time was the introduction of "work-based" courses for the less academic pupils. The purpose of these courses was to motivate the pupils and to prepare them for the world of work. The first of these courses were Building, Engineering and Food Education, with the emphasis on catering for the holiday visitor. Local businesses helped out where they could: the Western Garage even donated a good second-hand car for the boys to work on. There was also an Intensive Commercial Course in the fourth year for pupils who would normally have left at fifteen to take up employment in local offices and shops. These courses, which were very popular, were the special responsibility of Mr Norman T Hardie.

These developments, the "common course" in first year and the "work-based" courses for the less academic pupils, were fundamental ones and from them has developed our present system of education.

Nor were these Mr Macintosh's only innovations. He abolished lines, which were becoming impractical with the growing pupil numbers and the spread-out nature of the school building. Perhaps he will be remembered best for the introduction of "Leisure Activities". From August 1967 the whole of Friday afternoon was devoted to "Education for leisure". Each term pupils chose from a list of varied interests which they could pursue. The list included football, shinty, hockey, rugby, netball, golf, photography, toy-making, knitting, embroidery, chess, Scripture Union, Young Farmers' Club, Community Service, piping, stamp collecting and many more. These activities were enjoyed by pupils and staff, who offered to teach some hobby of their own. The purpose of leisure activities was to educate pupils in the proper use of leisure in a world where the working week was becoming gradually shorter. Certainly many pupils were introduced to hobbies and interests which, left to their own devices, they would never have explored.

There were a few other changes. Previously the dux of the school was chosen from the sixth year. Now, because of the diversity of subjects studied by the sixth year, it was decided to chose the dux from the fifth year, where most pupils had a common core of subjects. Accordingly, 1967-68 was a transitional year, with a sixth year dux and runner-up and a fifth year dux and runner-up. From 1969 we have the pattern which is followed today, with dux and runner-up chosen from fifth year.

In August 1968 Mr Macintosh set up a "School Council" - not to be confused with the Lorn Schools' Council which existed in the years preceding the formation of School Boards. This consisted of fifteen pupils and one staff representative. At a time when there was a great deal of student unrest, it was felt to be a good idea to give pupils a sense of involvement and participation in various matters affecting the school.

Unfortunately, Mr Macintosh was not to remain long at Oban High School. He left in February 1972 to take up the post of Rector at the Royal High School in Edinburgh. As well as being a distinguished scholar and teacher - while at Jordanhill he gained the prize for the best student teacher of his year - he also did a great deal of committee work. While he was at Oban High he was a member of the SCE Examination Board, of which he later became Chairman, Vice-President of the Headmasters' Association of Scotland, Convener of the Education Sub-Committee of the Highlands and Islands Development Board and Chairman of the Board of Governors of Jordanhill College of Education. He also co-operated with the Scottish Education Department in a pilot project on the new structure of promoted posts and the introduction of the guidance system, both still features of our secondary schools. Despite all this committee work he did not neglect his duties at Oban High School and often worked until ten o'clock at night.

Even in retirement Mr Macintosh is very active: he has undertaken the chairmanship of both the Trustees and the Academic Council of the Gaelic College in his native Skye. He became an FEIS in 1971 and in 1992 has been given an honorary doctorate by Edinburgh University. Those who worked with him remember him with affection and respect. As a former member of staff once said, "He was a scholar and a gentleman."

The main problem which faced Farquhar Macintosh and John Maclean before him was that of accommodation, both classroom and hostel. In August 1960 the school had 880 pupils and this rose to an all-time record of 1,037 in September 1971. Even in the early 1960s accommodation was a problem. In 1960 there were still five classes from Rockfield using classes in the High School building. By the summer of 1961, however, temporary huts were built in the playground of Rockfield and Oban High was able to reclaim these rooms.

A few years later, when it was announced that the school-leaving age was to raised to sixteen in 1970 (it was in fact delayed a couple of years) it become obvious that more classrooms would be needed to cope with this. Accordingly, as early as 1964, the Director of Education, Mr T G Henderson, visited the school with some Inspectors to discuss preliminary plans for the new extension. As the existing back playground was earmarked for the new extension it was necessary to obtain more space for a playground. Eventually the Authority was able to convert a piece of ground belonging to the Argyllshire Gathering into a playground.

As is often the case the were delays in starting the building. In September 1968 it was announced that, because of financial restrictions imposed by the Treasury, the proposed new extension, which it was hoped would go out to tender that autumn, had been delayed by about a year. *Plus ça change. . ..*

Eventually the building did get under way in 1971 and it was opened the next year. In the years preceding this the school was bursting at the seams. The appointment of an extra member of staff caused difficulties; when Mr Archie Robertson was appointed to teach Religious Education in 1967, Farquhar Macintosh had to make a request for the conversion of a suitable cloakroom into a classroom. Later another cloakroom had to be converted, and at one time, classes were being taught in a corridor.

At a time when just over sixty pupils, the total number who live away from home, are accommodated in one hostel, it seems hard to believe that at one time it was anticipated that Oban would need an extra four eighty -bed hostels in addition to the existing ones. The source of the problem was Oban's position as a natural focus of secondary education for the whole of the North Argyll area and the problem was aggravated by the tendency for the pupils in even more distant parts of the country to prefer Oban to either Campbeltown or Dunoon even if Oban was less conveniently placed.

Certainly there was considerable strain on hostel accommodation, Kilbowie, opened in 1956, had places for 34 boys, and the longer established Craigard had places for 45 girls, but there were regularly over 100 pupils in lodgings. In January 1963 there were 65 boys and 59 girls in lodgings; a year later these figures had risen to 69 boys and 68 girls, while in September 1964 there were 72 boys and 74 girls in lodgings. This rise reflected the increase in the number of pupils transferring to Oban High from the junior secondary schools after the introduction of the "O" grade examination in 1962. It was thought too that with the closure of the Ballachulish line in 1966 and its replacement by a bus service, which would be slower, several pupils who travelled by train might choose to stay in Oban rather than face a long bus journey twice a day.

It had been suggested early in 1963 that there should be a new girls hostel at Kilbowie, but there were several objections to this, and the Education Committee therefore decided to go ahead with an extension at Kilbowie for a further 40 boys and to continue to search for a suitable site for a new girls' hostel. Through some confusion between the Education Department and Argyll Education Committee permission was actually given for an eighty-bed hostel and building went ahead.

The new extension at Kilbowie was opened in August 1968. With the new building came a new staff structure. Previously, the Matron, Miss MacBride, was in overall charge, but now there was a Warden, who was also a part-time member of the school staff. The Warden was in charge of the two hostels with Miss MacBride as Senior Matron responsible for the physical well-being of the boys. She was based in the old Hostel building, where the junior boys lived, the seniors being in the new building.

The new extension was built to a standard design promoted by the Scottish Education Department to speed up the process of building hostels in places where they were needed desperately. The girls' hostel, which was eventually built on a site at Glencruitten, followed the same plan. The official opening ceremony for Glencruitten Hostel was carried out in September 1971 by Mr (now Sir) Hector Munro MP, the Under-Secretary of State for Health and Education. In the course of his speech he remarked that he had been stationed in Oban during the Second World War when he piloted Sunderland and Catalina flying boats operated by Coastal Command.

Hostel life had, of necessity, to follow a fairly strict timetable. In Craigard, where the Warden was Miss MacLean, a lady who took her duties very seriously, the girls had a rota for ringing the bell at 7.30 am each morning, 8 o'clock on Saturdays and Sundays. They made their own beds and on Saturday mornings were not allowed out until they had changed their beds and cleaned their rooms, which were sometimes inspected. They also had a rota for corridor duty and pantry duty, where they had to help the maids with the dishes etc. On weekdays they had to be in by 5 pm and after tea they had study from 6 to 8 pm. Miss Anne MacPhail, who had lived in the Hostel when she was a pupil herself, was the resident teacher who supervised study. The girls were allowed out on Saturday mornings and afternoons and until about 8.30 at night, which was about the time the cinema came out. Anyone going to the School Club could come in slightly later. On Sunday mornings everyone had to go to church. Most went to the Parish Church where they occupied the balcony, as did the Hostel boys.

As a special treat the girls were allowed out on an evening before they were sitting a Higher exam. In case of any deception Miss MacLean demanded a copy of everyone's exam timetable in advance! They were also allowed out into the garden on summer evenings. As one might expect there was the occasional rebellion, usually minor rather than major. From time to time there would be a "beanfeast" after "lights-out" (9.30 pm for juniors, 10.30 pm for seniors). Sometimes girls sneaked down the fire escape. This was the normal escape route for anyone going to the unofficial end-of-session "beanfeast" at the Hydropathic. It is doubtful whether beans were ever actually consumed on these occasions, although certain other things were. If Miss MacLean was suspicious she would put catgut across the top of the fire escape to catch the miscreants on their return. Fortunately Craigard never had any fire which necessitated the use of the fire escape for evacuation purposes on these occasions.

The normal punishment was being "gated" on the following Saturday. For serious offences girls would, of course, be reported to the Rector. Girls were also kept in if they had been unwell during the week, in which case they might also have been subjected to a dose of salts or a kaolin poultice, both favourite treatments.

Although the Hostel was kept spotlessly clean, with its brown linoleum floors well published, it was somewhat spartan. Certainly by the 1960s it had central heating and was very warm. The food was really quite adequate. Sometimes in the evenings the girls would make toast on the electric fire in the lounge and spread it with butter surreptitiously removed from the kitchen.

For entertainment there was one radio allowed downstairs at night for the juniors and one for the seniors. Television did not reach Craigard until 1967. The girls' favourite programme was *Top of the Pops* and there was always a stampede to see this. On a more cerebral note, newspapers were left for the sixth year in there lounge. At Christmas there was dance or "Hostel Hop" which the girls arranged entirely on their own. They were also allowed to go to school dances.

As you might expect, with 45 girls in one building, there was always a shortage of hot water in the morning. Moreover, everyone had one night a week allotted for a bath and hairwash. It was too bad if your night was Saturday and you wanted to go to the school dance the next Friday!

In Kilbowie, which held 34 boys, the routine was very similar. There, in the early 1960s, the water problems were not confined to the hot water supply. A water supply which had been sufficient for a private house was inadequate for the needs of 34 boys and associated staff. They often had a shortage of water in dry spells. In early 1963 the situation became so difficult that the boys had to fill buckets with sea water in order to flush the toilets. They had to wash and shower in the school and have tea there before walking home to Kilbowie. For a couple of weeks the junior boys were sent home to ease the pressure. There were major problems again in 1964 and 1965, when it was decided to link Kilbowie with the Oban water system. Even after this there were sometimes problems as Kilbowie was right at the end of the supply pipe.

The temptation to sneak out by the fire escape was not so great at Kilbowie because of the distance from the town. It was also quite eerie walking down the Gallanach Road in the dark. However, the boys did make the effort for really important events such as the beanfeast at the Hydro.

The distance from the town also made it difficult to keep staff. The maids, who were very poorly paid, were frequently lured away to better jobs in the town. The boys were transported to and from school by bus, a service for which their parents had to pay. The skill of the bus drivers in turning the bus at the Hostel gates, where there were only a few inches to spare, was a source of wonder to the boys.

The matron of Kilbowie, Miss MacBride, an Irish lady, was awarded the BEM in the New Year Honours List of 1968. She was a remarkable lady, who was very motherly towards her boys and appreciated the problems involved in being away from home. Rather deaf, she had a hearing aid attached to her glasses, and if things became a bit noisy she switched it off. Now in her eighties, she is still alive and well and living in an Eventide Home in Limavady in Ireland. During the Second World War she took an active part in aiding survivors from convoys who were landed in Londonderry. She came to Kilbowie in 1956, the year that it opened, and retired in 1970.

As Kilbowie had spacious grounds the boys were able to make use of these for playing football. The older boys would organise activities for the younger ones. In the summer some of the boys went rowing in the school boots, which were kept at Kilbowie. As in Craigard there was a "Hostel Hop" at Christmas and the boys were also allowed out to school dances and the School Club.

Generally life ran smoothly at Kilbowie, as it did at Craigard. There was the occasional piece of mischief; on one occasion Mr Cushley, the master-in-charge at the time, was counting heads at a fire practise. It was only when he reached around 44 that he realised that something was not quite right: some of the boys had been going back into the hostel through the conservatory and back down the fire escape to be counted twice.

When the new extension opened in August 1968 it seemed luxurious compared to the old Hostel. The boys were now in three-bedded rooms, while the prefects had their own rooms. The prefects also had a room where they could make their own cups of tea. This building also had its own laundry room, complete with washing machines, so that the boys no longer had to send home their parcel of dirty washing each week, as had been the custom and was still the custom in Craigard. Another feature which was greatly appreciated was the Games Room. Television had come to Kilbowie in 1965, but the boys still enjoyed games such as "Monopoly" which occupied them for hours at a time.

Unfortunately, for a short period not long after the Hostel opened there was a considerable amount of vandalism. Around this time too, the food deteriorated, in quantity rather than quality, so much so that some boys used to buy old toasters at the Auction Mart and make toast with loaves they bought. Needless to say, they were not supposed to use electrical equipment of this nature. Most boys had contacts in the town, friends or relatives from home, and they were able to visit them for meals and some home comforts. These people made a big contribution to the lives of the pupils who lived away from home. Pupils would also go along to the sales at the Auction Mart to meet people from home. Island pupils would meet the boat on a Saturday for the same reason.

Although there were many drawbacks in living away from home there were some bonuses. Many good friendships were made. No doubt, too, for those going on to further education their time in Oban was in good preparation for the future. Some of the things they learned in the Hostel were of a dubious, if not illegal, nature. For quite a while the Kilbowie boys were able to get free phone calls home. There were several phones in the new extension and it was discovered that if you tapped out numbers on the receiver rest you would get through without paying. Sometimes the boys on the upper floor would open their windows, someone would whistle out or play the chanter, the boys below would open their windows to see what was going on and they would immediately be soaked by buckets of water emptied on them from above. One Assistant Warden, a spinster lady, had a particularly hard time. Whenever the boys did not want to be disturbed in the pursuit of some nefarious deed they would persuade one of the younger boys to remove all of his clothing and walk up and down the corridor outside her room. As soon as she opened her door she saw this boy and was so embarrassed that she closed the door at once. The mischief went on undisturbed.

The opening of the new extension at Kilbowie with its eighty beds meant that the boys who had been in lodgings in the town were able to move into the Hostel. As a result it was easier for girls to find lodgings. It was to be another three years before Glencruitten Hostel was open. Most parents preferred their children to be in a hostel, probably because they knew that they would not be allowed out too often and would have study supervised. At one time too pupils in lodgings had to pay for their school meals whereas hostel pupils had their meals paid for them.

Towards the end of 1960 Mr Maclean requested of the Education Committee that they appoint an Attendance Officer who would also look after the welfare of the pupils in lodgings. He wrote "She would be expected to assist in finding lodgings for pupils during the summer holidays and to see any arrangements made in regard to pupils changing lodgings. She would deal with complaints, whether from landlady or pupil, and would look into such matters as bad behaviour, undesirable friendships, as well as unsatisfactory food and heating. One or two evening visits per week to pupils in lodgings would be part of her regular duties." Most of her day would be taken up by problems connected with attendance. Mr Maclean added that one of his own staff had been carrying out welfare work in her own time and in addition to her teaching duties. During the summer holidays she had dealt with 31 requests from parents for help in finding accommodation.

As a result of this letter the Education Committee decided to appoint a full-time woman Attendance Officer. Mrs K Cameron was appointed to the post in May 1961 and she was succeeded a year later by Miss Campbell, who became Mrs MacCalman. It must have been reassuring for parents to know that someone would be keeping a watchful eye on their children, who at the age of eleven or twelve, were away from home for as much as two months at a time. In those days many pupils were able to go home only at long weekends and holidays.

Parents would apply to the Attendance Officer, who would supply them with a list of lodgings. It was then up to them to visit the lodgings of their choice and make the final arrangements. Some landladies had a tradition of taking pupils from certain places. No doubt pupils who were leaving would pass on the name of their landlady to pupils from their home village or island. There were a few lodgings where pupils felt somewhat regimented but most landladies treated the pupils well and many have kept in touch over the years. The Attendance Officer made regular visits and even used to bring grapes for anyone who was ill. Farquhar Macintosh himself also made occasional visits.

John Maclean and Farquhar Macintosh might never have thought that a time would come when Oban would have a surplus of hostel accommodation, but this is, in fact , what has happened, with all hostel pupils now accommodated in Glencruitten Hostel.

Apart from the hostel and lodging pupils a considerable number travelled to school every day. Most came by bus, as they do today. It is surprising how few days were lost because of bad weather. Occasionally buses were delayed as a result of icy roads or a sudden fall of snow and there was an odd day when buses did not get through at all. The day after the great January storm of 1968 was one such day although, strangely enough, the Taynuilt bus did manage to complete its run. On that day the problem was caused by fallen trees blocking the roads. Fortunately the damage to the school itself was not too severe. Kilbowie Hostel was without electricity and water for most of the day and the boys had to have their tea in the school canteen.

Undoubtedly, as far as school travel was concerned, the main event of the decade was the closure of the railway line between Ballachulish and Oban. Announced by Dr Beeching in 1963, the closure eventually took place, after a public inquiry, in March 1966. There were many objectors to the closure. Some felt that the projected time of 1 hour 50 minutes for the bus journey was too optimistic as the road was narrow and twisting, and busy with tourist traffic in the summer. A point made by Mr Maclean was that pupils could do their homework on the train but not on the bus which was to replace it.

Despite all the objections the line did close on Saturday, 26th March, 1966. The last train left Oban at 9.35 pm with a crew from Ballachulish and then made the return journey with an Oban crew - driver Kenneth MacIntyre, fireman David Strachan and guard Ian Black. On board were Mr J G Mathieson, Convener of Argyll County Council for many years, and Provost Spence, previously Principal Teacher of Physical Education at Oban High. The pupils obviously felt that it was the end of an era for them too, as they had clubbed together to buy a present for the guard, Mr Hugh MacNeill, and this was presented to him at Connel Station.

Travel on the Ballachulish train was, to quote one who travelled on it, "an education in itself". The trains were steam hauled and the carriages did not have corridors. Sometimes pupils would walk along the running board to get from one compartment to another. There was a tradition whereby boys and girls did not mix - there were male compartments and female compartments. There were, of course, members of the public on board too. One man is remembered for always insisting that the pupils should take out their books and do their homework. In very dry weather some of the pupils would throw lighted horse-hair, which they had pulled out of the seats, on to the track. Forestry workers had to follow the train to put out the fires.

It was a long day for the pupils. The train left Ballachulish about 7 am. It also served Kentallen, Duror, Appin, Creagan, Barcaldine, Benderloch and North Connel. The arrival in Oban at 8.40 am gave the pupils adequate time to walk up to the school. If the train was a bit late the pupils made the most of it. On one occasion the train reached Oban station at 8.55 am. All the pupils took their time and reached the school at 9.20 am with the exception of one, a son of the manse, now a distinguished cleric himself, who ran up the road and arrived in School at 9 o'clock. All the others were sent to detention that day. This was possible because the train home that day did not leave until 4.50 pm. Usually the pupils spent the time between 4.10 pm and the departure of the train looking around the shops or having a walk round the pier.

British Rail did not waste any time once the line was closed. The rails were lifted by that autumn. One benefit was that tolls were lifted from Connel Bridge, but there were losses. A round trip popular with tourists was to travel by train to Ballachulish, by MacConnacher's bus from Ballachulish to Glenetive and by boat down to Achnacloich where they joined the train again to return to Oban. (Achnacloich was another of the stations axed by Dr Beeching). The Royal train had been on the line during the reign of Edward VII. He sailed down from Kinlochleven to Kentallen where he joined the train.. The American General, later President, Eisenhower also travelled on the line during the Second World War when he came to inspect the American fleet assembling in Loch Linnhe prior to the invasion of North Africa.

During the period 1960-72 the school had a very active social life, with many activities run for the benefit of the pupils by members of staff. Many of the activities were of a sporting nature. Oban High had an outstanding record in sport in the 1960s. The PE department led by Mr Spence and his successor, Mr MacWilliam and by Miss Jean MacDonald organised football teams, shinty teams, hockey teams, netball teams, and later, rugby teams. Mr Spence, who came to Oban High in 1954, had brought the school out of the athletic doldrums. It was due to his energy and hard work that the school achieved a level of success it had never enjoyed before. The school team entered the Schools Football Association Shield competitions, boys entered the Scottish Schoolboys Athletics Championships, pupils were sent on coaching schemes and on climbing and outdoor training schemes.

As well as the school teams there were also clan teams, who competed against each other. Even those who were not athletically talented were keen spectators at the school sports. Everyone cheered enthusiastically for their own clan, especially at the relay races, which took place right at the end of the sports. There were many individual successes in the sports over the years and many records were broken. One of the best years was 1963 when several new records were set : Alasdair MacArthur in the Senior Boys High Jump; Hugh MacLean in the Senior Boys Discus; Dennis Hill in the Intermediate Boys 220 yards and 440 yards; Henry Silkowski in the Junior Boys High Jump; Archie MacDougall, Neil Maclennan and Ian Donn all exceeded the previous record in the Shinty Ball; Ann MacGillivray in the Senior Girls Discus. The Intermediate Boys Relay record was also broken.

Nineteen sixty-three was also the year when the first ever Inter-School or County Sports were held. It cannot be denied that Oban High dominated their section in the sports. They won both Senior Championships and one each of the Intermediate and Junior Championships as well as six Relay Races. They continued to do extremely well in subsequent years.

In 1964 the first ever County Schools Cross-Country Championships were held and Oban High won all three Championships. They went on to take part in the Scottish Championships at Pitreavie and acquitted themselves creditably there.

One of the most exciting moments was indubitably in 1966 when the senior shinty team won the MacBean Trophy by beating Inverness Royal Academy 3-1 in the final. The senior team had already won the Murchison Trophy and the junior team the MacPherson Trophy. This was the first time that any school had held all three trophies at the same time. To celebrate the occasion the teams were entertained to tea by Oban Town Council.

The year 1965 saw the formation of the school's first rugby team. Rugby had never been encouraged before as Mr Maclean was afraid that boys would be less keen to play shinty if there was a rugby team as well. Fortunately this was not the case as rugby is now well established in the school and shinty is still popular. In their first "friendly" match against Oban Lorne, Oban Lorne won by 21-5, a score which, according to *The Oban Times* was not an entirely accurate reflection of the performance of the schoolboys.

Football was always popular with the boys and under Mr Spence's influence the School had a busy fixture list with a fair degree of success. Mr Spence was the inspiration behind games like "Argyll versus North of Scotland" and "Argyll versus Rest of Scotland". Several Oban boys were usually picked for the Argyll team. On more than one occasion Oban boys were included in trials for the selection of the Scottish Schoolboys International Team. Alasdair MacArthur, now a member of staff, was the first boy from the school to gain a place in this team.

133

There were other sports which were perhaps minority interests but nevertheless added to the life of the school. Very often these depended on a member of staff being interested and taking charge of the sport. There was a Basketball Club, a Tennis Club, a Badminton Club, a Climbing Club, a Rowing Club, a Ski Club, a Golf Championship and a Gymnastic Team. When Farquhar Macintosh introduced "Leisure Activities" on Friday afternoons in August 1967 many of these sports could take place then. It was very useful for the PE staff to have team practices then, as many pupils travelled home as soon as school finished and many others had after-school or Saturday jobs.

One of these clubs which developed into something much bigger was the Badminton Club. In the school session 1961-62 it become the School Club and now included activities such as table-tennis, basketball, netball, darts, chess and draughts. The Club was now open to fourth year as well as fifth and sixth. The meetings, as before, were held on Saturday nights during the winter months. The Club could not have existed had it not been for the generosity of the staff who gave up their Saturday evenings to supervise. Staff, presumably volunteers, took turns at supervising, but from about the mid-60s onwards most of the burden fell on Mr Bill Davidson. The Club was enjoyed greatly by the pupils as there was not a lot to do on Saturday nights. There was the cinema, but in those days films tended to be quite old before they reached Oban.

The Club's main reason for existing was to entertain hostel pupils at the weekend, although many local pupils went too. After the new extension to Kilbowie Hostel was opened the boys had their own Games Room and were less inclined to come to the School Club. As a result the membership dropped until it was not worthwhile continuing it.

The Debating Society underwent a major change in 1960. Previously it was compulsory for all members of the fifth and sixth years to attend and take their turn to speak. Now the constitution was changed so that attendance was no longer compulsory. This had the advantage of attracting only those who had a genuine interest in debating. (By the 1963-64 session a Junior Debating Society was also formed). On the other hand the new form of the Society was less successful in overcoming the reticence of the typical West Highland pupil, who now stayed away.

The School Cadet Company, formed in the school in 1952 under Captain (later Major) William Clark flourished throughout the 1960s. On average there was a membership of thirty to fifty boys each year. They met on Thursday evenings and Friday afternoons and there was an annual camp, usually in the first fortnight of July. The aim was to develop character and to prepare boys to join the army. Quite a number of boys did in fact do this. At the Thursday evening meetings the boys could play games, such as billiards and darts, and they could shoot on a .22 rifle range. They also practised drill, map-reading, field craft and weapon training, as well as taking part in sporting activities such as football, athletics and sailing on *Elk*, the yacht gifted to the Company. On one occasion the boys acted as film extras when *The Idle Prawn* was being filmed at Glencruitten. On the death of Major Clark in 1967 the Company was taken over by Captain Page (of the Modern Languages Department), who was promoted to Major. These two, along with Captain George MacKay (of the Technical Department) were the backbone of the Company during the 1960s, but they were assisted by various others, such as Mr John Clark, Mr Norman MacDonald, Mr H Cameron and Mr C Malone.

The Cadet Company was one of the organisations which prepared its members for the Duke of Edinburgh's Award. The first person in Oban High to receive the Gold Award, in 1965, was Angus Gordon, the son of Mr William Gordon, Principal Teacher of Art, and at that time a fifth-year pupil. Angus, who had hitch-hiked to Vienna and back with his older brother at the age of eleven was remarkable individual. A keen mountaineer and cross-country runner, he was chosen to go on the British Schools Exploring Society's 1964 expedition to a cold and desolate part of Central Iceland. The party consisted of sixty-seven British schoolboys and representatives chosen from industry. Angus was the youngest of them. The expedition, which lasted seven weeks, was gruelling. It involved marches where the boys had to carry loads of sixty pounds, wade through ice-cold rivers and sleep in tents in temperatures which fell as low as fourteen degrees of frost. Sadly, Angus died while still a young man, a few years after gaining a degree in Psychology at Edinburgh University.

The first girls in Argyll to win the Gold Award were Mairi Morrison, daughter of Mr Donald Morrison of the Gaelic Department, Margaret MacDougall, Jennifer MacAulay and Rosamond MacAulay. They received their awards in January 1966, not long after they had left school. The girls were members of the "Campaigners", a youth organisation of the Free High Church. There were also several Bronze and Silver awards for other "Campaigners" and Cadets.

The Scripture Union was another organisation which had a good following in the School. As well as the meeting on Wednesdays at 4.10 pm there was a branch at Kilbowie which held its meetings, thanks to Miss MacBride, on Sunday evenings. The High School Branch was split unto senior and junior sections in 1963. Teachers involved were Mr M MacArthur, Mrs MacLune, Mr George MacKay, Miss Norma MacDonald and Mr Glass.

The Climbing Club was started in 1959 by Mr Murray, Principal Teacher of History. The boys spent many Saturdays climbing and sometimes stayed overnight in Youth Hostels. Mr Spalding of the Technical Department later formed a Climbing Club for the younger boys and he kept the Club going when Mr Murray's health deteriorated. Mr Spalding devoted a lot of time to the Club and sometimes took groups of boys away for a week at a time.

The Rowing Club, whose boats were kept at Kilbowie, was run by Mr Turner, who taught Geography (there was not an actual Geography Department in the early sixties). As well as the enjoyment of rowing, the boys and girls experienced hard work in looking after the boats. Miss MacBride co-operated here too and allowed the Hostel boys to help and take part.

In the summer of 1964 four canoes which had been built by the Technical Department were launched at Kilbowie. Quite an occasion was made of it. The School closed early and classes four, five and six were invited to attend. After the launching there was a race, which was won by Clan Somerled. A barometer, which was to be competed for every year, was presented to the winning crew by Mrs Maclean.

For those whose interests were musical rather than physical there was Mr Garth Kay's Recorder Group, who performed at numerous school concerts and on other occasions. At one time, too, there was a Dramatic Club, which performed three one-act plays in the Dunollie Hall in 1961. There was also a Film Club at one time.

One of the highlights of the pupils' year was the Christmas dance or "Musical". There were other dances in the course of the year but the Christmas one was special. The Musicals were always well attended by staff and pupils. Many people worked hard to make them a success. The Art Department made Christmas decorations for the Hall and Canteen and the Domestic Science Department (now known as Home Economics) provided the supper, which was set out nicely in the Canteen. The finishing touch was the pupils being piped along the corridors from the Central Hall to the Canteen, often to the strains of *The Glendaruel Highlanders*, Mr Maclean's favourite pipe tune. Music at the dance was mainly traditional, Billy Ford being a great favourite.

Up until 1969, first year pupils did not have a dance. Instead they sometimes had a film show or, later in the decade, a beetle drive and party. Another innovation came in 1971 when the Senior Musical was held in the Corran Hall since the Central Hall, where all dances had been held before this, was too small for the numbers involved. This dance was for fourth, fifth and sixth years. Previously the fourth year had had their own separate dance.

There were other dances too, mostly organised by the Clans. As Mr Maclean did not wish pupils to go to dances in the town, there was usually about one dance a month in the school for the seniors. The Clans organised other activities too. One regular event was the "Ossian Concert". They also challenged the other Clans to a quiz. Perhaps the most adventurous undertaking was when Clan Diarmid chartered *King George V* for a mystery cruise in June 1964. There was music and dancing on board. Altogether it was a very successful event. Each year the Clan Trophy was awarded to the Clan judged to have done the most for the School.

In 1992, the centenary year of the Mod as well as of the school, it would be impossible to ignore the place of Gaelic in the School and the success of the Gaelic choirs and individual pupils. Trophies were won by the choir on several occasions. The premier trophy, the Oban Times Challenge Shield was won in 1961, 1963, 1964 and 1965. Perhaps the choir's finest performance was at the Perth Mod in 1963 where it also won the Mrs Campbell Blair Trophy, the Angus M Ross Trophy and the Mrs Hobbs Cup, the latter two for Gaelic. That year, too, Margaret Macleod from Ardnamurchan won the girls' Silver Medal, with Sandra Fjortoft the runner-up. The boys' Silver Medal was won on two occasions, in 1966 by Niall Brown and in 1968 by Duncan MacFadyen. Both boys came from Colonsay. In 1962 the youngest ever ladies' Gold Medallist was Anne Gillies, who proved that she was as talented musically as she was academically. In 1970 the men's Gold Medal went to a former pupil Duncan MacDonald.

These Mod successes were a tribute to the hard work of the Music and the Gaelic Departments. Mrs Kelday was an enthusiastic music teacher who had even produced an opera, *HMS Pinafore*. When she returned to her native Orkney in 1964 as Organiser in Music, she was succeeded by Mr Brownlie Henderson, who had great success at his first Mod in Aberdeen, although he was not himself a Gaelic speaker. The Gaelic input came from Mr Donald Thomson and his assistant, Mr Donald Morrison, both natives of Lewis. Mr Maclean and Mr Macintosh, from Raasay and Skye respectively, also took a great interest. Donald Thomson would surely have been proud to know that two of his former pupils are now Professors of Celtic, William Gillies at Edinburgh University and Donald Meek at Aberdeen. Indeed, even when Donald Meek was in sixth year at school he did some Gaelic broadcasting.

On a slightly less exalted note, the school team, comprising Donald Meek, Mairead Thomson (Donald Thomson's daughter) and Iain Kennedy (now a Solicitor in Oban), won the Gaelic Quiz Competition in 1967 after defeating teams from Inverness High School, Inverness Technical College and the Nicolson Institute, Stornoway.

In 1971 Oban High achieved national fame after appearing on the television quiz show *Top of the Form*. The Team, which consisted of Stuart Ross, Kenneth MacIntyre, Mary Nicol and Ann Hay, did extremely well. In the first round they defeated Kirkwall Grammar School, and in the second round Harrogate Grammar School. They were however narrowly beaten in the semi-final by Kenilworth Grammar School. As they were one of the top three teams they were chosen to represent the United Kingdom in the *Transworld* competition. In this they won their morning match against Minneapolis but lost in the afternoon to Baltimore, the eventual winners.

Two years earlier, in 1969, Mr Iain MacCormick of the History Department, along with Mr Pat Robertson, Headmaster of Rockfield School, and traffic warden Mrs Alexandrina MacDonald, had brought great honour to Oban by winning another television quiz programme, *Quizburgh*.

Although Oban High is somewhat isolated geographically, many school trips were made to broaden the pupils' outlook. These varied from trips to the Playhouse to see Olivier's *Hamlet* to foreign holidays. Some pupils took part in cruises to places as far apart as the Azores and Leningrad. The inspiration behind the trips in the early 1960s was Mr William Gordon, who took pupils to places of culture such as Paris, Vienna, Brussels, Amsterdam and Italy. One school magazine describes such a group as "a part of artists and adventurers in the ratio of one to ten". This is probably an accurate description of all such groups. There are many happy memories of these trips. On one occasion, when the assorted pupils were being taken through Montmartre en route to the Sacré Coeur, Miss Isa MacInnes was accosted by a Frenchman whose persistence she finally quashed by pointing to the pupils and repeating "mes enfants, mes enfants!". This had the desired effect; he departed at once. Isa ran the office on her own until 1963 when she had some part-time assistance from Mrs MacLellan. The office, now the Depute Rector's room, was very small. The present office was Mr Gordon's art room. Always cheery, Isa did her best to smooth the way for anyone in trouble.

Mr Gordon retired in 1970 after serving in Oban High School since 1947. Even those who were not artistically gifted could enjoy his Art Appreciation classes in fourth year (architecture) and fifth year (painting). Enjoyable at the time, they were of great educational value. Mr Gordon also produced plays, some in Gaelic, and designed and painted sets for them. A member of Oban Gaelic Choir, he also took part in some of the local Operatic Society productions. He is also remembered for his superb dancing at the Christmas Musicals. Also, unlike many art teachers, Mr Gordon actually painted pictures, some of which have been exhibited.

An interesting trip to Oberammergau took place in 1970 under the leadership of Mr Archie Robertson, who taught Religious Education for some time. Perhaps the greatest adventure was the exchange visit to Nova Scotia in May 1971. Eight senior pupils spent three weeks in Cape Breton, where they lived with the Canadian family of their opposite number. The Canadian pupils made the return visit to Oban in August. The Oban pupils were entertained most hospitably in Canada, even although on one occasion they were thrown fully clothed into a lake. Oban High, in its turn, went to a great deal of trouble to entertain the Canadians. There was a weekend trip to Aviemore, a buffet in the School Hall and a barbecue to mark the Canadian guests' last evening.

There were various differences between the Canadian School and Oban High. One of these was the lack of school uniform in the Canadian school. The Canadians felt that they looked brighter in their casual clothes but admitted that there was an element of competition. In Oban High at this time uniform was still worn by most pupils. The wearing of uniform had been encouraged by Mr Maclean. It is to be hoped that the new school uniform will be a success, although it will long seem strange to these of us used to the navy and yellow of the past, which at some point mysteriously changed to black and gold. An interesting fashion note is that as the sixties progressed the boys' hair became longer and the girls' skirts became shorter.

The 1960s saw the start of many things which we take for granted today. Television, black and white of course, arrived in the school in 1964, shortly after the BBC mast came into operation in the summer of 1963. Calculators also made their first appearance in these years. In the spring of 1966 Mr James Troup, Principal Teacher of Mathematics, and Mr Bill Davidson went to see some calculating machines at an exhibition in Glasgow. Shortly afterwards the school obtained some of these mechanically operated calculators, which were to prove very useful.

Since the School now has, for the first time, a Principal Teacher of Computing, Mr J Milligan, it is worth noting that the school's first experimental course in Computer Studies was introduced in the Session 1969-70. Mr Bill Davidson took on much of the work involved in this. Paisley College of Technology funded it substantially and granted the School postal access to their computer. Later Jordanhill College took over and, later still, the School obtained its own computer.

With the arrival of Mr Sandy Elliot in November 1967 Oban High had another "first": it was the first school in Argyll to have a Laboratory Technician. Now no Science Department could manage without one.

Just as some subjects become fashionable, others become less so. Nowadays, alas, there is no Classics Department as such, nor is there a Navigation Department. Within Oban itself some other well-loved institutions of the 1960s have gone. No more do Oban's youth spend their Saturday afternoons in the George Cafe or their Saturday evenings at the Playhouse Cinema. There is no longer Joe Boni's with his delicious ice-cream, not to mention a supply of Askits for a certain teacher. Nor is there a holiday for the Games; that stopped in 1967 when the Games were held in August for the first time.

Another feature of the school of the sixties was the end-of-term visit to Church, the Old Parish, Argyll Square or the Free High. The pupils walked there and back in crocodile fashion. School uniform was worn, and the girls wore navy berets, at least until the mid-sixties. Separate provision was made for Roman Catholic pupils then as now.

The Prefects in those days had various duties. They supervised the boys' and girls' lines, while the School Captains took them in and read out any announcements. Prefects were posted along the corridors and on the stairs, to make sure that pupils kept to the right and proceeded in good order. The girl Prefects had to collect the dinner money in the canteen, not a pleasant task. At one time the staff had to take turns doing this. The boy Prefects took turns at supervising. The main privilege was access to the JS (Junior Study), a separate one for the boys and girls, where the Prefects could have tea and biscuits at the interval. The girls JS was quite cosy, with a coal fire. There was the occasional scare when a mouse appeared out of a corner but on the whole it was a pleasant room, despite the colour scheme of cerise and turquoise after the girls painted it one weekend.

Politics have always been high on the agenda at Oban High. Whenever there was a General Election there was usually a Mock Election in the School and the pupils were allowed to parade their political prejudices. Two teachers from the 1960s managed to reach the House of Commons and one of these is now a member of the House of Lords. Mr Iain MacCormick was SNP member for Argyll from 1974 until 1979. Mr John J MacKay, who was Liberal candidate for Argyll in the 1960s, changed his political allegiance and captured the seat for the Tories in 1979. He served as our MP from 1979 until 1987 and for some of that time was a Scottish Office Minister. Recently he became Lord MacKay of Ardbrecknish, a title which betrays his Argyll origins. Although John Smith, the present leader of the Labour Party, was not himself educated at Oban High, his mother was a pupil, as were his sisters Mary and Annie, who both left during the 1960s.

On a local level, too, the staff took an active part in politics. Mr Donald Thomson was elected to Oban Town Council in 1954 and twice served as Provost. Mr E T F Spence also served on the Council, twice as Provost. He later became a County Councillor. Another staff member who was a Town Councillor was Mr John J MacKay. The school's tradition of political activity has continued to the present day - Mr Ian Smyth of the Mathematics Department represents one of the Oban wards on the District Council.

Politics is not the only vehicle to fame for pupils and staff. Few schools in Scotland, if any, could boast of having a teacher as distinguished in the field of literature as Mr Iain Crichton Smith, who came to Oban High in 1955. He was responsible for most of the school magazines produced. According to one magazine editor, he did most of the work. He has had poems, short stories and novels published and broadcast in English and Gaelic. He is a writer of international renown and in recent years has travelled widely to give lectures on his work. He left teaching in 1977 in order to devote more time to writing. Oban High was lucky to have him on the staff[1].

It was as the champion of Gaelic that Mr Donald Thomson, Depute Rector after Mr Lees retired, was honoured with the award of the OBE in 1970. He was elected President of *An Comunn Gaidhealach* in 1962 and worked tirelessly for the Gaelic cause. At the time of the 1970 Mod, which was held in Oban, Concorde was making test runs down the west coast of Scotland. A team from Glasgow University and various pieces of technical equipment were installed in a house at Millpark Terrace to measure the effect of Concorde's sonic boom on a typical council house. Donald Thomson wrote a letter requesting that there should be no flights during the finals of the Mod. His request was granted.

Another recipient of an award, this time the MBE, was Mr Norman T Hardie, who built up the Technical Department from one teacher at the time of his arrival in 1938 to a large Department fully involved in the new work-based courses of the late sixties. For may years he was active in the EIS and he was appointed to the Executive in 1962. In 1963 he was made a Fellow of the Educational Institute of Scotland. He was elected Vice-President for the year 1969-70 and in 1970 he was elected to the newly-formed General Teaching Council.

It would be impossible to name all the staff who made Oban High the excellent educational establishment that it was in the years 1960-72 and no offence is meant to any who are not mentioned here. There are, however, some people who retired during this period after many years of service in the school.

One of these was Mr A H Davidson, Principal Teacher of Science, who came to Oban from Wick High School in 1931. During the First World War he had joined the forces straight from school and he returned to active service as a Major in the Royal Engineers in 1939. His war work was recognised with the award of the MBE in 1946. He had been a keen sportsman, who had played in the Highland Football League. Music was also an interest of his, as was scouting. In fact he was District Commissioner for ten years. He put his many interests to practical use in the service of the School. In 1955 he became Depute Rector and ran the school efficiently when the Rector was absent because of illness. Before he retired he was made a Fellow of the Educational Institute of Scotland to mark his work in education. Many of his pupils will remember him for his reference to "Davidson's alley" namely the gutter, where he complained of having to walk on his way home from school.

He was succeeded as Depute Rector by Mr W Lees, Principal Teacher of Commercial Subjects. When Mr Lees retired in June 1967 he had served thirty-seven years in Oban High School, longer (just!) than any of his colleagues. He came from Lanarkshire and had worked as a miner when he was young. As well as his School duties, which he performed ably, he taught evening classes from 1930 until 1962 and was head of Further Education. When Mr Maclean took ill in October 1965 Mr Lees found himself in charge of the school. A strict man but fair, he ran the school very efficiently until Mr Macintosh took up his position in January 1967.

No former pupil can fail to remember Mr James Troup, who came to Oban High School from Glasgow in 1931 and taught there until he retired in January 1968. In 1940 he became Principal Teacher of Mathematics. He was a strict disciplinarian whose reputation went ahead of him with the result that, by the 1960s he had little need to exercise his discipline. Although he came down hard on anyone who misbehaved, he was very helpful to anyone in difficulty. He used to give extra lessons after 4.10 pm to his Higher Maths classes in the weeks preceding the exam. Woe betide any pupils who looked in the door as they passed; they were hauled in to observe the class! Mr Troup was popular in the staff room and he was a good sport. For many years he was a stalwart member of the Staff Hockey Team which played the senior girls' team each year. It was very rarely that the girls won, thanks to the dubious tactics employed by the staff. He also had a keen sense of humour. Those who made stupid mistakes were not allowed to forget them in a hurry. One pupil who worked out that a car would go one mile on thirty-nine gallons of petrol was reminded of this mistake regularly, even when she was in the Higher Maths class.

Another teacher famous for his jokes was Mr Henry Dobbins, Principal Teacher of Modern Languages. Unfortunately, like most teachers' jokes, they were repeated year after year. "Don't worry, it's one of ours", he would say when a plane passed overhead and the whole class looked towards the window of Room 34. Each year the Modern Languages Department had a French student. These students had quite a hard time. Usually they were given a whole class for a period or half a period. Nowadays they take a few pupils from a class at a time. This system seems much more beneficial for pupils and student alike.

Mrs Stuart of the Art Department retired in 1967. She was very modern in her outlook. Present-day pupils would have been at home in her classroom. She believed that Art needed an atmosphere of freedom and she made her room such a place. A very cheery person, she neither believed in nor made use of corporal punishment, yet few pupils took advantage of this.

Miss MacNaughton came to Oban High in 1946 and taught there until her retirement in June 1969. She was enthusiastic and concientious and always willing to lend a hand at school functions. Having Mull connections herself, she often turned a blind eye when pupils came in slightly late on Monday morning after taking a weekend at home.

Mr Ewen MacDonald, Principal Teacher of English left in 1961 to become Rector of the Gordon Schools, Huntly, a job described by himself as "the muckin' o' Geordie's byre". Mr Greig Anderson who came to the Science Department in 1962 had been teaching in Huntly previously. Strangely enough, when he was a pupil at Aberdeen Grammar School, Mr MacDonald taught him English. Mr MacDonald's successor, Mr John Clark, also left to become a Head Teacher, this time of Auchterarder Junior Secondary. He was an excellent teacher who took part in many activities in the School and the town. He achieved outstanding results in Higher English - 75 passes out of 75 in 1967, the year he left - but was not only interested in certificate classes. In 1965 he took one of his classes to Appin to visit the scene of the Appin Murder which was being studied at the time.

Many other excellent teachers left during the years 1960-72 - Mr Magnus More, who has just retired as Director of Education for Fife Region, Mrs MacKenzie, wife of Rev Donald MacKenzie, the School Chaplain and member of the Education Committee, Miss Norma MacDonald, Mr Glass, who also became a Rector, as did Mr Blake, Mr Little, Mr Hegney, Mr A C P Smith, the very popular Mr MacWilliam, Miss Anderson, who ran the Junior Debating Society, Mr Torquil MacLeod, who exhibited paintings in London and elsewhere, and several others.

When Mr A J Murray retired prematurely through ill-health in 1967 it was, in his own words "because I can no longer give of my best". This was typical of a man who never spared himself as far as his pupils were concerned. He came to Oban High in January 1949 and was promoted to Principal Teacher of History in 1956. Mr Murray, however, had not always been a teacher. After graduating from Gonville and Caius College, Cambridge, he took up social work among the unemployed and lectured for the Workers' Educational Association in Yorkshire. When he was invalided out of the Army in 1940 he worked as an accountant in Glasgow. It was only in 1946 that he started teaching. His previous experience helped to give him the keen insight into human nature for which he is remembered. He was an excellent teacher, ahead of his time in many ways. Even in the 1960s, before the advent of the more modern methods of history teaching, he tried to get his pupils to think things out for themselves rather than learn facts by rote. To this end he even wrote his own textbooks. He was undoubtedly a brilliant man, but he was also humane and understanding, with a good sense of humour and a fund of amusing stories. Before his illness affected him Mr Murray was very active in the school. As recounted in the last chapter, it was he who took a party of pupils to Dresden in 1956. In 1959 he started a Climbing Club for Senior pupils but had to give this up in 1961. That he soldiered on in school until 1967 is a tribute to his tenacity.

Mr Murray did not have a long retirement, although he did manage to write a book about his famous ancestor, Frederick Huth. When he died in March 1969, an address prepared by him was read at the school end-of-term service. Eight prefects acted as pall-bearers at his funeral in the Parish Church, where he had been an elder. The next day pupils attended a memorial service in which Farquhar Macintosh read the lesson and John Maclean gave an appreciation. In it he said, "He was, I think, the best-loved teacher I have ever known".

By this time Mr Maclean himself had retired. He took ill in October 1965 and never returned to work. It is very difficult for those of us who left before this time to imagine the school without him. His spirit pervaded the whole school. Most pupils will remember him standing outside his office when classes were changing. He would stand there, hands on his lapels, and pick out various people as they passed, to enquire either after their own progress or that of brothers and sisters who had left school. He had a marvellous memory and knew everyone by name. He not only signed all report cards but issued them personally. At one time, when he was responsible for the Primary Department as well, he would administer reading tests to Primary 2 children when they were being streamed for the next year.

A brilliant scholar, he had gained a First Class Honours degree from Edinburgh. He then went to Cambridge, and thereafter came a period of post-graduate study in Vienna. As preparation for this he taught himself German in the summer months before he went there.

Without a doubt he could have had a distinguished university career, but he chose instead to go in for teaching. After teaching in Edinburgh and Inverness, he became an Inspector of Schools, in which post he showed helpfulness and understanding, attributes not common among the Inspectorate in those days. He became Rector of Oban High School in 1950 at the age of forty.

The School's Bursary Competition successes have already been noted, but it must also be said that most of these were due to himself and Mr Cunningham Irving, the Principal Teacher of Classics. Mr Irving was a first class teacher but did not have enough time on his timetable to take all the Latin classes and Greek as well. In the 1960s he was helped out in Latin by Mr A J Macleod but it was the Rector who taught much of the Greek as well as some Latin. He amazed his pupils with his ability to recite from memory large tracts of the *Iliad* and *Odyssey*. It was common for him to send a short poem in Greek to anyone about to sit their finals.

When he retired Mr Maclean did some work on Glasgow Unversity's Gaelic Dictionary and he also translated the *Odyssey* into Gaelic in a very short time, an incredible feat. It is, however, for his humanity and care for all his pupils that he is remembered. While he was keen for all his pupils to do their best, he often emphasised that it was more important to be a nice person. He knew all that was going on and, as far as the staff were concerned, he was a hard taskmaster. Yet he never expected them to do anything he would not do himself. Although he was strict with his staff, he was also kind. At Christmas he would buy Christmas cakes for the men's staffroom, the ladies' staffroom and the Prefects. Any parents who called were warmly received.

When Mr Maclean died suddenly in September 1970 many tributes were paid to this great man. Mr T G Henderson summed Mr Maclean up precisely when he said "He was one of the most complete Headmasters we have ever known. Complete in the sense that he had a scholarship second to none in his own particular field and complete in his management of the School and in his relations with the community".

NOTE

1   Editor's note: It is regrettable that in such a prestigious work as *The Cambridge Guide to Literature in English* (CUP, revised edition, 1992), the statement is made on page 927 that Iain Crichton Smith "worked as a schoolteacher in Clydebank from 1955 until 1977, when he became a full-time writer". No mention is made of Oban High School.

The years 1972-1981

NEIL A MACINTOSH

"If I could be the Rector
I think it would be fun
I'd put my feet upon the desk
And sit upon my * ! * "

OHS School Magazine, 1975, extract from *School* by Sheila Lawrie

Sometimes maybe! But not very often, to judge by the activity and achievements within and around Oban High School in this decade.

In the 1970s Oban High School said farewell to a distinguished Rector, Farquhar Macintosh, and to a good number of senior and long serving staff, some leaving to retirement, others to promotion, and two to the House of Commons, no less. The School welcomed Terence Twatt as its new Rector, and "Captain of the Ship" to quote E T F Spence at Mr Twatt's installation as Rector on 13th April, 1972. Also welcomed were many new staff, some to stay for several years, some to the present, and others, for example, the Modern Languages Assistants, for but a year. There were more pupils too, with the roll first passing 1,000 in the session 1971-72, and comfortably exceeding 1,400 by the middle of the decade. The Raising of the School Leaving Age (ROSLA) - to sixteen - and pupils' willingness to stay on, "hungry for highers" in Farquhar Macintosh's phrase, encouraged this development.

The impact of Government was felt beyond ROSLA, for this was the decade of local government reorganisation and also of Parent Teacher Associations and of Schools Councils. The demise of the County Council and the creation of Argyll and Bute District Council within the new "super" region of Strathclyde, the largest unit of local government in Western Europe, were part of this impact. At the last meeting of the Argyll County Council Education Committee, the Committee's Chairman E T F Spence, urged the new regional authority to meet all the commitments and long term plans that had been made for education in Argyll, including the building of more hostel accommodation for Oban High School. The new structure undoubtedly changed the climate in which Oban High School operated, and whilst something was lost, something was also gained.

Of more immediate, if similarly debatable, impact on pupils and teachers was the abolition of corporal punishment. This change took place in the second half of the decade. Overnight, reputations for being "good with the belt" disappeared, leaving only myth and legend to impress generations of up and coming secondary pupils.

The increase in pupil numbers threw into sharper focus the School's perennial problem - shortage of accommodation. The "New Building and Games Hall" had been scheduled for completion to coincide with the implementation of ROSLA, on 1st September, 1972. This did not happen. In his first entries into the School Log, Mr Twatt noted his concern, commenting, "the accommodation situation is chronic". He was also worried about the potential fire hazard that this posed. Relief came only in the third term of session 1972-73, when the new buildings were finally occupied by the Science, Geography, Music, Home Economics, Art and PE Departments. The School also gained a brand new Canteen. Some months later, a fire drill and safe evacuation were completed in two minutes and twelve seconds, and Mr Twatt wrote, "I was very relieved and impressed".

The completion of the new Language Lab (distorting the equipment budget by £3,000) and the later enclosure of the ground floor of the "New Building" to make more classrooms completed the only significant other building work undertaken in the School in these years. The "temporary" wartime HORSA Huts remained in full use throughout (and to the present). In addition, Oban High School acquired extra classrooms when "old" St Columba's was occupied in 1975, following the opening of a new primary school in Soroba.

The Twatt era brought more than a change of Rector. Visible and audible changes were quickly evident when Mr Twatt launched the Absentee Sheet, a daily news-sheet and list of absentees - always with a *Thought for Today*, and introduced a system of bell signals to indicate the start and end of periods and intervals. (A selection of the "best of" *Thought for Today* is produced through the rest of this chapter). A later visible change came when the Rector set up a traffic light like set of lights outside his office door to indicate when he was in and available, in and engaged, and when he was out, and giving a whole new meaning to the phrase, "the lights are on, but there is nobody in".

Thought for Today (First Absentee Sheet, 11 January 1973) ...

"It is what you learn after you think you know it all, that counts"

There were, of course, more substantive changes. Mr Twatt outlined his approach at his first prize giving speech in 1972, referring to the centenary that year of the 1872 Education Act, and saying, "Our task is to eliminate all that is bad, and to build on sure foundations for the future, a system which will cater for the needs of all children - each according to his or her ability - to give an education that is, above all else, comprehensive in the true meaning of the word." Two years later, in an article for the School Magazine, the Rector reiterated his consistent theme and goal - education in its broadest sense. "Examinations", he wrote, "are merely the measurement of academic success, not a guarantee that an education has been received."

The School established an impressive Guidance and Careers structure to ensure that "the needs of all children" were identified and best met "each according to his or her ability". The involvement of the local community was a critical aspect of this approach, through parents, councillors and the School Chaplains. In this regard, Oban High School was especially well served by the Rev John MacLeod and Mgr Thomas Wynne.

The substance of most of the rest of this chapter is a measure of just how successful Mr Twatt and Oban High School were in giving an education "that is, above all else, comprehensive". The roll of achievement at Oban High School in these years is, quite literally, as broad as it is long - but both too broad and too long for a short chapter to do it justice. Instead, the following selection is offered to illustrate and demonstrate the point. In this case, the selection is perhaps conclusive that Oban High School offered an education which was comprehensive in every sense of that word. The emphasis of the selection is eclectic, rather than exclusive ... but there is so much to choose from.

Education for Leisure

Football - Table Games - Badminton - Chess - Flower Arranging - Photography - Ski-ing (both locally and with trips to France and Austria) - Sailing- Canoeing - Debating - Drama - Shinty - Hockey - Rugby - Army Cadets (including a visit to the Argyll and Sutherland Highlanders in Germany, at Osnabruck) - Country Dancing - Cookery - Choreography - Vehicle Maintenance - Electronics - Rod Making - Guide Company - Scripture Union - Guitar - Continental Club - Biology Club - Model Making - Sea Cadets - Woodwork - Young Farmers Club - Embroidery - Opera - Young Ornithologists - Swimming - Volleyball - Golf - Social

Thought for Today ...

"Anybody who still thinks the sky is the limit, is short of imagination"

Service Group - Duke of Edinburgh's Award - Hill Walking (locally, in North Wales and in the Lake District) - Scouts - Basketball - Orchestra (Woodwind, String and Brass) - Air Training Corps - Yoga - Athletics - Tennis - Angling - Exploring Oban ("Please bring waterproofs ...") - Piping - Boys Brigade - Camping (locally, in North Wales and in Brittany) - Film Society - Radio Lorn - Gaelic Choir - Bee Keeping - Sculpture - Reel and Strathspey - Puppet Making - Short Story Writing ...

This list (not exhaustive) of activities and clubs cannot be read by any former pupil or teacher of Oban High School in the 1970s without some strong recollection of at least one activity or club, the other pupils involved and the teachers or other individuals (for example, Flight Lieutenant Bill Coutts of the ATC) who led the group. Pupils and teachers from earlier or from later years may understandably enough read this list with some envy. These activities and clubs really represent the richest vein of personal and group development running through this decade. A lode of achievement, marked by diversity, almost universal participation in something or other, and, above all, by massive commitment on the part of so many of those involved. It was also, of course, by and large, great fun!

The good Lord took the fifth day to create the fish in the sea and the birds of the air: at Oban High School, the fifth day - or half of it anyway - was for long given over to "Education for Leisure". This innovation was to the credit of Farquhar Macintosh. The Friday afternoon session continued to be given over to it well into Mr Twatt's Rectorship. Only later in the 1970s, following a major timetable reorganisation, did Friday afternoon give way to become simply a couple of periods. The organisation of "Education for Leisure" at Oban High School had indeed earlier been the subject of an MEd thesis by Andrew Dunn, a Classics teacher at the School, who left early in the decade to take-up the post of Principal Teacher of Classics at Campbeltown Grammar.

"There was a young lady called Bess
who had 64 squares on her dress
Some thought it was queer
but she said, "It is clear
My Leisure Activity's Chess."

(OHS School Magazine, 1973, Anon)

Thought for Today. . .

"The kindly word that fails today may bear its fruit tomorrow."

Gold, Bronze and Lunch with the Council

In 1973 the School celebrated a first when pupil Rae MacCallum was awarded the Gold Award under the Duke of Edinburgh's Award Scheme. Rae, together with Mandy Anderson, a Bronze Award recipient, was entertained to a lunch by Oban Town Council, held in the Great Western Hotel, on 6th September, 1973.

Summer School

Not Oban High! The Scottish Youth Theatre, instead, was where three successful applicants from the School spent part of their summer in 1979. Karen Crow, Joseph Baah and Steven Thom were all accepted by the Youth Theatre, when hundreds of others from all over Scotland were turned down.

"OHS Corporate Video"

The corporate video, such a feature of 1980's business and management communication, was much earlier a feature of an imaginative and innovative approach to promote Oban High School. In 1976, Mr Laurenson and his Film Studies Group, produced a 20 minute film, *Oban High School, An Introduction*, aimed at the following year's intake of first year pupils. The film "starred" Mr Twatt, Mr Mitchell and several first year pupils as they followed their timetable. Although nobody gave up the day job, the film was a great success.

... Screen Test

Fred MacPherson, of 1B3, and James Campbell, of 1B1, who both saw Mr Laurenson's film as part of its target audience, took part in the BBC quiz programme *Screen Test* in 1977. Fred successfully made it through to the semi-finals which were shown on 10 June 1977.

Thought for Today. . .

"When one burns one's bridges, what a very nice fire it makes."

Two Rooks and A Gold Medal

David Powell, of 3B3, won a Gold Medal in 1974, not on the chess board, but for his painting of two rooks building their nest, in a major art competition held at the Kelvingrove Art Galleries. There were over 3,000 entrants in the competition. In addition to his medal, David also won the junior J D MacGregor Memorial Prize.

David's achievement was but one of several successes enjoyed by Oban High School pupils, both within and without the School. In 1979, for example, the winners of a bank sponsored Art competition for drawing, photography, ceramics and painting were: Seniors, 1 Tracey McKenna, 2 Amanda Twatt, 3 Catriona Boase, and Juniors, 1 Stephen Starling, 2 Robert MacLeod, 3 Sara Brown.

You Have Been Watching ...

Mak the Sheep Stealer (1972) ...*Trial by Jury* (1974) ...*The Demon* (1975) ...*The Pirates of Penzance* (1975) ...*The Gondoliers* (1976) ...*St Jerome and the Lion* (1976) ...*Oliver* (1977)...*Half a Sixpence* (1978)...*THOR*... *Oban High School in Concert* (various) ...*Annual Christmas Carol Service* (every year!)

This medley of musical and theatrical talent, shows and performances would have delighted any and all of the Nine Muses. It certainly impressed Mr Twatt. Of his first experience of *Oban High School in Concert* the Rector enthusiastically writes that he feels "exceedingly proud to be a member of staff in such a happy and progressive school, where the impossible takes a few seconds, and miracles take only slightly longer".

Mr Twatt's comments may have veered slightly towards mild exaggeration. They are, however, quite representative of the numerous compliments paid to the School by the parents, teachers, guests and VIPs who attended these and the many other shows and performances presented by Oban High School throughout the 1970s.

A particular and attractive community-minded feature of Oban High School's many shows was the consistent effort made to invite and facilitate the attendance of pensioners. This commitment by the School included, for example, recording School Christmas Carol Services to play them in the local hospitals.

Thought for Today. . .

"If you think you're always right, you're wrong."

150

The sheer success, entertainment and plain good fun enjoyed by these varied performances had two simple common denominators: commitment and co-operation, without which nothing much will ever happen. The volume and quality of performances, quite simply, implies COMMITMENT writ large. In everyday terms, this meant, for example the hard graft of rehearsals and practice and evenings and weekends given up by pupils, teachers and parents. The role of co-operation was in bringing together individuals and departments to make a script written on paper come to life. The Music, Art and English Departments will spring readily to mind, but in reality the whole School co-operated to achieve success. Think of a show and think of the work *behind the scenes* - lighting, stage direction, costumes, seating, catering and the rest - and the true measure of co-operation, not to say involvement, becomes evident.

The considerable demands placed on the School Orchestra must also be evident from the great number of performances presented. The pupils' talent, skill and dedication were recognised, applause apart, by regular success in the Trinity College Music Examinations (fifteen pupils in 1977 alone, for example) and by places won on the Strathclyde Region Schools Orchestra. The growth of the School roll in the 1970s was matched by that of the School Orchestra, which had already passed fifty by the middle of the decade. The teachers responsible for leading this achievement and for coaching the orchestra were the quartet comprising Betty Beath, Norman Nicholson, David Mason, and their leader Brownlie Henderson.

"Thoromania"

In the age of the Bay City Rollers and their like, "Thoromania" was a phenomenon peculiar to Oban High School. The band "THOR" brought together five highly distinctive styles and talents, who individually taught PE, Geography, Mathematics and Art, but who were, by night, collectively the most successful teachers' band in the School's one hundred year history. Indeed, assuming that lightning does not strike twice, the School's second century is unlikely to produce anything to rival "THOR".

This pre-eminence was duly recognised in 1977, when the School Magazine devoted what would, but for being a few pages out, have been a centre-fold exposure of the band and its members.

Thought for Today. . .

"The smartest people we know are those who ask our advice"

Ted Heath, PE (qualified) and vocalist (self-taught), advised readers, "without any hesitation", that the greatest influence on his music was Scottish and Newcastle Breweries. Inspired by frothy liquid, it was then perhaps appropriate that Mr Heath's comment about the group was "At the moment we are bubbling below take-off point...".

Ian Gowdie, Art (qualified) and lead-guitarist (self-taught), claimed *The Muppet Show* as his biggest influence. He was sufficiently confident of the band's future to hope for a million seller for their first released single, before the first Sunday in September, but was decidedly more reticent in predicting in which year this might be.

Donald Campbell, PE, advised that he could play, "the musical wellie and anything else that requires hitting". Mr Campbell credited Ian Gowdie with the original idea to form the band. Mr Gowdie, however, gave the credit to Mr Campbell - perhaps, again, the influence of Messrs McEwan and Younger shaping the very formation of the band.

Tom Laurenson, Geography, guitar, Jew's Harp, penny-whistle and the paper and comb, told magazine readers that he enjoyed playing in a band that ranged upward from the musically incompetent: the word "upward" was clearly printed in the article.

Finally, Maxie Campbell of Mathematics and another guitarist graciously opined that Ian Gowdie was good for his age, and regretted that Ted Heath did not share more of Tom Laurenson's effervescent personality, that of a "court-jester".

Under the influence of their diverse inspirations, this quintet, later a quartet when Mr M Campbell left, themselves had an inestimable impact on the pupils and colleagues who listened to their music from the mid 1970s onwards. In the new decade, in March 1981, the Absentee Sheet could still speak of "Thoromania"...

The persistence of "Thoromania" as a social, cultural and, above all, a musical phenomenon should not, however, diminish the fond recollection that pupils and staff of this era may have of other, if sometimes less distinguished, performers. *ASYLUM, KRAAKEN* and *Billy Ford and His Band* will spring readily to mind on the band front, and perhaps also *RIF RAF* and *LIVE MUZAK*. The *Crystal Heaven Disco* and *DIY and DISCO* offered a contemporary

Thought for Today. . .

"To ignore the danger is to deserve the disaster"

alternative to these live bands. All combined with general success to entertain at Christmas, St Valentine's, Halloween and other suitable social occasions, some maybe best forgotten, but most well remembered.

Two great musicals...

If gold-plated Oscars were available, then two of Oban High School's musicals would have been in line for an award.

Oliver, Lionel Bart's musical, made famous by the film with Mark Lester in the title role, was produced by Oban High School in 1977. Long months of preparation and rehearsal came to a spectacular fruition and the musical was an outstanding success when presented in the Corran Halls in March of that year. The principal parts, bar one, and all other parts were played by pupils. Iain Forgrieve played Oliver, Colin Felgate the brutal Bill Sykes, and Janice Munn the tragic Nancy. The late John Sharples gave a virtuoso performance in the role of Fagin.

Mr Sharples was, indeed, no stranger to the boards, having been one of the regular players in many of the decade's performances, from the title role in *Mak the Sheep Stealer* onwards. In that part, he earned himself the custard-pie-in-the-face so beloved of slapstick comedy. When not acting and teaching French, John Sharples also contributed enormously to ski-ing and camping as School activities, using both to combine language practice in France.

The School made everything used in *Oliver*, including all the costumes and all the scenery. Brownlie Henderson was Musical Director, and Mrs Morven Boardman was the Producer.

The following year, the team of Brownlie Henderson and Morven Boardman repeated their success, with the School's adaptation of the musical *Half a Sixpence*, which was set at the turn of the century. The other well known adaptation of this musical starred Tommy Steele.

A cast of twenty-nine, were supported by a chorus of fifty-five, and an orchestra of thirty-five - well over 100 pupils on stage - a remarkable achievement. The lavish set and costumes (and perhaps the "Coke and Crisps Party" held afterwards) drove the price of tickets up, from, adults 90p and children 60p for *Oliver* to £1.20 and 80p respectively.

Thought for Today. . .

"Duty, too often, is the thing that one expects from others."

The Senior Depute Director of Education wrote Mr Twatt to thank him for his invitation to the show, and to say that he was"extremely proud of Oban High School and its staff and pupils. Well Done!"

Half A Rainbow...

The School Clans "tartans", red, green, yellow and blue - were not of the warring variety (at least, not normally). They, as earlier, competed less with claymore and targe, rather with sporting, debating and theatrical prowess, where, in all three arenas, the cut and thrust could be every bit as deadly and grim.

The highpoint of inter-clan competition was, of course, the annual School Sports, but the 1970s also introduced some other highlights too. This was very much the case with the *It's A Knockout* style *Clan Clash* or its variant on a theme, *We Are The Champions!* The honours over most of these occasions were fairly evenly spread by the Clans, although a particular Clan always seemed to be to the fore at any given point in time. One of the greatest acts of persistence in Clan history paid off in 1980, when Fingal won the Relay for the first time in nineteen years, three full school generations and more after their last success!

The opening of the town's new swimming pool in 1975 brought Clan colours to the fore, when boys were requested to purchase a pair of trunks in their Clan colour. Girls, in this same year that the Sex Discrimination Act came into force, were requested to wear a (sensible) one piece navy swimming suit.

The inter-clan debates were always topical, and often humorous, as Fingal and Somerled demonstrated, for example, in 1978, when they debated the motion, "That TV and newspapers have put far too much importance on the World Cup". (Remember Ally MacLeod and his good lady advertising carpets, cars and ...and ...and ?) Fingal, proposing, were triumphant, and went on to win the tournament and the coveted Gowdie Gavel.

Humour, pathos, high melodrama and a whole lot else were abundant in the turns, sketches and playlets contributed by the Clans to the many School concerts and functions held in the decade - and there were very many of these. Fund raising for Clan and other worthy causes was an additional motivation here.

Thought for Today. . .

"No matter what you do, someone always knew you would"

"Great chieftain o' the pudding race"

School Log, 23rd January, 1975, "the excellent first" annual Burns Supper was held by Oban High School. Ted Heath, impresario and PE teacher, organised the event, with Jean Black addressing the main course, and "Oban High's own Bard" Iain Crichton Smith, making a witty speech of reply. The next day the School presented a lectern, made by John Thomson, to the Burns Club of Oban, at their Supper in the Regent Hotel. Iain Crichton Smith, incidentally, was awarded the Queen's Jubilee Medal in 1977.

Four Records

The School Sports in 1976 proved to be a record breaker, including a double for Alan Cathro. Alan threw discus and javelin 34.05 m and 41.97 m respectively. William Thomson set a new record by throwing a weight (6.25 kg) a distance of 8.6 m, and Graham Crerar did likewise with a triple jump of 10.97 m.

Another Record

The turn of the decade, found the School competing to spin the turntable, with the launch of an extended play (EP) record to raise funds. *Oban High School in Concert* featured the Gaelic Choir, the Pipe Band and the Orchestra and was recorded in October 1979 - and all for £1.40.

The record was the idea of Joe Rhodes, Depute Rector, and was sold in a cover designed and printed by the Art Department.

Fund Raising ...

"OBAN HIGH SCHOOL PLAN MASSIVE FUND RAISING VENTURE"
(*The Oban Times*, 22nd June, 1972)

Raising School funds in general was an activity rich in diversity and effort throughout this decade, of which the School EP above was but one example.

Thought for Today. . .

"Knowledge comes but wisdom should linger"

Mr Twatt's rectorship opened with a tremendous burst and variety of fund raising activity This was all ably directed by Betty Scott, Mathematics, a teacher well able to count the pounds shillings and pence! The first term of session 1972-73 found pupils and teachers variously engaged in a Fashion Show, a slideshow of *Oban, Old and New*, a Sponsored Walk, a Sale of-Work, a Car Treasure Hunt, a Concert, a Raffle, and a Sponsored Chop. This last activity produced a frantic request on the Absentee Sheet of 14 September for bush saws and small axes "to enable this event to take place". The request did not go unanswered and pupils chopped nearly 700 bundles of firewood for distribution to local pensioners. The aptly named "Beaver Lads" - Duncan Lamont, George MacKain, and David Campbell - cut the most bundles, with a total of 37.

The generosity of Provost Ian Jackson, Master Butcher, provided the main course - a whole sheep - for a Barbecue held on 21 September 1972. This day was immortalised on the front cover of the following years School Magazine, with a picture of Alistair Miller, English complete with smock and beret, turning the sheep on an impressively large spit. Admission to the Barbecue was 15p. All told, this particular fund raising campaign raised several thousand pounds.

"RECTOR GOES TO GREAT LENGTHS TO RAISE MONEY"
The Oban Times 27th February, 1975

The opening of the town's new swimming pool in 1975 inspired the Rector both to raise funds and to promote a healthy activity - a Sponsored Swim. Mr Twatt, *The Oban Times* reported on 13th February, 1975, commenced, "a fortnight's strict training" in preparation for the event, to complete as many 25 m lengths as possible in ten minutes.

On the day, the Rector was piped to the pool side, with Finlay MacLeod, School Captain, playing Handel's Water Music. Whether it was the fortnight's training or the magic of the pipes resonating around the building we will never know, but Mr Twatt completed an impressive 13 lengths in the given time. He was followed into the water by a good number of pupils and teachers, raising altogether the sum of £1,276.27. (Two years later, incidentally, the same music was played by the School Orchestra raising funds on an end of term cruise to Lismore on the *Columba*). The Rotary Club and the Round Table provided prizes for the pupils who completed the greatest number of lengths and for those who raised the most sponsorship. With an outstanding 23 lengths completed in ten minutes, Marion MacKay of

Thought for Today. . .

"Absence of occupation is not rest"

1G2 and Charles Paul of 5B2 collected the trophies awarded. The top eight fund raisers each received savings stamps. All the winners, with the Rector and the organisers, were pictured on the front page of *The Oban Times* on 1st May, 1975.

The following year, the life saving value of being able to swim was demonstrated by Oban High School pupil James MacDonald, of 2B1, when he made an heroic attempt to save three people swept out to sea near St Andrews. *The Oban Times* reported that the shy hero left the scene, saying only that he came from Oban. Shortly afterwards, on that same east coast, Malcolm McKillop, James's classmate, and Marion MacKay of 3G1, both completed the Tay Swim of one mile in the sea.

"24 miles, 1,449 feet and one inch..." The decade's most heavily advertised fund raising event, was also one of its most unusual. Sixty very generous prizes were offered by local businesses - including, a fish supper a week for a year! - for the correct or nearest guesses as to how far a moped would travel on one pint of two-star. The moped travelled just over 24 miles when the event was staged on 30th September, 1976. The money raised was part of an appeal to raise £25,000 to build an Outward Bound Centre in order to extend further the scope of the School's extra-curricular activities.

"Clearance Sale ... 7,283 packs of cards". Not the playing, gambling variety, rather Christmas Cards. This was the number of packs of five "designer" cards sold by the School at 5p per pack in 1980. In 1979, the cards had gone on sale at 25p per pack...

The fund raising decade that had started with a Fashion Show was drawing to an end in 1980, when Lawrie Campbell, of 4B2, won a prize for accusing a teacher of attempted murder - Greig Anderson, Physics, was the "correct" answer in the School's "Who Shot JR?" competition. In the intervening years, the pupils and teachers of Oban High School had raised thousands of pounds for School funds, and provided no little entertainment and interest to the local community. All manner of sponsored activities were sold to the good citizens of Oban and around - spelling, walking, dancing, swimming, chopping, silence (!) and even slimming (Mr Twatt lost almost two stones over the summer holidays in 1978 to help buy a rescue craft for the Sailing Club). In addition, goods and services from hot dogs and tablet to car wash and valet were offered for sale by enthusiastic pupils at various Fetes, Shows and Sales-of-Work.

Thought for Today. . .

"As long as you live, keep learning how to live"

The tremendous support given to and by the local community in all these efforts was a marked feature of this decade's fundraising by Oban High School. That Mr Twatt was a good sport must also be quite evident.

"... the greatest of these is charity." Notwithstanding these efforts to raise money for the School, the record of giving at Oban High School in this decade was one of which the School could be even more justly proud. It is a splendid testament to the goodwill and generosity of so many pupils and teachers over the years, in giving both to their own local community and to the world at large. All of the following charities and good causes benefited from time given and money raised by Oban High School:- The Red Cross - Leukaemia Research - Save The Children - British Sailors Society - Action For The Crippled Child - Oban Hospital Radio - UNICEF - Vietnam Relief - SHELTER - Barnardo's - RNLI - The Earl Haig Fund - Annual Blue Peter Christmas Appeal - Guatemala Earthquake Disaster Fund - Indian Cyclone Disaster Fund - Cancer Research - Queen's Silver Jubilee Appeal - East African Emergency Appeal ... and many more.

Extra-mural and evening classes

"WHO ARE THE SCOTS?"
"ROMANTICS, REALISTS AND IMPRESSIONISTS"

(Extra-Mural Classes, advertised in *The Oban Times*, 6th January, 1972)

The local community benefited, of course, not just from the involvement of the School in the community through fund raising and charitable activity, but also from the involvement of the community in the School.

These extra-mural classes, for example, sitting in perhaps inspired juxtaposition, were but two of a very broad range of cultural, educational and interest classes that were offered to the community throughout the 1970s in and by Oban High School. An "O" grade in Arithmetic a revived and stimulated interest in Gaelic or a course in Art appreciation, all of these and many more were made available to the community served by Oban High School. Here, as for the "normal" pupils of the School, study, preparation and application to the various courses by parents and other adults were rewarded, as appropriate, with formal certificates and qualifications or by education in its broadest sense.

Thought for Today...

"If you brood over your troubles, you'll have a perfect hatch"

The Rector and his staff were keen that the School's facilities and resources be put at the full disposal of the community. The steady expansion of evening and extra-mural classes throughout this decade is perhaps the best measure of just how successful the School was in achieving this.

The achievement, ability, commitment and - so important too, the social dimension - friendships that arose from literally hundreds of local people attending evening and extra-mural classes are yet another area adequately to cover which is beyond the scope of this short chapter. But it is essential to mention it. It clearly defined and demonstrated Oban High School as very much a "community school" long before that phrase became a fashionable aspiration.

<u>Shinty</u>

'In it ...
... there is
an entirely new
shinty ball
made of wool
so it does not hurt you".

(OHS School Magazine, 1975, extract from *My Head* by Angus Campbell.)

The shinty ball made of wool never materialised, but a shelf load of cups and trophies were earned by the School teams using the caman against the real thing. The players may have sometimes come off the field gouged, bleeding and sore but, so often, they were also victorious in this most ancient game.

The decade started in the session 1971-72 with a visit, led by Ian Beath, to Dublin to play the Blessed Oliver Plunkett Secondary. Victory went to the Oban High Under-15s, 11 to 2. This was followed by a meeting with the Irish Prime Minister, An Taoiseach, Jack Lynch, where the party, to quote the School Log, enjoyed "hospitality on a very generous scale". The two schools made a number of return visits to play each other and in 1973 Mr Twatt himself accompanied the pupils to Dublin. This visit was profiled for the 1974 School Magazine by

Thought for Today. . .

"When trouble goes to sleep, don't set the alarm clock"

159

that doyen of shinty correspondents, G Y Slater. The Rector, readers were informed, mightily impressed his many hosts by his rendition of *These Are My Mountains*. On the field of play, a single goal separated the teams, Oban High losing 11-10 in the closing seconds of the game. For Oban, Donald Black was described as having had "an immense game", with Duncan Forgrieve and substitute Joe MacIntyre joining him on the scoreline.

On native soil, Oban High School several times won the following trophies: the MacPherson Cup, the MacBean Cup and, at the turn of the decade, the Hugh Lawrie Cup. The dozens of successful and competing players of the 1970s would surely complain if recognition were not given to some of the individuals who, off the field of play, contributed so much to Oban High School Shinty. Ian Beath and G Y Slater have already been mentioned, but the list would be incomplete without acknowledging, in particular, Eddie Cooper, Larry Forgrieve and, on the teaching staff, Greig Anderson, Physics.

Rugby

"It had all the makings of a fairy story, there were GIANTS and UNDERDOGS, big teams and country cousins, tragedy and glory. This one came true."
(OHS School Magazine, 1976, Match Report)

The players probably would not have thanked you for the comparison with fairies, but they would have relished the idea of being giant-killers. The game was Rugby, and these were the glory years.

In Elgin, in March 1976, competing for the first time in the North of Scotland Schools Rugby Association Sevens Championships, the Oban High School team were triumphant with three resounding victories, beating Elgin 12-0, Lossiemouth 26-0, and crushing Lochaber 28-0 in the final. The winning team, of I MacLean, R Robb, A McColl, D MacDonald, W Thomson, M MacFadyen, J Driver and I Berrie, were pictured in *The Oban Times* on 25th March, 1976, flanked by their coaches, Brian Mitchell, Physics, and Charles Robertson, History.

The engraving "Oban High School" became very common on rugby silverware and trophies in these years. The School's teams travelled - and won - the length and breadth of Scotland and beyond, even to the home of Rugby, to test their prowess. The commitment and enthusiasm of the players and their teacher coaches, Ian Thomson, also History, joining Brian

Thought for Today. . .

"As long as you live, keep learning how to live"

Mitchell and Charles Robertson just mentioned, produced victory after victory and achievement after achievement. In September 1979, the School fielded no less than five full teams: seventy-five players, all wearing School colours - badges courtesy of the Art Department and stitched-on by Home Economics. In November 1977, Oban High School won a match by its most convincing margin, hammering Wick 58-0. In this game, Michael Grace scored a personal record of six tries.

The principal competitions and trophies won by Oban High School at various times included the following: the Lochaber and Lorne Trophy; the MacKelvie Shield (U 13), the President's Challenge Shield (U 14), the Bon-Accord Cup (U 15) and the Dounreay Cup (Senior) - all North of Scotland Schools League Championship Cups; the Bruce Cup (U 13), the A J Slashen Cup (U 14), the J M Ryan Cup (U 15) and the C Wilken Shield (Senior) - all in the Elgin Seven-a-Side Competition; the Highland Shield (U 13), the Grant Cup (U 15) and the Highland Cup (Senior) - all in the Highland RFC Seven-a-Side Competition.

This outstanding record was marked in December 1979 by a Civic Reception, hosted by Argyll and Bute District Council, in the Corran Halls. This Reception, perhaps, inspired the School to even greater heights in the following year. The new decade was barely a couple of weeks old when Oban High School won four straight home matches against local rivals, Lochaber High School. *The Oban Times* commented particularly on a "classic drop kick" by Alan MacPhail, the School's U-15 Stand-Off. The new decade, indeed, witnessed Oban High School's finest hour, with a clean sweep across all four leagues - Senior, U-15, U-14 and U-13: the Grand Slam! "... (a) remarkable performance, unique in the history of Scottish Schools Rugby ... a fitting tribute to the effort and commitment of the boys in the club, and their coaches", to quote *The Oban Times*. The following year, Oban High School was only seven points away from a repeat of this superb achievement, although the Dounreay Cup (Seniors), The President's Challenge Shield (U-14) and the Mac Kelvie Shield (U-13) were all retained.

"The games people play ..."

The most successful competitive sports in these years were Shinty and Rugby, but they were far from being the only sports played by pupils.

Thought for Today. . .

"The only thing most people get out of life is experience"

Oban High School, for example, filled seven out ten places, and both reserves, on the County Badminton Team in 1979, with Flora McGill, Margaret Ferguson, Anne Ford, Moira MacIntosh, Billy Hay, Robert Dairon, Joseph Baah, Robin Seggie and David MacDougall all picked. Boyd Robertson, Gaelic, led the Badminton Club.

In November 1977, the still quite new Basketball Club, coached by Mrs MacLean, made it through to the second round of the Scottish Cup. The team of Ruth Graham, Judith Paget, Maureen Tindall, Angela McLauchlan, Sheila Lamont, Penny Warwick, Isabel Smith, Jackie Driver, Christine MacMillan and Morag McColl losing to St Andrews Academy.

On the Athletics field, the Oban High School team swept the board at the County Championships held in June 1981, bringing over 30 district titles and records back to the School.

Football, Netball, Volleyball, Hockey, Swimming, Ski-ing, Golf, Tennis and Sailing were just some of the many other team and individual sports actively pursued at Oban High School. Brothers Lake and Keith Falconer came first out of eighteen competitors to win the Laird Trophy for Sailing in October 1979. This, the last race of the year, brought a successful season to a close for Oban High School Sailing Club. June 1977 saw Alison Clark and Iain MacIntosh the winners of the Nestle's Ladder Tennis Tournament. In June 1979, perhaps in response to larger events in the country in May, Cricket made an appearance on the PE curriculum.

Gaelic

"We look forward to hearing that he has introduced Gaelic into the curriculum."
(OHS School Magazine, 1972, on the departure of Farquhar Macintosh to the Royal High School, in Edinburgh.)

The writer is unclear as to whether this blessing was bestowed on the pupils of the Royal High School: the record is, however, emphatic that Oban High School continued to rejoice and excel in its Gaelic tradition. And what could be more natural for the town that was the birthplace of *An Comunn Gaidhealach* and home to the first National Mod in the very year that Oban High School opened its doors to secondary education.

Thought for Today. . .

"When something defies description, let it"

The Local, Provincial and National Mods in this decade all rang with applause for the performance of Oban High School pupils in verse, song, prose and on the magical instruments of our heritage, the bagpipes and the clarsach. Soloists, duets, groups and choirs all enjoyed success and tremendous participation. In 1973, for example, more than one in eight pupils took part in the Local Mod. The Rev Norman MacDonald, Glenrothes, wrote to Mr Twatt in March 1973, to say "Last Sunday, I listened to the part your pupils took in the Gaelic broadcast, and they are a credit to their school, their teachers and to the County of Argyll." These words of appreciation were wholly typical of the many compliments paid to the School for the quality of its distinctive Gaelic culture.

Applause and compliments were, of course, not the only things gained by Oban High School pupils. The following is a brief selection of some of the prizes and trophies won in the National Mod:- James C MacPhee Memorial Medal, (1976), Alastair Barnett; Silver Medallists 1978), Karen Matheson and Steven Jamieson; First, Junior Folk Groups (1979), Na Latharnaich; First, Piano (U-12) (1979) Donald Shaw; Turriff Trophy (1980), Karen Matheson; Donald MacLeod Memorial Trophy (1980), Gordon Barr. In both 1977 and 1980 OHS Gaelic Choir won the Hugh MacPhee Choral Trophy, the Dugald Cowan Trophy, the Rona MacVicar Trophy, the Donald. D MacIsaac Trophy and the Dugald MacDonald Quaich, while in 1979 the Choir won the Dugald Cowan Trophy, the Rona MacVicar Trophy and the Miller Trophy. Successes at the Provincial Mod included the following:- MacLennan Shield (1976), Neil Johnstone; First, Chanter (1980), Fiona MacLeod; First, Piping (1980), George Bell; Catherine Campbell Cup (1980), Joan MacLachlan. There were many, many more ....

The natural talent and application of the pupils was, however, only a part of the explanation for this consistent success. The perfectionism and diversely inspirational coaching skills of, in particular, the Gaelic Department completed the explanation. Donald Thomson, Donald ("Dan") Morrison, Boyd Robertson and Catherine Morrison were the four Gaelic scholars most readily associated with this success, but the Gaelic Choir was also of great credit to, in especial, Mrs Catriona McCrindle.'

Thought for Today. . .

*"It is important to think about what we are thinking about
and then think again"*

The Pipe Band

"SALUTE TO OBAN JUVENILE PIPE BAND"

(OHS School Magazine, 1975)

As the language of "Tir nan Og" thrived at Oban High School, so too did its distinctive music, that of the bagpipe.

The Oban Juvenile Pipe Band, formed in 1970, marched far and wide and, also, returned to Oban with prizes and trophies. The early and mid 1970s were particularly good years. The Band, for example, won two firsts at the World Championships held at Stirling in 1974, one for playing and one for marching and discipline. The Band Leader then was Pipe Major Angus MacLennan, and the Tutors were Pipe Major R MacCallum and Drum Major S Pearson, a formidable and successful team.

OHS School Magazine

The wealth of material available between the covers of this annual publication is perhaps indicated by the frequency with which it is quoted here. This indication alone, however, would be but a poor guide to the true volume and quality of the features, short-stories, poems, interviews, drawings, photographs, competitions, limericks and crosswords that were crammed between the covers every year.

In this decade, for example, you could read interviews with Lord MacLean, Mr Miller, the Director of Education, Ian Cuthbertson of *Sutherland's Law* and Anne Lorne Gillies, a former pupil (1955 to 1962). "We would not have dared to wear them in my day," was her comment about girls wearing trousers to school. Alternatively you could choose a topical subject, as in 1975, when Lynne Ferguson wrote a hard-hitting critique of the Raising of the School Leaving Age.

Hard-hitting of a different kind was the subject of Derek Morrison's poem, *The Belt And The Pane* in the same edition, of which this is an extract:-

Thought for Today. . .

"No-one is old enough to know better"

164

"The teacher slowly opened his desk,
out came the black Lochgelly
The poor kid's hands were shaking
and his legs were just like jelly.

"He took the six and went to his seat
looking as brave as ever
but soon he started to howl and cry
from the taste of the dreaded leather."

The following year, in 1976, Peter MacQueen, the Head Janitor, contributed his Ten Commandments, breaking any of which could have led to a "taste of the dreaded leather". Here are two of them:

"YAEZWULNAEWRITEFINGSONRAWALLS"
"ANFINEULYDINNAPLAYRAGEMMWIRATEACHURSANJANNIES"

By the middle of the decade the School was able to produce and print the entire publication in-house. This perhaps accounted for the decline in the number of advertisements carried in the magazine, for example from twenty-six pages in 1972 to ten pages in 1977. The material was almost all produced in-house, the exception being a section devoted to contributions from the local feeder primary schools. A notable feature of the magazine was the significant proportion of material that was in the Gaelic.

The key to the achievement was, once again, the familiar theme of commitment, co-operation, hard work and good fun! Each year an editorial board, or a magazine committee, was formed from the pupils to publish the magazine. And each year, as is customary in all good publications, they thanked a long list of people who had contributed material, time, help and advice, especially members of staff.

Islanders, Hostellers and Travellers

"The following pupils have permission to travel on the paper boat..."

Thought for Today. . .

"There are always ten better things to do than to give up"

A perilous journey! This, and others like it, was all part and parcel of attending Oban High School for generations of island pupils. In 1972, for example, there were about 200 pupils from the islands at the School. The largest single group - over 60 - at that time came from Mull, Iona and Ulva, with a good two dozen from Coll and Tiree, down to six pupils from Luing.

The hijinks, and occasional excesses, of these pupils at sea were a regular, if not quite a standing, item on the Absentee Sheets. The rest of the School was left, briefly, wondering what lay behind announcements like, "All pupils who were passengers on the Columba ferry at 1.00 pm on Friday 17 [November 1972] report to the Depute Rector in the Central Hall at 1.25 pm today." The record suggests that nothing *major* ever actually happened in any of these incidents, but the accompanying stories were often of a nature to remind you of the exploits and catchphrase of an earlier master mariner on the West coast - "If Dougie was here he would tell you himself."

The record is, however, clear enough on one thing, that once in Oban, it was a major preoccupation of senior staff to make sure that the islanders were neither late coming to the school nor early leaving it. In November 1976 the Absentee Sheet thundered, "It has been observed that many of the pupils disembarking from the Mull ferry on Monday mornings are MAKING NO EFFORT TO REACH THE SCHOOL ON TIME." Quite the reverse was observed at the end of the week, when considerable ingenuity was displayed by these same pupils in requesting and justifying permission to leave early. Probationary teachers were particularly vulnerable.

The vagaries of wind and wave often disrupted and prevented journeys to and from home, legitimate or otherwise, at weekends and at end of term. These problems were sometimes exacerbated by timetable difficulties. An entry in the School Log in October 1974 reads as follows, "Inundated today with requests from pupils to leave early for Island destinations. There is an acute problem with winter timetables ...." A meeting was shortly afterwards arranged with MacBrayne's, the parents and the School.

If, however, individual problems were resolved, then there remained throughout the decade a pattern of travelling difficulties to the frustration of all concerned. *The Oban Times*, for example, carried a series of letters in March and April 1976, debating "The Lost Weekend".

Thought for Today...

"Culture is not a substitution for life, but the key to it"

In this instance, a journey to Kilchoan by land and by sea, about 30 miles as the crow flies, took a gruelling fourteen hours. In June, the parents involved were invited to a meeting with the Lorn, Coll and Colonsay Schools Council, but the weekend was never "found".

"One of the many MacLeans
who stays on an island called Staines
who was always off school
but said, "As a rule
I can never get back by MacBrayne's"

(OHS School Magazine, 1973, Anon)

Incidentally, the Rector himself was not immune to sailing difficulties, as the School Log reported in February 1973. Then Mr Twatt was stormbound in Stornoway, having travelled to celebrate the centenary of another great Highland school - the Nicolson Institute.

In 1976 a survey was made of the cumulative impact on island and other pupils of leaving home, travelling back and forth and staying, as they did, in hostels and lodgings, relative to their peers who either lived locally in Oban or who travelled daily from Dalavich, Connel and the like. This survey indicated that, in general, island pupils were the least successful in academic terms, coming behind the locals, who in turn came behind the daily travellers. The Rector, as *The Oban Times* reported, was quite concerned and very keen to ensure that island pupils attended lessons for a minimum of twenty-seven and a half hours per week. The report added that, to make this happen, island pupils might be "ordered" to spend less weekends at home.

Whatever the accuracy of this "snap-shot" survey, the Examination Board itself remained unimpressed by the peculiar difficulties that might easily affect a sizeable minority of Oban High School pupils. In 1981, for example, the Board advised, "A ferry difficulty of any kind will not be accepted by the Examination Board as a valid reason for being absent from an examination."

Thought for Today. . .

"Ten good words are worth a hundred bad ones"

Craigard, Kilbowie, Glencruitten and Lodgings

Away from ferries, late, stormbound or on time, and away from exams and the like, there was, of course, another aspect to the life of the islander pupil. That, as just mentioned, was life in hostel or in lodging, the hostel being the case for most.

The official opening of Glencruitten Hostel, in September 1971, by Hector Munro MP, Under Secretary of State for Health and Education, completed the family of Hostels accommodating Oban High School pupils.

The family itself - 'two sisters and a brother' (Craigard and Glencruitten for females, and Kilbowie for males) had an active staff of Wardens, Deputes, House Parents, Domestics and Supervisory Teachers to discharge the formidable responsibility of acting *in loco parentis* for around 200 pupils. At peak, over 100 were at Kilbowie, about 80 at Glencruitten and at Craigard, very much smaller, some two dozen pupils. This population was made up of islanders, with an infusion of pupils from, mainly, Lochgilphead and Tarbert, who were "staying on at school" after completing their fourth year at Lochgilphead High School, which was then a four-year school.

The parents with the 2.2 children at home, so beloved of the ad-men, can do the simple arithmetic and multiply the trials and tribulations, the successes and the failures, the intensities and the exasperations of their own teenage brood a hundred-fold and begin to appreciate the challenge - and the satisfaction (!) of the Hostel staff. The ultimate mark of their success *in loco parentis* is in the many achievements and accomplishments of former Oban High School hostellers in almost any walk of life that one may care to mention. The personal and the shared reminiscences of hundreds of pupils and staff who lived in the Hostels in the 1970s that lie behind this success are really beyond the scope of this chapter, but there is room for some brief details of events and individuals.

The accommodation itself comprised mainly dormitories with a small number of single rooms for senior pupils, who "supervised" their juniors in return for this privilege. There is no indication that the Hostels bred any West Highland counterparts of the luckless Tom Brown or of his tormentor, Harry Flashman.

Thought for Today. . .

"You cannot build a reputation on things you are going to do"

Up-grading of accommodation and building work took place throughout these years. There was major disruption, especially at Kilbowie, in the mid to late 1970s, when Strathclyde Region acted to meet new fire regulations. The Fire Brigade had established that the dropped ceilings at Kilbowie were potentially a fatal fire hazard, as had tragically been the case in several well publicised fires of the time elsewhere in the UK.

Hostel life offered pupils the opportunity for a quite vibrant and active sporting and social life. This was ever more the case as the decade moved on, and as facilities were steadily improved - for example, a mini-bus for activities, a music room at Kilbowie and a better TV/Games room at Craigard.

A very regular social feature, advertised on the Absentee Sheet, was the Kilbowie Disco, dependent entirely on visitors for dancing partners. The same, of course, was also true of the "Boogie 'n' Bite Nites" at Glencruitten Hostel. Every year, the Hostels all hosted Christmas Dinners, with turns by pupils and staff. Here characters like Cathy Gillies and Jean MacDonald, of the Catering and Domestic Staff at Kilbowie, really came into their own with contributions and compositions long remembered. Cathy Gillies was, incidentally, one of the last children to leave St Kilda in the 1930s.

The breadth and the daring of hostel sports and physical activities - from canoeing and sailing, climbing and diving, to swimming and ski-ing - owed a great deal to two members of the PE Department, Ian Beath and Donald Campbell. Mr Campbell's willingness to have-a-go at (almost) anything, in fact, earned him the nickname by which he was then and ever since known. Less active and (occasionally) more cerebral pursuits were led, at Kilbowie, by, amongst others, Tom Laurenson, Geography, Alex Hamilton, History/Modern Studies, Ian Young, Chemistry, and later by John MacKenzie, Mathematics. John McGlynn, of St Columba's Primary, contributed on both counts.

A particularly strong influence on hostel life, was Bill Gray, the Warden of Kilbowie, who, like Mr Twatt, took-up his appointment in 1972. Kilbowie was physically the most distant and remote of the Hostels and was therefore also the most self-contained. The Hostel Bill Gray inherited in 1972 was in need of some attention, in respect both of its appearance and of its standards: the attention that Mr Gray gave to these is to his great credit. This era coincided

Thought for Today. . .

"There is no knowledge which is not valuable"

with a major television series about a notorious German castle, used as a POW camp in the last war, and Kilbowie picked-up a fond (?) nickname from it. There were, however, no (recorded) successful "escapes" from Kilbowie.

At Glencruitten, Miss Ann Colthart, later of Home Economics, was the first Warden, with Miss Margaret Menzies and Miss Gwen Menzies, respectively her first appointed Matron and Assistant Matron. Two of the Matrons at Craigard in these years were Miss Janet MacKinnon, who had been Assistant to Miss MacLean, Matron for twenty years to 1970, and Miss Jan Inglis, formerly of Kilbowie Hostel, who later married the Rev Brian Wilkinson, one of the School Chaplains.

A final word on accommodation is due to the landladies and landlords who looked after the much smaller number of island and other pupils who did not stay in the Hostels, but who, instead, lived in private lodgings or, perhaps, with relatives. These pupils made a brief annual appearance in the School records, being asked to report to the School Nurse. With Oban's reputation for Bed and Breakfast and other hospitality, this check-up was perhaps to see that the lodgers were not being too well looked after! However that may be, the School and a fair number of its pupils (and teachers) in these years had good cause to appreciate private lodgings in Oban.

Daily Travellers

"All Dalavich pupils report to the Office at 11.00 am prompt. They are being sent home." (Absentee Sheet, 1 December 1976)

The season is the clue which indicates that this was not a mass act of discipline: more simply, it was snowing and not to have left early would have stranded these pupils in Oban. Just over a week later, the Absentee Sheet had this notice,"Owing to weather conditions, the following buses will be extremely late today:- Easdale, Dalmally, Barcaldine, Benderloch and Ballachulish." These, and announcements like them, were one of the most regular features in the Absentee Sheet.

The pupils concerned were the daily travellers, that large part of Oban High School's roll who were bussed from the various towns, villages and scattered communities which completed the sprawling catchment area of the School, a catchment area which, even after the reorganisation

Thought for Today. . .

"A mistake is evidence that someone has tried to do something"

f local government had removed the likes of North Appin and Morvern to Highland Region, as the largest of any school in Britain. How well this justified the innovative "roadshow" approach taken by Mr Twatt and his senior staff to ensure that informed advice and guidance about their children and the School was made available to all parents, wherever they lived. This fact of geography was undoubtedly one of the most significant influences and recurring themes in the distinctive character of Oban High School.

also affected the pupils. It was the lot of the daily travellers to rise early - from 6.00 am on and to return home late. The drivers and the liveries of Highland Omnibus, MacColl's, Stewart's, MacDougall's and other bus lines became very familiar to these pupils, as they were the first and the last sights of their official school day (homework excepted!).

These bus journeys, some long enough to impress even a hardened London commuter, apparently did not quite lend themselves the opportunities for "carry-on" afforded to the island pupils on their ferries - perhaps a 6.00 am start was a natural dampener. Nevertheless, mass meetings before the Depute Rector of all pupils who travelled on such and such a bus were far from unheard of. The early start, of course, meant an early or even a missed breakfast and, November 1977, the School introduced tea and biscuits in the Canteen, for 5p, for those who had travelled 18 miles or more, one way, to be served from 8.30 to 8.45 am. The significance of an 18-mile exclusion zone was never explained.

Two Hundred Years And More - In A Decade!

Not a riddle, rather the total service of a small number of long serving staff who retired from Oban High School in the 1970s. These are just some of them - with apologies to those others omitted for lack of space. Generations of Oban High School pupils will have good cause to remember them - fondly, or otherwise!

In 1972, presiding at his first School Prizegiving, Mr Twatt asked the question, "What manner of man is this? In the best possible sense of the word he is a character, one of the few real larger-than-life characters left in this age of social uniformity." Donald Thomson, Depute Rector, twice former Provost, Gaelic personality and polemicist, was the subject of Mr Twatt's question and remarks. This on his retirement after forty years service at Oban High School, and, to quote E T F Spence, the Chairman of the Education Committee, "a lifetime service given to the County of Argyll".

Thought for Today...

"Take time to be friendly - it is the road to happiness"

Two years later, in 1974, two longstanding colleagues of Donald Thomson's joined him i retirement, Miss May MacLaine and Norman Hardie.

May MacLaine had first come to Oban High School as a teacher in 1939, having previousl served in twenty-one County Schools as an itinerant teacher. She was a member of the Englis Department until 1958, when she was appointed the School's first Woman Advisor. In 197 she was promoted to Assistant Rector and finally retired, as Acting Depute Rector, in June c that year.

The previous session, Norman Hardie, Depute Rector, had retired, after some forty yea service in education. His achievments had earlier been recognised by his profession in 196 with his award of a Fellowship of the Educational Institute of Scotland, and later by the Crow with his award of an MBE in 1966.

In 1975 the School Magazine reported the retiral of Garth Kay, Principal Teacher c Chemistry, after twenty-seven years at Oban High School, commenting that he would t remembered, "for his remarkable enthusiasm for his subject, and the Artic conditions h fostered in his laboratory..."

December 1975 brought the retirement of two stalwarts of the language departments - Donal ("Dan") Morrison, Principal Teacher of Gaelic, and James Page, Modern Languages.

"Dan" Morrison, a native of Lewis, was described in the School Magazine as, "an all roun champion in sport", who in 1931 had smashed the record for throwing the hammer by a fu six feet, representing Glasgow University in London at the British Universities Champior ships. His championship of the Gaelic language was also formidable (with a voice to match' He was for a number of years the Chief Gaelic Examiner of the Examination Board. Servic with the First and the Eighth Armies preceded his twenty-eight years service at Oban Hig School.

"...soldier, scholar, linguist and musician" was how John Sharples described his colleague James Page. Jim Page came to Oban High School in 1951 with an active service record behin him in The Royal Scots, commissioned as Captain. Indeed, to these roots he remained true ending his long teaching career with the rank of Lieutenant Colonel of the Argyll Cadet Force

Thought for Today . . .

"The weaker the argument the stronger the words"

The same year, 1975, Betty Scott, formerly Mrs McClure, retired from the Maths Department, having come to the School as a "temporary teacher" in 1942. Unfortunately, ill health borne of so many years working, cut her retirement to six short months and she died in 1976. "Ma Scott" was noted for her somewhat disconcerting habit of running round a first year class and telling many of the pupils that she had taught their parents!

Tragedy also visited the School in this decade, when two fine and committed teachers lost their lives in drowning accidents. Cunningham Irving, Principal Teacher of Classics, died along with his wife in the summer of 1974, and Alistair Miller, Principal Teacher of English, died in 1977.

Both men were influential teachers of their own subjects and both contributed significantly to the School's extra-curricular activities. Cunningham Irving formed and led the highly successful Photography Club. Alistair Miller, for example, accompanied a party of pupils on an educational cruise on the SS *Uganda* to Norway, Sweden, Denmark, Russia and Finland in 1973 - and by all accounts, "party" was the right word!

On a happier note, Oban High School furnished Rectors for three other Schools in the decade Farquhar MacIntosh to the Royal High School, Edinburgh, in 1972, John MacLeod to Wick High School in 1976, and Joe Rhodes to Dunoon Grammar School in 1980. Iain MacCormick, Scottish National Party, and John J MacKay, Conservative, left the School to travel a bit further - to Westminster, and the House of Commons.

Around Scotland - Oban - Why Here?"

(BBC Schools Film, August 1979)

This is a fair question, and one which the film tried to answer by exploring the reasons for the town's development, with the enthusiastic help of Oban High School pupils. The film was made on Lismore and Luing, as well as in Oban itself. With the town developed the High School, and with it all the issues of transport, by sea and by land, and accommodation in hostel and lodging, just recounted. The success and achievement of the School in meeting and overcoming these issues and in serving so far flung a community are marked in the success and achievement of all its pupils and teachers both in school and in later life, be they islanders, daily travellers or locals. In 1978 a group of Canadian educationalists visited Oban High School to see at work a living model for the education and development of their own remote areas and offshore islands. Imitation is truly the sincerest form of flattery!

Thought for Today . . .

"Facts not theories, govern the world"

Impressions of the Eighties

This chapter comprises the personal impressions of people connected with the School various capacities.

(i)

Education in the Eighties by Alex Hamilton

The 1980s in Scottish schools, including Oban High, were not years of simple trends ar straightforward development, but rather they saw much stress and trauma brought about t conflict between assorted forces. The alliances and enmities between these forces change from time to time sometimes creating the strangest of bedfellows. This has led the School its centenary year to be much different from its form and structure a mere dozen years ago 1980, never mind 1892. Whether the pendulum will swing back only time will tell, but muc of the philosophy and deeds of the 1980s is likely to be with us for a long time.

The 80s were of course the Thatcher years, when the Conservative government decided overthrow the traditional ideas of Academia and the philosophy of "education for its ow sake" and to introduce some of the discipline of the market place into schools with the fin purchasers of the educational product - the world of business- having a much greater say c school activities. Thus disappeared the respected dominie of the flowing gown, the high status of "academic" subjects, apart from a small but shining outpost, the Department of Lat and Greek, which had for so long been a major power within the school. The perceive changing needs of the economy led to the demise of the "manual" subjects like Woodwor and Metalwork and the establishment of what is perceived as one of the major successes the 80s. A series of High-Tech courses were introduced. The Technical Department was re equipped with tens of thousands of pounds worth of computers and a separate Department Computing began to grow. Links between School and the "real world" of business and wor were established and have become a most significant feature of Oban High. Many employe have generously given of their time, experience and expertise to come into the school to assi pupils and to welcome pupils to their place of work.

Efforts were made to apply market forces to the teachers themselves by making them mor accountable to their Council employers and to the other purchasers of the products, th parents. Consequently a detailed contract was prepared with precise conditions of service la down threatening much of the voluntary nature of the traditional professional. School Boar were recreated to give a greater say to those parents who wanted a direct influence on th policies of the School. To suggest that right wing thinking held total sway would be a exaggeration. Not only were these changes enforced by a Labour controlled Strathclye Regional Council, but what was probably the biggest change in education in the 80s cam about initially as a result of the much more socialist thinking of the 70s, when a series of repor were published which set the ball inexorably rolling towards certification for all. For too many years most pupils had left Oban High with few formal qualifications (up to 1972, when the School Leaving Age was increased to 16, most pupils left school at the end of their third year, before Lowers and Ordinary Grades were sat). The spirit of equality was in the air saying that maximum development should be sought from all pupils and indeed extra effort should be devoted to those with more difficulties with positive discrimination in favour of the underprivileged, and that the achievements of all should be recorded. Thus, admittedly among considerable controversy, Standard Grades were introduced. More resources were devoted to pupils with learning difficulties with many classes being equipped with a second teacher to assist such pupils. At the end of the decade an extra specially trained teacher was employed to assist those children with particular social and emotional difficulties.

Along similar lines and responding to the disappearance of traditional apprenticeships, increasing unemployment and the mushrooming of the role of tertiary education, the School Leaving Age has been effectively increased to 17. In 1980 the senior school of fifth and sixth year pupils was almost exclusively an academic preserve. Little was provided for the non-academic. By the end of the 80s a whole series of new courses certificated by SCOTVEC ranging from English Communication to Enterprise Activities and from Photography to Travel and Tourism was introduced.

Over-laying all of these processes was the all-pervading influence of bureaucratic centralism. Decision after policy after dictat after memo came showering down from an increasing number of officials, committees and "educationists". While some gems were included in this, it added to the stress and conflict within the School and was at least partly responsible for the growing demand for increased autonomy aided once again by the market economics principle of treating each school as a competitive unit selling a product. Thus as Oban High School enters its second century it is becoming largely responsible for its day to day financial management leaving only major strategic decision-making to Council officials.

There was yet a further layer of change in the 1980s and that was to the role of the teacher; and it was much greater than simply the disappearance of the academic gown. As pupils were no longer seen as empty vessels to be filled by the omniscient dominie but rather as future citizens and workers capable of independent decision-making, teachers moved from being pontificators to managers of a wide range of learning processes with different pupils in the same class undertaking different work depending on their individual needs. This change is not only a reflection of the altering structure of the national economy with a diminishing demand for manual workers and a greater requirement for a flexible and creative workforce, but also of a new social order as the children of the swinging 60s have now become the parents and the opinion formers with a different perception of education.

The challenges of the 1980s were considerable and they were accepted by the staff so that the School is now all the more able to deal with the 90s.

A Pupil's Reminiscences by Marion MacKillop

I started school in 1983 as a "heater girl", progressed through Central Hall and up to C Floor, to return in 1992 in the role of student teacher in the Biology Department.

Everyone will remember how territorial we all were at school. There were those who frequented the heaters outside the Central Hall, otherwise known as the "heater girls"; there were the "Maths Corridor crowd", who had to be carefully negotiated while you went from A Floor to B Floor as two rows of eyes stared at you willing you to trip; and there were the girls who took up residence in the "old toilets" which smelt permanently of smoke. This area was considered out of bounds, as it had to be if you wanted to attend your next class unscathed. Over in the new building could be found the "A Floor Cloakroom girls", the "A Floor Toilet girls" and the "C Floor Mob" - or perhaps they called us other things!

By my third year, I had discovered that my niche in the territorial stakes was at C Floor, where those pupils from third year upwards who played an instrument were allowed to congregate at break. There, we had the use of two very comfortable solo rooms equipped with pianos and, joy of joys, even a mirror! The only drawback with this set-up was that, if you wanted to be absent from orchestra practice at lunch-time, you had to be very careful that "Harry" couldn't find you. There wasn't really any point in hiding on C Floor because he could seek you out wherever you hid!

Some of my happiest memories were spent in the Music class with "Goblin": glorious whole double periods spent listening to *The Four Seasons* or gathered around his grand piano, singing parts of *The Creation*. Some days he would take us out (ten of us in the Landrover!) to see various church organs and then he would buy us all ice cream.

School lunches were another major part of school life for me. There were the wonderful motherly dinner ladies who gave you large helpings and big thick slices of chocolate chewing gum. The biggest problem was surviving the dinner queue when the most feared teachers were on duty. You simply did not breathe when "Techy" Thomson, "Psychi" and Ziggy" were in charge.

History class with "Carrot Tops" deserves a mention. I well remember the day he reprimanded Marion MacKay for talking and issued her with a hundred lines. Incensed that Marion should smirk on being the recipient of such a punishment, he promptly dealt out a further hundred. By now completely losing the head because she was still smirking, he served a hundred more and I was moved to intervene. "But Mr Thomson, it's not Marion's fault," I ventured, only to be silenced with an instant punishment of yet another hundred. The moral of this tale is that if you should have the misfortune to wear a brace which makes it look like you are smirking, take it out in "Carrot Tops" class!

Another memorable incident occurred in Dave Waltho's (Aah! - the agonies of an adolescent crush) class. Having been otherwise busy over the lunch-time break, neither I myself nor Nicola Robertson had availed ourselves of the opportunity to go to the lavatory. On explaining our predicament and requesting his permission to leave the room, Mr Waltho obviously decided to teach us a lesson. He refused to let us leave and promptly went round the entire science lab turning on every water tap! Suffice to say, we were glad to leave the class at the end of the period.

Certain teachers in Oban High have perfected their own individual methods of punishment. One particular Geography teacher's mean act consisted of standing beside your desk, relieving his flatulence, smiling, and walking away, leaving you dying under the table! How many of you out there also suffered at Tom Laurenson's desk when out to get your work marked? I vividly recall the time when he flicked my head with his finger nail for chattering. But I had the last laugh: he moved me to the back of the class as a punishment and put me right beside Jamie McColl, my teenage sweetheart!

One of the high points of my time at school was the School trip to St Malo in France. One day, several of us surreptitiously purchased some alcohol in preparation for a midnight party, only to have it immediately confiscated by the attending staff. For purposes of security, it was duly deposited in a wardrobe in the bedroom occupied by two of the male staff. However, late at night, a plan was hatched to retrieve our supplies. Several of us donned our shortie nighties and crept upstairs to their room, knocked on the door and entered. There they were, all tucked up nicely in bed for the night. We sat ourselves down on their beds and proceeded to chat. The poor men were terrified! Confident that we had temporarily immobilized our prey, we gave the others the nod and they crept along the floor and recovered our goodies. However, we were caught in the act by other staff members who were not so easy to fool and our plan was foiled.

Is there a teacher somewhere who recalls going for a leisurely swim and ended up having his swimming trunks removed? You deserve a medal for taking the whole episode in such good spirit and for not sending us all straight back home! As the staff present had nervous breakdowns on their return from France, may we former pupils now belatedly apologize for our behaviour and assure you that we had a wonderful, unforgettable holiday and have many, many happy memories.

(iii)

Art and Design by Eric Strachan

Hindsight is a fascinating indulgence: our selective memories paint pictures of delightful happy times in the past without the frustrations and almost insurmountable problems facing us in the present. However searchingly we look back though, the 80s were indeed halcyon days for us in this department. We had a definite feeling of direction and we were achieving success. There is no better recipe for a happy department and total staff involvement. We also felt appreciated. The Rector at the time, Terence Twatt, was a curious but welcome ally in

177

our endeavours. Curious because we knew very well that much of what we were doing he did not fully understand and yet he seemed to have total faith in our "knowing what we were doing". His measure, as he once said, was the effect on the pupils, our clientele. His perception and his faith were greatly appreciated. His interest in the drama and grand schemes led us into areas where we would not normally have ventured. One such was a design, which we still have on paper, to convert the Games Hall into a multi-purpose space for drama productions without in any way reducing its effectiveness as a games area. The project was professionally surveyed and approved but did not materialise for the usual reason, cost. The cost of the black-out blinds for the translucent roof to enable day-time productions proved prohibitive. All was not lost, however; as with most of these great plans there was usually a spin-off. In this case, it was a modular stage. The staff designed a set of modules which could be bolted together in innumerable permutations to provide a flat stage, a stepped stage, a cat walk etc, etc. They also made a model to convince sceptics. The Technical Department made a beautiful job of constructing the modules and improved the design of the locking bolts. Those modules are still in use.

Terence's greatest plan of course was to redesign the entire school. He haunted the Art Department during this period and one design after another was produced and put to death. One plan however did seem to be attractive and an artist's impression of the finished scheme was made into a Christmas Card which he sent to various interested bodies. They remained merely interested. It is interesting to note that the new school, which is now being built in phases, includes several important features from our own design, which the authorities at that time had said could not be done.

The 80s was the decade of the great Christmas Dance decors. Each year the Art staff selected a theme, usually literary in origin, though occasionally illustrating a period or a saying. An overall plan was drawn up by the Principal and the components farmed out amongst the staff. The scale of the work was enormous: a 14 foot Alice falling down the rabbit burrow, a 40 foot dragon whose eyes glowed brighter according to the noise level, a 16 foot "bronze" statue of Charles Dickens with a flock of London pigeons flying round his head and huge backdrops appropriate to the subject, canons that fired balloons, birds which laid eggs whilst in flight, an oil rig which had struck balloons. Pupils were totally involved in the productions at which even visiting theatre companies were amazed. Sadly it is extremely unlikely that this type of work will ever be repeated in schools on such a scale. Although the Art Department was the nucleus for these happenings the exercise was one of the finest examples of inter-departmental involvement in our experience. The lighting was engineered by Tom Laurenson, head of the Geography Department, all manner of gadgets were produced by the Technical Department, hoists, ropes, clips etc were loaned by the Navigation Department, etc, etc, Heady Days!

While on the subject of theatrical decor we must not forget the large School productions in the Corran Halls. These were not our productions of course but inevitably we were called upon to produce backdrops, flats, props and sometimes special effects. One of our special advantages is the speed at which we can "knock up" a huge rock, an eighteenth century fireplace, a suit of armour etc. This means that last minute ideas by producers can usually be catered for. All art departments can and should be used in this way.

Oban High School has never had areas suitable for the safe display of art work. It has always been a source of envy for us to visit other schools with wide access spaces, social areas, entrance halls etc, irresistible invitations for displays of work. Consequently when Angus Simpson, Manager of the Bank of Scotland, offered us the opportunity to display work in the foyer of the Station Road Branch of the Bank each year, with the added incentive of cash awards to the most outstanding exhibitors, we were absolutely delighted. In this situation the work was completely safe, did not require invigilators and was exposed to a wide public, who may not otherwise go to see School work. This was a far-sighted concept from a very public spirited man.

The Art Society gave us exhibitions in the Reading Room of the Corran Halls. These were also very successful and appreciated, though the out-of-town situation inevitably reduced public awareness despite the Society's use of the press for publicity.

The 80s saw the rise and fall of "computer reporting". This would hardly be worthy of a mention here were it not that Art and Design drove one of the biggest nails into its coffin. Each subject was allowed to choose a very limited range of comments from a "Dictionary" provided. Not to bore you with all the details we showed that with the great variety of skills taught in this subject we would need the whole dictionary. Needless to say the all purpose, all powerful, all knowing computer failed to compete with the personal and precise comments required for this exercise.

During the 80s the number of pupils opting to study this subject at all levels rose to a phenomenal level. In 1987 we had over 120 'O' grades and 40 Highers. No year passed without our contributing to the first year Degree Courses in the various Art Colleges, several going on to study Fine Art at the universities. Quite a number of pupils, usually one a year, went to study Photography in Edinburgh or Glasgow.

The Department had taken full advantage of the TVEI programme and the staff fleshed out modules in photography, ceramics and video. These courses became immensely popular. The late 80s saw the introduction of SEB Short Courses. We immediately embarked on these in Jewellery, Textile Printing and Photography.

The lay-out of the Art Department changed quite dramatically in the 80s as a result of the lift installation. Initially it meant the total destruction of our most important specialised spaces, the process camera/photo screen room, the dark room and the print and screen-wash room. No provision had been made to replace these facilities. Eventually it became clear that the print room would escape but that the other two spaces would be lost. Some swift work on the drawing board by the Principal and some impressive negotiation by Mr Brian Mitchell and one or two sympathetic members of the Local Authority led to the construction of a much larger dark room and the conversion of the lift entry into a gallery area. This was achieved in a remarkably short space of time.

The year 1989 saw our last presentation at O grade. Standard Grade, which had already been introduced into many other schools, would take its place. We in Oban High School Art and Design Department had always been in favour of the philosophy behind the new course, but we had made many critical submissions to the SED about the clumsy and inevitable costly mechanisms for assessment. The intransigence of the SED in the face of overwhelming contrary advice is at times beyond belief. Suffice it to say here that the cost factor is gradually but inevitably forcing them to think again.

Finally, have you ever heard of *Stone Soup*, the film? You haven't! You haven't lived! It was mentioned earlier that one of our most popular courses involves video production. When we got our first video camera the staff decided to spend an in-service opportunity to produce an introductory film with the intention of inspiring the pupils. The whole film was produced in two days and all the props, effects, animation, costume, location shooting, interior lighting etc were done in that time. Ian Gowdie's knowledge of the camera, George Hamilton's experience of drama, John Nicol's impressive way-over-the-top acting, Jim Guthrie's hairy hands and fine timing and Eric Strachan's (one of the best fakers in the business) props, produced a memorable film. Ahem. The point of this account is that it sums up one of our most important objectives, to teach people to make the most of what they happen to have. With a bit of imaginative innovation we can all improve our lot to a remarkable degree.

(iv)

School Trips by Alex Hamilton

The records of the High School suggest that at the beginning of this century the furthest school trips were expeditions to the heights of Ben Cruachan. As the decades passed and the Second World War came and went school cruises to foreign shores were organised, as were cultural visits to Rome and Vienna and language visits to France and Germany. In the 1980s, undoubtedly inspired by Mark Twain ("travel is fatal to prejudice, bigotry and narrow-mindedness") but presumably unmindful of Robert Benchley's "there are two kinds of travel - first class and with children", there was a marked increase in the level of foreign travel from Oban High School.

In what may have been the death throes of Classics as the structure of the curriculum changed, two fascinating and enjoyable trips to the Roman sites of Pompeii and Herculaneum were made in 1984 and 1986. The highlights of such trips are somewhat unpredictable but a bottle of elixir from the ancient Pantheon - otherwise known as Coke - after a forced march through the streets of Pompeii under a burning sun must rate high. For one group of pupils Coke and discos in Sorrento were outvoted by a tour round the stadium of Napoli and being able to stand on the turf hallowed by the then-time wonder, Diego Marradona. The remains from 79 AD were also quite good!

The 1980s saw the beginning of a regular series of study visits to the Battlefields of the First World War in Belgium and France. During the decade over 200 pupils have followed in the path of the original tours by Thomas Cook to the slaughter grounds of Ypres and the Somme. Seven decades may have passed since the end of the Great War but it is a limited mind which is not moved by the huge monuments inscribed with the names of a quarter of a million British soldiers who were killed but have no known grave and by the many dozens of beautifully tended cemeteries which dot the countryside. Trips which are not enjoyable are not successful but the Battlefield tours are clearly not all fun. The emphasis is very much on attaining an understanding of the awesome events which tore Europe apart and on provoking thought. Hopefully there are quite a number of homes in the Oban High area which still have a well-used copy of the eighty-page Battlefields workbook which is completed by all participants.

This decade saw visits even further afield. In 1983 forty pupils travelled via London to Moscow and Leningrad in the Soviet Union. Everything was carefully controlled by the Soviet authorities, the Intourist guides being most displeased if any of our group wanted to do anything 2% different from the average. The seeds of change were to be seen even then and small events like an Oban Venture Scout exchanging scarves with a Russian Young Pioneer may have made its contribution to pulling away the Iron Curtain. On the School's second trip to the USSR in 1987 Gorbachev was in power, corruption and the black market were more evident and more young -and not so young - minds were opened. The School's links with Russia have now become strong with the home-to-home exchanges beginning in 1990 with School No 14 in Rostov-on-Don. As the 1990s progress hopefully foreign travel from Oban High will continue and expand. Next stop Africa - or perhaps India?

(v)

A View from the Library by Pauline McKiernan

April 17, 1983 - my first day as Oban High School Librarian, when I was presented with the prospective library, which still included blackboard and desks and was roughly divided into classroom and "library"(?) by antiquated, glass-fronted bookcases.

Seriously wondering what I had let myself in for, I contemplated starting a library from scratch to be ready for the beginning of the next session in August, never having worked in a school before, having been out of libraries for thirteen years and having no knowledge of the Scottish education system!

The School left me to get on with it - having appointed a specialist, it was assumed I knew exactly what I was doing. However, my previous experience in public libraries and my training did not desert me, my confidence grew and with tremendous back-up from Mike

Sargent, Principal Education Librarian for Argyll and Bute and the staff at the Cowal Teachers' Centre, I made it. Not in four months, as we refused to open until the room was carpeted and decorated, but in six. Oban High School Library finally opened in October 1983.

In the first three weeks ALL the pupils were given an introductory talk on the library: I had almost lost my voice and we were in business.

Almost ten years on it is salutary to look back; and being positive I will mention only some of the good things: the friendliness and support of the staff; the help and fun of a succession of pupil librarians; Aggie's cups of tea; book-buying trips to wholesalers (usually including a lovely lunch); pupils returning books saying "that was smashing, Miss"; and the feeling that, with the changes in education, a library is now an essential feature of the School.

Exciting things are also in store for the future with a new library/resource centre planned, including a computerised catalogue and issue system, a bank of computers for staff and pupil use, extended use of databases, a greatly expanded stock including videos, CDs, periodicals, cassettes, more storage space and, wonder of wonders, an office for the Librarian!

(vi)

Change in the School Office by Margaret Comely

The period of the 1980s proved to be a decade of change: it saw changes in staff, changes in technology and changes in workload.

Notably Miss Isa MacInnes, whose coming to the School is noted in Chapter 4, retired in 1984 after no less than 38 years' service. In addition, in 1989 Mrs Alice Dunn, who had worked in the Office since 1975, left to move to Fife and Miss Diane Cameron left to get married. In 1985 Mrs Anne May was appointed as second auxiliary and in 1989 Mrs Kathleen Smith and Mrs Ann Scott were appointed as clerical assistants. Despite the departures, the loyalty and stability of the staff have continued.

In 1983/4 the manual typewriters were replaced by electronic machines and 1988 saw the installation of the first Office computer, used for Registration and Attendance.

With the many changes in education the already heavy workload of the Office increased considerably. In particular the introduction of Standard Grade meant for the auxilliaries a massive amount of additional Xeroxing. Additional work has been generated by ethnic monitoring, the creation of School Boards, TVEI, Industry Days and the monitoring of APT and C staff absences.

More recently, 1990 saw the introduction of a Multimate Word Processor. The three clerical assistants have all received in-service training for the operation of this computer, but since there is still only one machine in the Office their expertise is unfortunately not fully utilised.

The introduction of Direct Purchasing in 1991 brought both great changes in administering the requisition and additional work for the clerical assistants. Hopefully this situation will resolve itself with the introduction of Delegated Management Resources.

(vii)

The Closure of Craigard and Kilbowie[1]

The arrival of regionalisation in 1975 sounded the death knell for the Hostels, although few people then could have foreseen the drastic changes in the education system and the effects on the Hostels. By June 1976 Oban High School and the Hostels lost all the Highland Region children when they were transferred to Lochaber High. Argyll County Council's policy had been to send secondary children from outlying areas to Oban High School. The Region's policy was completely different: the building of some schools and the upgrading of others to six-year status at Islay, Tarbert, Lochgilphead, Tiree and Tobermory meant that fewer pupils required accommodation at Oban. Tobermory was the last High School to be completed and August 1988 saw the arrival of the last thirteen pupils from there to attend Oban High.

With the decline in numbers Craigard closed as a Hostel at Easter, 1986. Lying empty for a few years it was finally sold to MacLeod Builders and converted into apartments. Outwardly the building remains unchanged, but it is hard to imagine the old cloakrooms as a small flat or a sitting-room in the coal cellar or pot cupboard! The noise of alterations must have disturbed the "Green Lady" or other ghosts that were said to stalk the corridors. One joiner who had occasion to work at night was not too happy there!

During the period of rundown, old Kilbowie Hostel also sadly closed its doors in 1986, the juniors transferring to live in the new block. It all ended in June 1990, when New Kilbowie closed. The few remaining boys transferred to Glencruitten, which is now being run as a mixed hostel.

(viii)

Hill-walking by Ian D S Thomson

The Hill-walking Club in the School was started at the end of the 1970s by Bob Boardman, a relative of Peter Boardman, who died on the North-East Ridge of Everest, and it continued, under the leadership of Ian Thomson, after Bob moved to Inverness Royal Academy as head of Physics in 1980. Also involved in the first half of the 1980s were Harry Thomson who had the unenviable task of teaching Religion to each class in S1 and S2 for one period a week before he fled to Peterhead Academy to be in charge of the subject there, mathematician Bill Clark, who soon abandoned the groves of academe for more fertile (and lucrative) pastures

183

selling Everest windows, and youthful teacher of English, Stuart Logan, who was promoted to Principal Teacher of Guidance in Rothesay Academy after a mere two years in the profession. From time to time other members of staff came for a day in the hills.

Sadly, the Club was forced into an early grave in 1986 through rules, promulgated by the regional mandarins, governing, *inter alia*, the certification of leaders of school parties and the ratios of pupils to adults. While it is clear that adults taking parties into the hills should be competent, these rules, which were almost certainly devised with the "townies" in mind, denied to pupils in Oban High School the enjoyment of a major recreational resource on their doorstep. Indeed, so experienced was Thomson's dog in route-finding and hillcraft that she could have led a party in complete safety - and at a speed rather more impressive than Thomson. One wonders what thoughts would have passed through the minds of those mandarins if they had seen a party of half a dozen Oban High School fifteen-year-olds working their way up a steepening Cruachan gully, whose snow became harder with height, with the leader in the rear finding his rucksack altogether a little on the heavy side.

Throughout its existence, the Club had a small, but devoted, membership who scaled most of the main peaks in an area stretching from Fort William in the north to Tyndrum in the east with the occasional expedition to more distant summits, such as Ben Lawers and Schiehallion. There were also two sorties to Glen More where use was made of the Forestry Commission camping site and less demanding recreation was found in the Aviemore Centre. Outings were normally made on Sundays, although, when Thomson was not engaged in his School rugby duties, Saturdays might be used as an alternative - and, occasionally, the Club took to the hills on both days resulting in a certain physical lethargy on the Monday morning. There were also occasions when the party included tyros, a few of whom sustained their interest in the hills to become regular members of the Club. On these occasions, the ascents were made at a more leisurely pace and encouraging noises were made on the steeper sections to keep the laggards on the move.

For those who needed them, waterproofs and boots could be borrowed from the School and ice-axes were provided for the winter outings, while transport was provided by the School minibuses. Hill-walks were made in most weathers and this gave the regular members a useful experience of the widely differing conditions which can be met on the hills and the opportunity to learn such skills as navigation and energy conservation. One group made a traverse of the Mamore ridge on the south side of Glen Nevis on a particularly hot and windless June day when water was scarce and flesh was suffering in the heat; another group had to abandon their attempt on Beinn Challuim when close to the summit because the wind became so strong that further progress was possible only by crawling; while a third had a particularly wetting experience in driving rain on Buachaille Etive Beag. This last outing was made memorable for one of the leaders when it emerged that a junior member had equipped himself with two anoraks instead of an anorak and a pair of waterproof trousers: the leader had to surrender his own waterproof trousers to the junior with the result that water could be wrung out of every article of his clothing, underwear included, at the end of the day. For the other leader, it was equally memorable. He reached the ridge rather bruised and battered by the elements some distance behind the rest of the party, who had waited for him. He was clearly a bit off form and muttered menacingly, "All I want to do is get off this bloody mountain." This he did, willingly taking up the suggestion that he could retreat to the minibus and use it to collect the rest of the party when they left the hill.

(ix)

Shinty by Greig Anderson

When Andy Dunn left the staff of Oban High School early in the 70s the School was left without any staff with shinty experience and Ian Beath, Principal PE, asked me, a friend of Andy, to take over the School teams with the coaching done at various times by John Fairlie, Larry Forgrieve, Eddie Cooper and Jim Felgate - all of whose services were much appreciated. During the 70s the School was highly successful on the shinty field, as is noted in Chapter 7.

In 1981 Oban Celtic Shinty Club kindly presented the School with the Peter Watt Cup for under-13 competition among Argyll schools to increase the chance of a game for first year boys. In that year also, Campbell Macleod, former Oban Lorn player, started to help with coaching the boys.

In 1983 a team from Freshford School, County Kilkenny, visited Oban and played a shinty-hurling game against an Oban High School team and stayed with the High School boys.

The following year, 1984, was an even more eventful one, for not only did Oban High School teams win the Murchison Cup (under-18), Wade Cup (under-16) and Peter Watt Cup (under-13), but also visited Eire accompanied by myself, John Boyle and Campbell Macleod to play shinty-hurling against Freshford School and a team from Malahide near Dublin. All those who went there remember the wonderful hospitality we received in Freshford, where we stayed with Irish families, and also the visit to Croke Park, Dublin, where a message of welcome to Oban High School was flashed up on the display board before the start of the senior hurling final we were there to watch. There was an unplanned bit of excitement at the end of the trip when the car carrying John Boyle, Campbell Macleod and two of the boys headed off for the wrong ferry terminal and only got back to the right terminal with two minutes to spare.

1985 saw a suspension of extra-curricular activities including shinty as a result of the teachers' industrial action, and unfortunately the effects of that dispute lingered on for years after.

In 1987 the under-16s defeated Kingussie High School to win the Wade Cup. I was delighted to see that success before I retired.

When I retired in 1988 John Boyle took charge of the shinty teams and Donnie MacVicar, former Oban Camanachd player and father of three sons who played for the High School and now play for Oban Camanachd, helped with the coaching.

In 1990 John Boyle organised a visit by a team from St Mary's School, Rathfarnham, Dublin to play shinty-hurling against the High School and to stay with the High School boys. That year also saw Oban High win the MacBean Cup for the first time since it was changed in 1986 from under-18 to under-13 competition.

In the autumn of 1990 John Boyle left to take up a post in Hastings and Mark McShane took charge of the shinty teams, although like John Boyle and myself not a shinty player. Mark continued the Irish connection started by John Boyle and in May 1991 I travelled with Mark McShane and several other adults along with the under-14 team to Rathfarnham where the boys played shinty-hurling against St Mary's School and against a Ballyboden boys team. It was another visit to Ireland memorable for the wonderful hospitality and we shared a civic reception at the Manor House with a party of primary school shinty players with Donella Crawford, President of the Schools Camanachd Association, in charge, who were also in Dublin that weekend to play shinty-hurling. Shortly after their return to Oban the under-14 team won the MacPherson Cup in an exciting final against Lochaber High School which went to extra time. This was the first time for fourteen years that Oban High had won that cup, although the under-14s had many times reached the final only to be beaten by a team from the North. At the end of session prize-giving Mrs Peter Watt presented the Peter Watt Cup to the captain of the under-13s, who were the finalists from the South but had been beaten by Portree High School in the final of the MacBean Cup.

In 1992 the under-14s reached their final only to see Lochaber High regain the MacPherson Cup. The under-13s did not make it to the final of the MacBean Cup and had to be consoled by the knowledge that the winners, Lochgilphead High School, were the only team who had beaten them in the South section.

In conclusion I ought to mention that there are others not named above who have on occasion helped the shinty teams with transport or in other ways, including Dougie Macintyre, one of the janitors, who is a Camanachd Cup medal holder and father of two former captains of Oban High shinty teams. Furthermore any success of the High School teams is built upon the coaching done in the primary schools, especially by Alastair Clark of Rockfield, Ann Cameron of St. Columba's and Duncan Forgrieve of Dunbeg. I have not named individual players as there were too many talented ones over such a period. Hopefully there will be many more in the future.

(x)

Rugby by Ian D S Thomson

For most of the 1970s and 1980s rugby was the premier team sport in Oban High School. In the early 1970s, Brian Mitchell formed a senior team which played a few matches with some of the boys playing also for Oban Lorne rugby club. In time, Oban Lorne was to become quite dependent on the High School as a source of competent and well-drilled recruits to the senior game. In 1973 there arrived in the High School a young, bearded teacher of History and

Modern Studies with an enthusiasm for the game and an earnestness to introduce it to as many of the boys in the school as possible. His name was Charlie Robertson and it was thanks largely to his influence that rugby developed so much in the High School during the rest of the 1970s. He was assisted by Iain MacCormick until the latter became a Member of Parliament in February 1974.

In season 1975-1976, an invitation was secured for a senior team to play in the North of Scotland Schools seven-a-side tournament in Elgin. Mitchell and Robertson knew they had a useful side - one which, having practised hard before the event, proved to be the surprise of the competition, winning the trophy at their first attempt. The two stars of that team, Billy Thomson and Angus MacColl, went on to play top class rugby furth of Oban before returning to be stalwart playing members of Oban Lorne RFC and the Isle of Mull RFC respectively. Following this seven-a-side success, an invitation for the School to join the North of Scotland Schools Rugby Association was soon received and membership of the Association brought with it the opportunity to play in the North of Scotland Schools leagues. This opened the door to guaranteed fixtures and over the next three seasons teams were formed at the under-fifteen, under-fourteen and under-thirteen age levels. The Oban teams had an immediate impact of the North of Scotland leagues

Oban High School RFC attained the pinnacle of achievement in season 1979-80 when they swept the board, being champions at under-thirteen, under-fourteen, under-fifteen and senior levels. That year, the league finals were held on the playing fields of Inverness Royal Academy, three of whose teams participated in the finals, the other (at senior level) being Elgin Academy. One after another the Oban teams won and memorable was the return journey with a special stop at the Clansman hotel overlooking Loch Ness. The Club was rewarded with a civic reception in the Corran Halls which marked not just their recent success but also the development of the Club since its inception. Ironically, by the time of this triumph, Charlie Robertson had departed from the High School to assume his duties as Principal Teacher of History in Kelso High School. So much was owed to the first class system of coaching he had developed before he moved to Kelso in September 1979. His translation to the Borders paved the way for Border tours by Oban to Jedburgh and Kelso whose schools reciprocated the visits. All this helped to maintain the high standard of rugby which was then being played by Oban High School. In the early 1980s, the senior team twice reached the quarter finals of the Scottish Schools Cup, taking some notable scalps on the way.

In the 1980s, in addition to Brian Mitchell, who took the senior team, a number of staff were involved in rugby, including Joe Rhodes before his elevation to Rectorship of Dunoon Grammar School, Ian Thomson, Ted Heath, Ian Cairns and Stuart Logan, who, like Thomson, was a non-rugby player who was persuaded to give assistance. Sterling service was given by Joe Black, who arranged the refereeing of the home matches and was in control of numerous games himself, while David Hutcheson of Soroba House Hotel very kindly laundered all the Club's strips for several years, a service much appreciated by the Club. The victorious season of 1979-80 was almost repeated the following season when all but the under-fifteen team, who were beaten finalists, were champions again. However, it was then decided by the North of

Scotland Schools Rugby Association to reduce the competitive nature of schools rugby by ending the leagues, the suspicion in Oban being that this was done because the leagues were dominated by Oban. There is little doubt that the leagues motivated the teams and encouraged the high level of commitment necessary if the Club was to flourish; the disappearance of the leagues may have been one factor which led to a decline in rugby in the School.

The Club travelled extensively and had fixtures on most Saturdays of the season. Apart from Lochaber High School where there was rugby at the end of the 1970s, the nearest schools offering opposition came from Inverness, Stirling and Glasgow, which meant a journey of almost two hundred miles and entailed leaving Oban at 8.00 am with a return in the late afternoon. With more distant venues, the day was even longer. The greatest distances were travelled in playing Wick and Thurso High Schools and the Nicolson Institute in Stornoway, these matches requiring two nights away. There were also two tours made to the Principality of Wales, the first organized by Charlie Robertson in 1978 and the second in 1980 by Ian Thomson and remembered for the fact that the driver of the second minibus was Marjory MacLean, the only lady member of the staff to drive for the Club. No matches were won but there was great jubilation when some points were scored against Pecoed in 1980. On both occasions visits were made to the National Stadium in Cardiff and photographs were taken on the hallowed turf.

Membership of the North of Scotland Schools Rugby Association gave the Oban boys the opportunity to play district rugby for the North of Scotland against the other districts. Such was the strength of Oban rugby for a few years that up to ten Oban boys might be playing in the senior North team. Angus MacColl was the first Oban player to appear in North colours and he was followed by too many to be named individually. Special mention has to be made, however, of the Malone brothers from Appin - Donald, Willie and Colin - all of whom played for the North. Tommy McQuade played for the North District for a total of five successive seasons at under-fifteen and senior levels. In season 1984-85, another singular honour came to the School Club when Colin Malone was selected to play for the Scottish Schools international team. Not only has he been Oban High School's only internationalist, he was also the first international cap from the North District.

The teachers' industrial action in the mid 1980s had a serious effect on rugby, which came to an end in most schools as an extra-curricular activity, although Oban did continue for a year playing such opposition as could be found. Unfortunately, the ending of the industrial action did not restore school rugby to its previous virility and there were many schools in which rugby was not restarted. Not so in Oban and efforts were made to operate teams at all the previous levels, albeit on a reduced fixture list. However, the old enthusiasm for lunch-time and after-school training sessions and the long Saturdays driving minibuses to distant venues - not to mention organizing fixtures, booking changing rooms, pitches and referees for home matches - had waned and, in the end, both Brian Mitchell and Ian Thomson decided to withdraw from school rugby when responsibility for the School teams was taken over by Oban Lorne Rugby Club.

Tennis and Squash by David Heath

With the redevelopment of five all-weather tennis courts at Dalriach Road, the erection of Oban Tennis Club's new clubhouse and the provision of two squash courts there, pupils were able for the first time to enjoy both sports and benefit from the coaching of Club members and staff of the School's PE Department. As a result of the teachers' industrial action team sports and inter-school fixtures were seldom available to pupils, who gravitated towards these individual sports.

Both sports provided a number of very good club-standard players of both sexes, including Rab McGill, Ian Barnett, Iain Morrison, Chris Smith, Kenny Drummond, Colin MacKay, Andrew and Ian Clark, Barbara Barnett, Jackie Wood, Margaret MacDougall, Fiona Morrison, Karen MacLachlan, Shona Campbell, Fiona Crawford, Marion MacKillop and Marie-Claire Robertson. Kenny Drummond, in particular, showed his versatility by achieving a high standard in the West of Scotland junior tennis and squash teams. In 1987 a High School team of Andrew Smith, David and Martin Heath and Nicholas Turner won the Scottish Schools Tennis title, while a team drawn from David and Martin Heath, Chris and Andrew Smith, Kenny Drummond and Ian Barnett twice finished in the top three in the Scottish Junior Squash Team Championships and the top side from a rural area.

International honours and a fair degree of success came to Andrew Smith at tennis and David and Martin Heath at squash. All three boys were involved in the first-ever triangular junior squash international between Scotland, Ireland and Wales which was held at the Oban Club, where Kenny Drummond and Rab MacGill, who were both too old to be included in the under-fourteen national side, made their debut as markers at this level.

Andrew Smith's achievement in being capped for Scotland at all junior levels was all the more remarkable as he took up the sport while still learning to walk again after a serious operation on his leg. Irene Wood, who introduced so many children to tennis at the local Club, recognised his talent and his burning ambition. In making remarkably rapid progress he soon found himself representing the West of Scotland junior team in British Counties Week. After a number of tournament successes he got his first national cap against Wales in Cardiff. While still at school he represented Scotland at the European championships in Belgium and at an invitation event in Holland.

After leaving school he was selected as a member of a professional tennis squad based at Arsenal Football Club. This consisted of six ranked British juniors who played in major tournaments as well as working at the Arsenal Sports Centre. One of the remarkable benefits which he gained from the membership of this squad was a month's intensive training at John Newcombe's ranch in Texas and a practice session with Gabriella Sabatini, one of the world's top women tennis players.

This year has been one of Andrew's most successful, since he has been runner-up in the Scottish Under-21 Championships and has represented West of Scotland at senior level in British Counties Week. He is now a member of the senior Scottish squad and hopes to gain his first national cap at this level very soon.

David and Martin Heath were introduced to squash by their father, Ted, a PE teacher at the school. Both of them showed considerable aptitude and Ted soon found himself driving them round Scotland to various tournaments at which they achieved a high degree of success. Through sound coaching from their father and from Mike Howard, Helensburgh, they were both capped for Scotland while still under fourteen.

Martin played squash seriously throughout his school career, but always found himself playing second fiddle nationally to the brilliant Aberdonian, Peter Nicol, who is now making a huge impact on the senior international circuit. Martin went to Glasgow University at the age of seventeen to study Physiology and Sports Science, joining his brother who was already there studying French. Under the skilful guidance of Alastair Duncan, one of Scotland's best qualified coaches, he established himself as the Number Two home-based Scot. In his final Under-19 International he completed a rare triple by defeating his English, Welsh and Irish opponents, a feat which very few Scots have achieved.

Early in 1992, having defeated Derek Ritchie, the top home-based Scot, Martin received his first senior national cap and was part of the side which won the European championships, defeating England in the semi-final and Finland in the final. This was one of the biggest upsets ever in the international squash scene and the pinnacle, so far, of Martin's career. On the completion of his degree Martin intends to turn professional, but before that he still hopes to be the first non-professional for many years to win the Scottish National Championship.

Meanwhile David, who has been teaching English in France for a year as part of his degree course, hopes that now he is back in Glasgow he can establish himself again as the Number Two player at senior level in the West of Scotland.

In conclusion, without the help and assistance of a number of teachers at Oban High and several members of Oban Tennis and Squash Club none of the young people mentioned in this article would have been able to reach the standards they have achieved and to enjoy their sports to the full.

None of us could have achieved what we have without the generous assistance of Irene Wood, Terry Macnair, the late Hugh MacFarlane, Marnie Clark and Mary McLean as far as tennis goes and in Squash Ted Heath, Billy Thomson, Alex Smith and Coll MacDougall, who masterminded our trips to the Scottish Team Championships in Edinburgh and, along with Ted, set up the West Highland Open Squash Tournament so that we could meet top players from all over the country.

NOTE

1   The information on the Hostels is extracted from two booklets printed on the occasion of the School centenary celebrations: *Craigard Hostel, a short history* by Anne MacPhail and *Kilbowie Hostel, a short history* by Anne M Gibb.

CHAPTER 9

The Glasgow Branch of Oban High School Former Pupils' Association

JOHN MACFARLANE[1]

It was in 1949 that the NATO treaty was signed in Washington DC, the German Federal Republic was formed with Bonn the capital, Joe Louis retired as World Heavyweight Champion and rationing of clothes, chocolates and sweets ended in Britain; but on Saturday 23rd April on a stormy evening a group of Oban High School former pupils were holding a reunion in the Lesser Hall of the Highlanders' Institute in Glasgow. Among those present at that meeting were Glasgow University students Moira Smith from Tarbert, Nan MacPhail from Oban and the son of the Oban post master, Gordon MacGillivray Roy Barr. More significant at that initial reunion were the names of Alasdair MacLeod (the son of the erudite Rector of Oban High School, Angus MacLeod), Duncan Robertson from Ballachulish, Alasdair Ogilvie, Tobermory, Annie Bonnyman and Elizabeth Buchanan, Achnaba, Benderloch. Although no Glasgow branch was formed at that time the seeds may well have been planted.

However it was eight years later almost to the day, 27th April, 1957, when a notice appeared in *The Oban Times* for a meeting on 2nd May, 1957 to be held in the Lesser Hall of the Highlanders' Institute to establish a Glasgow Branch of the Oban High School Former Pupils. The instigator behind this meeting was the former School Captain, Malcolm Black from Tobermory, who had approached the Rector, John Maclean. The latter approved the idea and suggested that the newly retired Depute Rector, George Milne, should address the meeting.

It was reported in *The Oban Times* that "such a large number attended the inaugural meeting that it had to be transferred to the larger hall" and the meeting, addressed by George Milne under the chairmanship of John A Smith (later to become Depute Director of Jordanhill Training College), was a notable success. The time was ripe for the formation of the branch: there was a large influx of FPs in the Glasgow area at the time who were scattered around the city and there was a keenness to find a focal point. The Glasgow Branch of the Oban High School Former Pupils was thus created with a strong committee formed.

As will become evident, each committee had its fair share of characters and this original committee was no exception. Its President was Rev Angus MacKinnon, originally from Tiree, but now minister at St Columba's Church, St Vincent Street; the Secretary was C J MacLeod; and the Treasurer was naturally a banker, Donald MacDougall from Oban. One of the best loved characters was Morag Edgar, a great organiser, who demanded the most from people

192

out in a kindly way. She was the Fund Raiser and later became a benefactor to the Glasgow Mid Argyll Shinty Club. Heather MacInnes, whose father was a gamekeeper at Ardchattan, was also a leading light, along with the architect from Oban, Eddie Swanson. Colin Palmer raised the tone of the committee as he was the Secretary of the Temperance Alliance in St Vincent Street, where later Committee meetings were to be held. Incidentally Colin in his schoolboy days was known as an expert in predicting examination questions, particularly in Higher English. Naturally he was well sought after by his fellow pupils.

The first function was a Ceilidh Dance Supper in Cranworth House with Rev A F MacKinnon as *fear an tigh* and musical entertainment provided by the Bone Trio (Anne Bone Maclean, still accompanies Highland Societies in Glasgow today) and Alastair Hunter on his tuneful box (the leader of the Lorne Broadcasting Band, but more of Alastair later).

The first meeting of the 1958 session found Colin Palmer installed as President and an evening billed as "A Song and a Story" with George Milne as the guest. This proved an interesting evening with the audience singing the old school song *Land of our Birth* the words of course by Kipling but the music by Julian Nesbitt, so long the Music Master at Oban High School. There followed songs from FPs and Mod Gold Medallists Helen T MacMillan and Hugh MacInnes, who was joined in a duet by Archibald MacGregor, formerly from the Shanghai Police.

However the most unusual contribution to the evening came from the Rev William Young, home on leave from Pakistan, who sang the 24th Psalm, *Ye gates lift up your heads on high*, in Punjabi. Incidentally Rev William Young was one of four brothers all of whom wore the kilt during their attendance at Oban High School. Their father, Rev John Young, was minister at Dunollie Road Church (later to become Christ Church, Dunollie) for twenty years from 1929 to 1949 and two of his sons, William and Ian, were duxes of Oban High School. The Rev William had an illustrious career, first as a missionary in Pakistan, then as Professor of Church History in Pakistan and finally as Bishop of Sialhot in Pakistan before returning to Scotland to become parish Minister for Resolis and Urquhart in the Black Isle. His brother Alex was a prisoner of war at the hands of the Japanese and wrote a tiny diary of the daily events in the camp, taking considerable risk in doing so. This diary is preserved in the Imperial War Museum, London. Alex later became an Art teacher in Kinghtswood Academy and was a staunch FP supporter. No doubt Morag Edgar's vote of thanks that evening covered the worldwide spread of Oban High School Former Pupils.

In 1960 a name from the original 1949 reunion emerged as President of the Association, namely Dr W Alasdair Ogilvie. Unfortunately Alasdair was heavily committed to his practice and held the office for only one year, but he has remained a committed and regular member ever since. Alasdair has for many years been closely associated with Glasgow Rangers Football Club, having been introduced into the Club by his friend and former classy left half George Brown, who later became a Club director. Alasdair stepped in as Club Doctor at times and his son Campbell is the present Rangers Secretary and a club director.

From 1961 to 1963 Donald MacNicol, originally from Taynuilt but a hotelier in Upper Largo in Fife, took over the reins as President and this rotund and jovial character was delighted to welcome a number of younger and not so young members, particularly from the St Andrews area, enthusiasts like Malcolm Black and Kennedy Cameron, to a social evening in the St Enoch's Hotel, sustained musically by FP Duncan MacDonald, the son of Rev William MacDonald, Oban Old Parish Church.

It was also at this time that the backbone of the Glasgow branch arrived in the form of three stalwarts, Tommy Ness, Alastair Duncan and Sam MacAskill. There is no doubt that the drive, enthusiasm and humour of these three characters sustained the OHS FP branch and ensured a continuity, if at times unsteady, for the next twenty years. Therefore it would be appropriate at this point to provide some background of these three redoubtable men.

Thomas P Ness provided a natural link with the Oban Branch of the High School FPs as his brother David was one of the founders in 1957 and one of the driving forces behind it until its demise in 1983. It is worth recording the tremendous work done by Ishbel Clark, the Secretary of Rockfield School and Secretary of Oban High School FPs Oban Branch for many years. David Ness however will be remembered by many pupils at Oban High School as the chief invigilator at examination times and the sound of his tackety brogues will be remembered as he walked between the desks in the Central Hall and Gymnasium during the examination periods. However as a background to Thomas P Ness, the following article appeared in the *Evening Times* in 1973:

"Nothing is more important to a newspaper than its readers - and in this case, I'm thinking not only of scores of thousands of Glaswegians who buy the *Evening Times* every afternoon.

You see, every newspaper also has a special category of 'readers' on its payroll - the readers whose job it is to check proofs and make any necessary corrections.

"For the past 17 years, the chief reader of the *Evening Times* has been Tommy Ness - and when he retires today, he will be ending a link with newspapers that goes back nearly 90 years. 'My father, the late Walter Ness, started as a printer on the *Dundee Courier* in 1885,' Tommy told me, 'and was head printer of the *Oban Times* for about fifty years.'

"Tommy himself hails from Oban and worked on the *Oban Times* before coming to Glasgow 39 years ago to join Outrams, publishers of the *Evening Times* .

"'I'm sorry to be leaving the many friends I have made here,' he told me.

"Tommy, whose home is in Clarkston, is one of the most highly regarded persons in newspapers in the West of Scotland.

"He and his wife, Margaret, have two married daughters.

"He told me - 'I've no particular plans for retirement, except to spend more time on gardening and golf'."

Tommy Ness's work as a proof reader with the *Evening Times* proved advantageous to a certain young estate agent who was setting up in business in Glasgow at the time, in that personal care could be taken in checking the adverts and in their positioning in the paper. Donald Skinner, later to step in and save the FP Association, was always pleased to receive advice from Tommy Ness on these matters.

The second of the three redoubtable men, who acted as President, Treasurer and Secretary in turn throughout the sixties and early seventies was Alastair J B Duncan. Alastair was born and brought up in Oban where his father, coincidentally, was a printer with the *Oban Times* along with Tommy Ness' father. Alastair attended Glasgow University, where he studied Geography, and he taught in Govan High School, rising to Assistant Head Teacher; but he took early retirement after suffering a stroke. He was a lively character who enjoyed life and after the early death of his first wife he married Betsy MacLennan, an FP from Islay and a nurse in the city. Together they were prominent attenders at all FP functions. Alastair was President in 1971 and 1972 but resigned from the Committee in 1974 due to ill health. He continued to attend the annual main function.

While Tommy Ness was undoubtably the most influential member of the three stalwart over a longer period of time and acted as President for five years from 1978 to 1983, Sam MacAskill's six years as President from 1964 to 1970 were active and happy times. Sam was born in Ullinish, Skye, in 1912. He was the youngest son of a sheep farmer, Allan MacAskill, who moved to a mainland farm, Barnacarry, just South of Oban, and Sam attended Kilninver Primary School.

In 1923 Sam went to Oban High School where his days were full of committing to memory vast amounts of English prose, poetry, maths and Latin. Corporal punishment was always in the background and "Scrimgeour", tawse at the ready over his shoulder for immediate action, was often the deterent to lack of work. Despite "Scrimgeour", Sam enjoyed the cameradarie and the dedicated teaching staff.

In December 1932 Sam joined the Metropolitan Police at Chelsea Police Station, where he was introduced to the delights of Mars Bars and a subsequent increase in weight. He resigned from the Metropolitan Police in 1936 and joined Crown Paints as a Sales Representative for the next forty years. However when war broke out in 1940 Sam enlisted in the RASC at Weymouth and within three weeks was promoted to Corporal because he could shout commands louder than the rest of the recruits! He was seconded to the Indian Army where he was commissioned in 1942, rose to the rank of Major and was mentioned in despatches for his part in the defence in Impbal, Burma, in 1944. There could not have been many people in Britain at that time who spoke fluent English, Gaelic and Urdu. In his later life in Glasgow Sam would love to go into an Indian or Pakistani shop and talk to them in their native tongue.

In July 1954, Sam and family moved to Glasgow where he continued his job with Crown Paints and became heavily involved with the Glasgow Branch of the Oban High School FPs, enjoying mixing with fellow Fomer Pupils.

With Sam MacAskill installed as President, Alastair Duncan as Secretary and Thomas Ness as Treasurer, the Branch was going from strength to strength with Saturday afternoon teas, Daffodil teas, Ceilidh Dances, May bus outings to Oban fitting into a busy programme; but the addition of an annual dance at the Highlanders' Institute added some very important new young members as well as much needed funds.

The Friday night dances at the famous Highlanders' Institute, being open to the public, presented a problem of stewarding. Tommy Ness had a solution in the person of Donald Skinner, who was starting his estate agent's business in the city at the time. Donald was also the dominating centre midfield player for Glasgow Mid Argyll Shinty Club and knew of at least eleven other young fit men who could act as stewards. Thus in return for a donation to the shinty club and suitable refreshments for the stewards on the night the stewarding problem was solved; or was it ? Unfortunately the back steps out of the Highlanders' Institute were quite steep and it was not unusual to see on these occasions one or two team members as well as officials from the OHS FP Branch having difficulty negotiating the steps in the early hours of Saturday morning. The shinty club results were never too good after these Friday night dances.

In 1964 the following new members were added to the committee Senga MacFarlane (formerly from Tarbert), Joyce MacKay, Duncan MacDonald, Angus Livingstone and Donald Skinner. They joined Annie Bonnyman, Dollie MacPhee, Duncan MacPhail, Chrissie Caldwell, Colin Palmer and Ishbel Lloyd (the sister of the Tobermory accordionist, Bobby MacLeod) and formed an energetic and active association. There were various additions and deletions to the Committee throughout the late sixties with, in 1966, the addition of district nurse Cathie Crawford providing another regular member for ten years. When she retired to return to Bunessan she promised she would return for each Annual Dinner. She has done so since, accompanying her nursing friend Cathie Henderson (née MacFarlane), from Hamilton and formerly Taynuilt, to each Annual Dinner. This is typical of the spirit of the Glasgow Branch. Although members may have moved away from the Glasgow area, they still endeavour to return for the Annual Dinner.

The first Annual Dinner, which has now become the highlight of the Association, was held in the Grand Hotel in 1966, where the now standard format for the evening was first developed. A guest speaker was invited from distinguished Former Pupils to reminisce on their school days at Oban High School. It was also important that the current Rector should also speak and three Rectors, Farquhar Macintosh, Terence Twatt and the current Rector, Brian Mitchell, have been fine speakers. However the first guest speaker was Alistair Skinner and the list of speakers includes Angus MacIntyre, Tobermory, Donald Thomson, Dugald MacArthur, Dr Archie Campbell, Mrs Mima MacVicar (née Greenshields), John Boyd, Dr Bobby Campbell, Rev Iain MacDonald, Tarbolton, Rev James Maitland, Anne Lorne Gillies, John Carmichael,

Dr Lorne MacIntyre, G Y Slater, Rev Gilliesbeag MacMillan, Erik Spence and Larry Forgrieve. There have been a number of years in which guest speakers have been unable to arrive, usually because of weather conditions. The speakers have added variety and flavour in their own styles to each Annual Dinner and at times they have received some adverse reaction from the audience, as when one controversial speaker made a scathing attack on the dress of teachers of today not realising the number of teachers who were in his audience, or when one speaker showed some slides of Old Oban to be confronted by William Lamont (known affectionately as Bill Peel) who gave considerably more background information to the slides as he was in his late eighties and still attended the Annual Dinner, brought along by the kind Dr Angus Greenshields. William Lamont's claim to fame was that he was the oldest member by a week (from Dan Nicholson) to play for Glasgow Skye shinty team, at the age of 64 years.

It would seem that the Association over the years had made steady progress but in 1972 Tommy Ness, Alastair Duncan and five Committee Members intimated their resignation and Mrs Anne Barr took over as President for one year, followed by the return to the fold of the very first President, Rev Angus MacKinnon, who remained until 1978. In 1975 "Babbie" Cameron and Morag Roxburgh joined the Committee and in 1976 Dr Elizabeth Milne became a Committee member, the Elizabeth Buchanan who attended the initial reunion in 1949. The late seventies showed a decline in interest in the Association, possibly due to the reduction in movement of Highlanders to the Glasgow area, and in 1978 a Special General Meeting was held with the motion moved to wind up the Association.

Donald Skinner and Neil McKichan moved the amendment to this motion and with six for the amendment and eight for the motion the two thirds majority was not achieved and the amendment was carried saving the Association. Donald Skinner then rejoined the Committee bringing also John Boyd, now the Queen's Inspector for Police, Scotland, and Donnie McGilp, the former Oban High School teacher and Tartan Wanderers star, now an Assistant Head at Knightswood Academy. Tommy Ness returned as President, Alastair Duncan, whose health was failing, returned as Secretary and the 1978 crisis was averted.

In 1979 Donald McGilp took over as Secretary from Alastair Duncan to remain in that position until 1989 and in 1980 John Boyd took over as Treasurer from Sam McAskill. The last of the stalwarts, Tommy Ness, resigned to move to Spain, his President's chair being taken by Dr Elizabeth Milne in 1984. The Annual Dinner was moved to a permanent date on the second Friday in March at the Bellahouston Hotel and following good publicity (usually via Alasdair Kennedy in his *Oban Times* "Glasgow Letter") the numbers at the dinner began to increase reaching a maximum of 164 in 1987. "Babbie" Cameron and Morag Roxburgh emerged at this time as the raffle ticket organisers with "Babbie's" top hat coming in useful for making the draw, which must have contained among the largest number of prizes, usually all kindly donated. It was also not unusual for the prizes to go east whence faithful attender Dr Kenny Murray brought a group of Edinburgh Oban High School FPs.

The increased numbers in the late eighties also coincided with an increase in the number from the Oban area. Members from Oban High School were enthusiastically brought along by the sadly missed Maureen Drummond.

In 1984 John Boyd resigned as Treasurer on his promotion to Chief Constable of Dumfries and Galloway and former School Captain John MacFarlane, originally from Taynuilt, took over. Irene Stewart (née Calderwood) at this time was doing sterling work in recruiting members to attend the Annual Dinner. In particular she recruited Anne Byiers, the daughter of a late Classics Teacher at Oban High School, Cunningham Irving, and Anne has become a committee member. In 1989 it was decided to change slightly the format of the dinner and to include dancing in the dining suite of the Bellahouston Hotel with the reception suite being used for non-dancers. This was a natural development as there were three superb accordionists regularly attending the dinner in Charlie Kirkpatrick, originally from Iona, Charles MacLean, originally from Tiree, and Alastair Hunter from Oban - the same Alastair who had played at the first function in 1957 in Cranworth House.

This new format, proposed by new Committee members Senga Smith (née MacFarlane) and Dr Christabel Fallon (née MacArthur), proved successful and seemed an ideal way of catering for the tastes of the wide age range of members who were attending from as far afield as Surrey Aberdeen, Edinburgh, Oban, Peterborough, Stranraer, Crieff, Mull and Islay. Dr Elizabeth Milne and Donnie McGilp had made some unsuccessful attempts to resign from the Committee. With reluctance their resignations were accepted in 1989 and Morag Roxburgh formerly from Dalmally, took over as President with Joint Secretaries Senga Smith and Christabel Fallon.

Donald Skinner, who had always been a distinguished Committee Member, always available when problems were to be solved, with his uncanny knowledge of names of Former Pupils and their background and his interest in genealogy of Oban, became President in 1991. This proved to be a vital move, as the Glasgow Branch (and Donald in particular) became heavily involved in the organisation of this centenary year. The Glasgow Branch of the Oban High School Former Pupils since its inception in 1957 has wound a rocky path involving many characters in evenings of friendship, camaraderie and good highland spirit. It is hoped it will continue to attract Former Pupils of the School.

NOTE

1   The author acknowledges the research assistance given by Donald Skinner.

CHAPTER 10

The Future

BRIAN R MITCHELL
Rector of Oban High School

Oban High School's centenary is being celebrated at a time of major changes in Scottish schools.

For those involved in the secondary sector the principal theme of recent years has been changes in the curriculum. The Standard Grade development programme followed by the consequential revision of Higher courses began in the early 1980s and is now nearing completion. This major reform has produced a massive change in emphasis, centred on the middle years of the secondary school. Teaching methodologies have shifted from teacher-led towards pupil-centred, the emphasis in learning has moved from the acquisition of knowledge towards the development of skills and, perhaps most importantly, pupils of all abilities have the opportunity to obtain Standard Grade awards in the Scottish Certificate of Education at the end of fourth year. The introduction of SCOTVEC modules as alternatives to Highers in fifth and sixth years, a process which has been underway since the mid 1980s, means that schools can now cater for the whole range of pupil abilities in the senior school. The staying on rate to fifth year in Oban is already over 80% and the continuing improvement of modular packages seems likely to increase this trend.

Even before the Standard Grade development programme has been completed an even more important change is already underway. This is the national review of the 5 to 14 curriculum. With its twenty-six associated primary schools the primary-secondary transition process has always presented special difficulties for Oban High School. The final goal of the 5 to 14 initiative of pupils following a coherent and continuous curriculum across the primary-secondary interface will, therefore, be hugely beneficial to the School. This programme will, in all probability, stretch on to the end of the century. However, early efforts in English and Mathematics are extremely encouraging with primary and secondary teachers working enthusiastically together to produce courses which effectively bridge the primary-secondary divide.

While the 5 to 14 programme is still going on it seems likely that further changes, this time to the upper years of secondary schools, will begin. The work of the Howie Committee has been well reported in the press, most probably because its recommendations threaten the existence of the Higher, the best known award of the Scottish Certificate of Education. The Scottish Office Education Department is presently considering reactions to the Howie report from interested parties, and an announcement will be made later in 1993. It seems likely that the Higher, as we presently know it, will be changed and that group awards will be re-introduced in the 1990s.

In the last part of its first century this school has enjoyed the benefits of new technology. The use of microcomputers is now implicit in several courses and the applications of word processing, databases, spreadsheets and interfacing are rapidly spreading through the curriculum. It is only a matter of time before microcomputers become a standard feature in all classrooms.

One special technological initiative involving Oban High School is just beginning. The Argyll and Bute Link in Education (ABLE), which is being funded by Strathclyde Region, European Community grants and Argyll and the Islands Local Enterprise Company, will create a telecommunications network between all the Argyll and Bute secondary schools and, eventually, link them to certain Further Education colleges. The intention is to develop this network to support students in further education and training. The link will also be available for adult learners in the community and will be used by the School to enhance the curriculum and assist teaching and learning. It will be fascinating in the years ahead to follow the development of ABLE. Clearly, using modern technology in this way has great potential for assisting in the delivery of an education service to rural areas.

Although a fair amount of the more immediate future of Oban High School can be predicted with a reasonable degree of confidence one important aspect has to be resolved. The structure of local government in Scotland is due to change with the present two tier local authority structure being replaced by single tier authorities. Strathclyde Region, which has served Oban High School very well, is likely to be dismantled by the mid 1990s. What new authority will Oban be placed in? Will the School's present catchment area be changed? Clearly the size of the School would be affected by a change in catchment area, but any major change would seem unlikely. Also, a change in local authority should not have a great effect on the management of the School as the Scottish Office has already issued guidelines to education authorities on how they should draw-up schemes for devolving the management of schools to the schools themselves. In this respect Oban High School is fortunate that from session 1992-93 it became part of Strathclyde Region's "Delegated Management of Resources" scheme which is very much in line with the Scottish Office guidelines. The scheme gives the School control over most of its budget and allows decisions to be taken at the local level to meet local needs. It is also clear that future arrangements will include an increased role for school boards, thereby giving parents more say in the running of schools.

For most of its first hundred years the public face of Oban High School has been the impressive two storey granite frontage facing Soroba Road. The single most noticeable change to the school early in its second century will be the replacement of this old part of the building by a new, modern block. This will be the final phase of the multi-million pound redevelopment of Oban High School which is already underway. A new two storey block built on the site of the old Technical department was occupied in 1991. Work has just begun on refurbishing and extending the 1956 block. This should be completed by October 1993 after which a new building will be added, wrapped round the Canteen and Games Hall on the south and west sides of the 1972 block to provide a new Technical department and extended PE accommodation. A further contract will see the upgrading of the 1972 extension taking place. Finally, if all goes according to present plans, in session 1997-98 all of the old granite building as well and the HORSA huts will disappear to be replaced by the final part of the re-designed school. The intention is to include a replica of the present bell tower on the front of the new school. Whereas there will be great sadness at the demolition of the old school there will also be great pleasure in having an Oban High School with accommodation and equipment as good as any in the country, well prepared for its second hundred years.

SCHOOL CAPTAINS

	BOYS	GIRLS
1950-51	Lamont MacKay	Cynthia Gray
1951-52	Archibald Boyd	Helen Ness
1952-53	Iain Sinclair	Barbara Leggett
1953-54	Norman MacGilp	Anna Smith
1954-55	Malcolm Black	Dorothy Walton
1955-56	Robert Reid	Margaret Pacey
1956-57	Andrew Noble	Ina MacAllister
1957-58	Donald MacLarty	Mary Mason
1958-59	Thomas Hunter	Ann Govan
1959-60	Gilleasbuig MacMillan	Maureen Hoey
1960-61	Duncan MacDonald	Margaret Robertson
1961-62	Alan Dallas	Katharine Troup
1962-63	Kenneth MacLeod	Anne Irving
1963-64	Alasdair MacArthur	Annie Cameron
1964-65	Alan Irving	Moira Beaton
1965-66	Andrew Robb	Hermonie Dawson
1966-67	Duncan MacLeod	Pauline Jackson
1967-68	John MacFarlane	Mairead Thomson
1968-69	Kenneth Scott	Mhairi Livingstone
1969-70	John Smith	Anne Struthers
1970-71	Duncan H C Robb	Mary A Nicol
1971-72	Hugh Beaton	Sheila D Whyte
1972-73	Lachlan J Beaton	Mary K Kenneth
1973-74	Allan Ritchie	Mary M MacCormick
1974-75	Finlay J MacLeod	Fiona C Wilson
1975-76	Ian C Ferguson	Mairi MacPhee
1976-77	E Gordon Kennedy	Catherine R Cameron
1977-78	Ewan J Kennedy	Lesley A Kettles
1978-79	James C MacDonald	Alexandra M Stewart
1979-80	Robert A Downie	Heather M Cameron
1980-81	Thomas McQuade	Margaret M McIntosh
1981-82	Alexander D Munro	Deirdre Michie
1982-83	Martin B MacLeod	Jacqueline Sutherland
1983-84	Lorne A Campbell	Fiona M McKie
1984-85	Colin Malone	Shirley Drummond
1985-86	Iain E Coates	Anna H Murray
1986-87	Kenneth T Drummond	Fiona M Sked
1987-88	Iain Danskin	Sheena MacDonald

1988-89	Neil Campbell	Angela Campbell
1989-90	Stuart Danskin	Victoria Murray
1990-91	Michael Raynor	Sheena MacDonald
1991-92	Craig Scott	Jennifer Pratt
1992-93	Iain MacIntyre	Pamela Campbell

DUX MEDALLISTS

DUX BOY   DUX GIRL

1893	Peter Campbell `	Christina B Corson
1894	Malcolm Hutton	Margaret H Robertson
1895	George MacGregor	Jeanie Paterson
1896	Alex D Robertson	Catherine Campbell
1897	William MacNaught	Henrietta Sinclair
1898	John Morrison	Katie Campbell
1899	Arch H McC Robertson	Mary Isabella MacKinnon
1900	Alex D Duff	Kate F Blacklock
1901	Charles E Duff	Margaret C Craig
1902	William A Munro	Flora MacMillan
1903	George Hope	Etta Duff
1904	Olaus M Martin	Margaret C McInnes
1905	Tom A Robertson	Mary Shairp
1906	Alfred D Duff	Christina MacDonald
1907	Henry L MacLennan	Isabella MacCallum
1908	Dugald Ferguson	Margaret B Martin
1909	Donald C Buchanan	Jane MacNaught
1910	Alex S McCallum	Margaret L Chisholm
1911	John C Dow	Mary H Cameron
		Mary M Martin
1912	John M Munro	
1913	Thomas R Duff	Jeanie Robertson
1914	Peter A Faichney	Janet M Calder
1915	Robert T Ross	Jean R Colthart

DUX OF SCHOOL

1916	Marion P Flemington
1917	Janet C Morrison
1918	Flora Kennedy
1919	Mary Cameron
1920	Mary Crerar
1921	Maggie MacKenzie
1922	Tearlach McG Whyte
1923	Ann M McCallum
1924	Helen M Campbell

1925	Margaret MacLean
1926	Minnie MacKinnon
1927	Alex M Henry
1928	Dugald MacArthur
1929	Elizabeth V Murray
1930	Allan McDiarmid
1931	Donald M MacPhee
1932	Hector W Cross
1933	Alexandra M Donald
1934	Donald McInnes
1935	Angus MacTavish
1936	William G Young
1937	Isobel M Wall
1938	Ian T Young
1939	Christina MacCorquodale
1940	Gilleasbuig Cameron
1941	John MacNeill
1942	Sheena M Yule
1943	Alasdair M MacLeod
1944	Jeannette Lowe
1945	Archibald Lamont
1946	Ian Duncan
1947	Ismay Firth
1948	Morag C Smith
1949	Anne J MacFarlane
	Donald J Campbell
1950	Elizabeth MacDougall
1951	James V Silverton
1952	Margaret G Campbell
	Allan MacLean
1953	Barbara J Leggett
1954	Alasdair J S Sinclair
1955	Robert A Reid
1956	Colin A Vincent
1957	Kathleen L MacKinnon
1958	Angus J MacIntyre
1959	Maureen M Hoey
1960	Gilleasbuig MacMillan
1961	William Gillies
1962	Anne Gillies
1963	Neil Beaton
	Kenneth MacLeod
1964	Alexander Morrison
1965	Ann Naismith

1966	Elizabeth A MacIntyre
1967	Hugh MacIntyre
	John MacAllister
1968	Veronica Hay
1969	Andrew Kydd
1970	Stuart M Ross
1971	David C Page
1972	Donald M Watt
1973	Carolyn M MacKay
	Susan E Brown
1974	Gavin Boyd
	Vivienne J Oatey
1975	Duncan J MacDonald
1976	Rosemary A Cameron
1977	Lesley A Kettles
	Catriona Brodie
1978	Andrew M Hall
1979	Alisdair W I Campbell
1980	Janet K Ansell
1981	George C Robertson
1982	Sara A Brown
	Jane Rayworth
1983	Patrick MacDowall
1984	Donald G Marshall
1985	Laura A Sharp
1986	Karen E May
1987	Martin C Gibson
1988	Helen M Leitch
1989	Barrie McKillop
1990	Alasdair MacGregor
1991	Alastair Proud
1992	Margaret Harrison

(i)

Personalia

This index does not include the names of people who only appear in the photographs or in the lists of Captains and Dux Medallists.

Alexander, John 112, 120
Anderson, Donald 61
Anderson, Duncan 61
Anderson, Greig 142, 157, 160, 185f
Anderson, John 44f
Anderson, Mandy 149
Anderson, Peter 61
Anderson, Miss 142
Anderson, Mr (janitor) 59
Anderson and Nisbet (Messrs) 28
Argyll, Dean of 65
Argyll, Duke of 5, 6, 7, 12; 70; 72
"Autumnbottom, Albert" 120f

Baah, Joseph 149, 162
Baily, Dr 54, 55, 56, 57, 65
Bain, G M 73
Bald, Claud 63
Balfour, Agnes 17
Balfour, Duncan 17
Balfour, Emily 17
Balfour, Lord 28
Balfour, Mary Jane 17
Balfour, Willie 17
Barnett, Alastair 163
Barnett, Barbara 189
Barnett, Ian 189
Barr, Mrs Anne 197
Barr, Gordon 163 192
Beath, Betty 151
Beath , Ian 159f, 169, 185

Beattie, Colin 45
Beattie, James 1, 29, 33, 36, 43, 45-47, 48, 49, 52, 61, 64f, 67, 75, 77, 80
Begue, Rev 28
Bell, George 163
Bennett, Major 74
Berrie, I 160
Biddulph, Colonel 104
Birkintyre, Mr, MP 39
Black, Donald 160
Black, Ian 131
Black, Jean 155
Black, Joe, 187
Black, Malcolm 192, 194
Blake, Mr 142
Boardman, Mrs Morven 153
Boardman, Peter 183
Boardman, Robert 183
Boase, Catriona 150
Bonnyman, Annie 192, 196
Boswell, James 6
Boyd, John (inspector) 25, 28f, 61
Boyd, John 196, 197, 198
Boyle, John 185f
Breadalbane, Lord 72
Brown, Donald 107
Brown, George 193
Brown, Dr Katie Anne 105
Brown, Niall 136
Brown, Sara 150
Brown, Colonel 74
Brown, Mr (school board) 13
Brown, Rev 28
Buchanan, Elizabeth (Dr Milne) 192, 197, 198
Burnett, James 114

Cairns, Ian 187
Calderwood, Andrew (Messrs) 28
Calderwood, Irene (Mrs Stewart) 198
Caldwell, Chrissie 196
Cameron, Ann 186

Cameron, "Babbie" 197
Cameron, Diane 182
Cameron, H 135
Cameron, Mrs K 131
Cameron, Kennedy 194
Campbell of Dunstaffnage 6
Campbell, Alasdair D 118f
Campbell, Angus 159
Campbell, Archibald (burgh fiscal) 44
Campbell, Dr Archibald 196
Campbell, Colin 87, 89, 92, 96
Campbell, David 156
Campbell, Donald 152, 169
Campbell, Rt Rev J A 92
Campbell, James 149
Campbell, J M (solicitor) 44
Campbell, Laurie 157
Campbell, Maxie 152
Campbell, Dr Robert 196
Campbell, Shona 189
Campbell, Miss (Mrs MacCalman) (attend-
ance officer) 131
Campbell, Mr (school board) 55
Campbell, Dr 28
Campbell, Dr 74
Carfrae, J A 29
Carmichael, John 196
Carter, John 13, 36
Cathro, Alan 155
Cherry, Alastair 2, 10
Clark, Alastair 186
Clark, Alison 162
Clark, Andrew 189
Clark, Iain 101
Clark, Ian 189
Clark, Ishbel 194
Clark, Ivor 119
Clark, Jean (Mrs Ferguson) 114
Clark, John 135,142
Clark, Mamie 190
Clark, William 183f
Clark, William J 88, 94, 104f, 108, 134
Clarke, Edward Daniel 11
Clarkson, J J 70

Cleaver, Iain 104
Clements Mr (school board) 53, 55
Coats, Agnes (Mrs Hardie) 87, 89
Colthart, Ann 170
Connaught, Duke of 71
Cook, John 94, 111
Cooper, Edward 160, 185
Cooper, Provost 28
Coutts, Flt Lt William 148
Cowan,Sir Robert 102
Craig, Mr (school board) 23, 24, 25, 26
Craik,Sir Henry 28
Crawford, Cathie 196
Crawford, Donella 186
Crawford, Fiona 189
Crawford, Mr (plumber) 60
Crerar, Graham 155
Crow, Karen 149
Cumming, Mrs 69
Cumstie, Mr (school board) 13
Cushley, Mr 129
Cutherbertson, Ian 164

Dairon, Robert 162
Dale, David 11
Davidson, A H 84, 87, 91, 92, 93, 95, 97,
109, 140f
Davidson, Annie (Mrs MacDougall) 90,
92f
Davidson, Iain 97
Davidson, William 134, 138
Davidson, Miss (schoolmistress) 20
Dent, H C 101
Dent, Helen (Mrs Davidson) 94, 111
Dobbins, Henry 94, 102, 107, 116, 141
Donn, Ian 133
Dow, Miss M A (Mrs Macfarlane) 86, 88,
94
Driver, J 160
Driver, Jackie 162
Drummond, Kenneth 189
Duff, Rev A 28
Duffy, Fraser, 119
Duncan, Alastair 190

Duncan, Alastair J B 194, 195, 196, 197
Duncan, Anne 105
Dunn, Alice 182
Dunn, Andrew 148,185

Edgar, Morag 192, 193
Eisenhower, President 132
Elland, Mr 32
Elliot, Sandy 139
Elphinstone, Bishop William 10
Ewart, Professor William 97

Faichney, Alexander 16, 26, 33, 37, 53f, 55, 67
Fairlie, John 185
Falconer, Keith 162
Falconer, Lake, 162
Felgate, Colin, 153
Felgate, James 185
Ferguson, Lynne 164
Ferguson, Margaret 162
Fisher, Robert 59
Fjortoft, Sandra 136
Forbes, Rev James 44
Ford, Ann 162
Forgrieve, Duncan 160,186
Forgrieve, Iain 153
Forgrieve, Larry 160, 185, 197
Fraser, David Munro 69
Fraser, Miss 26, 32, 34

Gabriel, William 93
Gall, Mr 64
Galt, Eric 94
Galt, George G 87, 94, 99
Gardiner, Florence 93
Gardner, Frances 77
Gibb, Anne M 191
Gillies, Anne 118, 123, 137, 164, 196
Gillies, Cathy 169
Gillies, William 118, 123, 137
Gladstone, Rev 28
Glass, Alexander 135, 142
Gordon, Alasdair 135

Gordon, Angus 135
Gordon, William 94, 110, 135, 137, 138
Gordon, Major 104
Gorrie, James (Messrs) 25, 28
Gowdie, Ian 152, 180
Grace, Michael 161
Graham, Donald 88
Graham, Helen 101
Graham, Kenneth 87, 88, 89, 93, 121
Graham, Ruth 162
Grant, Mrs, of Laggan 5, 7, 67
Gray, Cynthia 101
Gray, William 169
Green, Mrs 69
Greenshields, Dr Angus 197
Greenshields, Mima (Mrs MacVicar) 196
Gregorson, Mr (school board) 13, 20
Guthrie, James 180

Hamilton, Alex 169
Hamilton, George 180
Hardie, Norman T 87, 88, 89, 93, 111f, 120, 124, 140, 172
Hardie, Dr Robert 105
Harris, Annie D 44
Hay, Ann 137
Hay, William 162
Heath, David 189, 190
Heath, Martin 189, 190
Heath, Ted 152, 155, 187, 190
Hegney, Mr 142
Henderson, Brownlie 137, 151, 153
Henderson, George, K B 86
Henderson, T G 100, 102, 126, 144
Hill, Dennis 133
Hoey, Alan 119
Hope, A E 86
Hope, George, 46, 51
Houston, Jan 116
Howard, Michael 190
Hunter, Alastair 193, 198
Hunter Mr (school board) 13
Hutcheson, David 187
Hutchison, Rev 28

Hutton, James 24, 26, 29, 58

Ingilby, Rev A 44
Inglis, Jan (Mrs Wilkinson) 170
Irving, Anne (Mrs Byiers) 198
Irving, Cunningham B 94, 108f, 143, 173, 198

Jackson, Provost Ian 156
Jackson, Miss (Craigard) 98
Jamieson, Steven 163
Johnson, Samuel 6
Johnstone, Neil 163
Jolly, William 13
Joynson-Hicks, Sir William 78

Kay, Garth 109, 136, 172
Kay, Miss 96
Kelday, Mrs 137
Kennedy, Alasdair 197
Kennedy, Donald 35
Kennedy, Iain 137
Kennedy, Thomas 66
Kennedy, William D 64, 67-75 *passim*
Kilgour, John (Messrs) 28
Kirkpatrick, Charles 198
Knox, John 2

Laives, Sir John Bennet 39
Lamont, Archibald 92
Lamont, Duncan 156
Lamont, Sheila 162
Lamont, William 197
Lang, Alexander (sen) 16
Lang, Alexander (jun) 16
Laurenson, Thomas 149, 152, 169, 177, 178
Lawrence, Martin Brydon 13
Lawrence, Robert 13
Lawrie, Sheila 145
Lees, William 87, 112, 140, 141
Lewis, George 8
Lindsay, T S 73, 79
Little, Mr 142

Livingston Mr (school board) 22, 44
Livingstone, Angus 196
Logan, Stuart 184, 187
Lowe, Catriona (Mrs McClements) 87, 89, 91
Loynd, George Melbourne 92, 95, 109f
Lynch, Jack 159

MacAllister, Provost 77
MacArthur, Alasdair 118f, 133
MacArthur, Christabel (Dr Fallon) 198
MacArthur, Dugald 76, 82, 99, 196
MacArthur, Helen (Mrs Ross) 90
MacArthur, M 135
MacAskill, Samuel 194, 195f, 197
MacAulay, Jennifer 135
MacAulay Rosamond 135
MacBride, Mary 117, 127, 129, 135
McCaig, Miss (landowner) 23
McCaig, Mr (school board) 13
MacCallum, John 89
McCallum, Rev M 44f
MacCallum, Pipe Major R 164
MacCallum, Rae 149
McCalman Dr 39
MacClure, Mrs Betty 108, 135, 156, 173
McColl, Angus 160, 187, 188
McColl, Helen 113
McColl, James 177
McColl, Morag 162
McColl and Graham (Messrs) 25
MacCormick, Iain 137, 139, 173, 187
McCorquodale, D 86
McCrindle, Mrs Catriona 163
MacCulloch, Maureen (Mrs Drummond) 97, 198
MacDonald, Alexandrina 137
MacDonald, Allan (parent) 30
MacDonald, Allan (teacher) 86
MacDonald, Dr C M 73, 74
MacDonald, Calum 104, 119
MacDonald, D 160
MacDonald, Donald A (translator) 121f
MacDonald, Donald Alastair 104, 119

MacDonald, Duncan 137, 194, 196
MacDonald, Ewan 106, 114, 142
Macdonald, Hugh 47, 85
MacDonald, Iain 196
MacDonald, James (pupil) 157
MacDonald, James (benefactor) 104, 119
MacDonald, Jean (Kilbowie) 169
MacDonald, Jean (teacher) 111, 119, 132
MacDonald, John 104, 119
MacDonald, Màiri 11
MacDonald, Peter 5, 6
MacDonald, Norma 135, 142
MacDonald, Norman 135
MacDonald, Rev Norman 163
MacDonald, Rev William 97,194
MacDougall of Dunollie, Surgeon (-Major)
-General Henry 28, 34
MacDougall of Dunollie, Colonel 24, 25,
27, 34
MacDougall, Agnes 47
MacDougall, Archibald 133
MacDougall, Miss C A 92
MacDougall, Coll 104, 114, 190
MacDougall, David 162
MacDougall, Donald 192
MacDougall, Dugald "The Horse" 78
MacDougall, Elizabeth 97
MacDougall, Grace 51
MacDougall, J and A (Messrs) 21, 22
McDougall, John 44
MacDougall, Margaret 135
MacDougall, Margaret 189
McDougall, Patten of Gallanach 44
McDougall, Miss 26
McDougall, Mr (janitor) 34
McDougall and McColl (Messrs) 21, 25,
26
MadFadyen, Duncan 137
MacFadyen, M 160
Macfarlane, Cathie (Mrs Henderson) 196
Macfarlane, Donald 86, 88, 93, 94
MacFarlane, Hugh 190
MacFarlane, John 198
MacFarlane, Mary Jane 49

Macfarlane, Robert 23, 62
MacFarlane, Senga (Mrs Smith) 196, 198
Macfarlane, Mr MP 39
MacFie the Younger, Mr, of Airds and
Oban 28f, 39
Macintosh, Fraquhar 124, 125f, 131, 137,
141, 143, 145, 148, 162, 173, 196
MacIntosh, Iain 162
MacIntosh, Moira 162
Mackintosh, Miss (Craigard) 98
Macintyre, Angus (Glasgow) 44
MacIntyre, Angus (sen) 77
MacIntyre, Angus (jun) 111, 118, 196
McIntyre, Archibald 16
Macintyre, Dougie 186
MacIntyre, Duncan 119
MacIntyre, Eric 111, 118
MacIntyre, Iain 119
McIntyre, James 16
MacIntyre, Joe 160
MacIntyre, Kenneth (son of Angus) 111,
118
MacIntyre, Kenneth (sen, train driver) 131
MacIntyre, Kenneth (jun) 137
MacIntyre, Lorne 111, 118, 197
MacIsaac, Provost Dugald 44, 64
McIsaac, Duncan 36
MacKain, George 156
MacKay, Colin 189
MacKay, Joyce 196
MacKay, George S 112, 120, 135
MacKay, John J 139, 140, 173
MacKay, Lamont 101
MacKay, Marion (swimmer) 156, 157
MacKay, Marion 176
Mackay, Mary 20, 21
McKechnie, Sergeant 35
McKechnie, Sheriff 39
McKelvie Dr 39, 44
McKenna, Tracy 150
MacKenzie, Rev Donald 103f, 142
MacKenzie, Mrs Donald 142
MacKenzie, John 169
MacKenzie, Rev (of Maryburgh) 28

MacKenzie, Mr (groundsman) 77
McKichan, Neil 197
McKiernan, Pauline 181f
McKillop, Malcolm, 157
MacKillop, Marion 176f, 189
MacKinnon, Rev Angus 192, 193, 197
MacKinnon, Flora 87
McKinnon, James 17
MacKinnon, Janet 170
McKinnon, Jessie 17
MacKinnon, John 91, 92
MacKinnon, Minnie 89
MacKinnon, Mr (school board) 22, 23, 24, 27, 32, 52
MacLachlan of MacLachlan, Major 72
MacLachlan, Joan 163
MacLachlan, Karen 189
MacLachlan, Lachlan 34f
McLachlan, Sheriff 44
MacLaine, May 86, 116, 172
Maclaine, Neil 36
McLaren, Lachlan 36
McLaren, William 34, 43
McLauchlan, Angela 162
Maclean, Anne Bone 193
Maclean, Calum 100, 121f
MacLean, Charles 198
MacLean, Hugh (first prefect) 101
MacLean, Hugh (discus thrower) 133
MacLean, I 160
Maclean, John 82, 95, 97, 100-103, 104, 106, 108, 111-122 passim, 123, 124, 126, 130, 131, 133, 136, 137, 138, 141, 143f, 192
Maclean, Mrs John 136
MacLean, Lord 164
MacLean, Marjory 186
McLean, Mrs Mary 162, 190
Maclean, Sorley 100
McLean, Miss (Craigard) 117, 127f, 170
McLean, Mr (school board) 22, 23, 33
MacLellan, Mrs (office) 138
MacLennan, Pipe Major Angus 164
MacLennan, Betsy (Mrs MacAskill) 195

MacLennan, Miss E 46
Maclennan, Neil 133
MacLeod, Alasdair M 90, 192
Macleod, A J 143
MacLeod, Angus 73, 74, 75, 80-82, 83, 84, 85, 86, 88, 90-98 passim, 100, 101, 108f, 115, 121, 192
MacLeod, Bobby 196
Macleod, Campbell 185
MacLeod, C J 192
MacLeod, Finlay 156
MacLeod, Fiona 163
MacLeod, Ishbel (Mrs Lloyd) 196
MacLeod, John 173
MacLeod, John (poet) 121
MacLeod, Rev John 147
MacLeod, Kenneth 123
Macleod, Margaret 136
MacLeod, Robert 150
MacLeod, Torquil 142
Macleod, Rev 28
McLucas, Donald 54
MacMillan, Christine 162
MacMillan, Gilleasbuig 118, 197
MacMillan, Helen T 193
MacMillan, Iain A 89
Macmillan, John 20
Macnair, Terry 190
MacNaughton, Baillie 77
MacNaughton, John 100
MacNaughton, Margaret 108, 116, 142
MacNeill, Hugh 132
MacNicol, Donald 194
MacNicol, Dr 44
MacPhail, Alan 161
MacPhail, Anne I 93, 112, 127, 191,
MacPhail, Duncan 196
Macphail, Dr James Calder 4
MacPhail, Dr Katherine 69
MacPhail, Nan 192
MacPhail, Mr (education committee) 98
MacPhee, Dollie 196
McPherson, Alexander 36
MacPherson, Fred 149

McQuade, Thomas 188
MacQueen, Alexander 21
MacQueen, Peter 165
MacQuisten, F A 78
MacRae, Kenneth 101
Macrae, Mary 36
McShane, Mark 186
McSporran, Sheila 101
Mactaggart, Samuel 93
MacVicar, Donald 186
MacWilliam, Mr 132, 142
Maitland, Rev James 196
Malcolm, Colonel Edward 44
Malone, C (teacher) 135
Malone, Colin 188
Malone, Donald 188
Malone, William, 188
Marshall, James 120
Marshall, Thomas 87, 89
Martin, Rev D J 28, 65
Martin Janet 117, 122
Martin, Sgt John 33, 34, 41
Mason, David 151
Matheson, Karen 163
Mathieson J G 120, 132
May, Mrs Anne 182
Meek, Donald 137
Menzies, Gwen 170
Menzies, Margaret 170
Miller, Alistair 156, 173
Miller, James 35
Miller Mr (Director of education) 164
Milligan, James 138
Milne, George 75, 78, 83, 86, 88, 90, 96, 97, 98, 100, 105f, 113, 192, 193
Milne, Peter 120
Milne, Mrs Peter 120
Mitchell, Brian R 149, 160, 161, 179, 186-188 *passim,* 196
Mitchell, Mr (of 1897) 28
More, Magnus 142
Morgan, Miss (Mrs de Gaye) 87, 90
Morrison, Catherine 163
Morrison, Chris (Mrs MacLachlan) 85, 111

Morrison, Derek 164f
Morrison, Donald 94, 103, 135, 137, 163, 172
Morrison, Fiona 189
Morrison, Iain 189
Morrison, Mairi 123, 135
Munn, Archibald 36
Munn, Janice 153
Munn, Sergeant 54
Munn, D and A (Messrs) 28
Munro, Bella 101
Munro, Hector MP 127, 168
Munro, John (d 1915) 27, 28, 39, 42, 44, 52, 65, 67, 70
Munro, John 100 122
Munsie, Sheena 95, 96, 107
Murray, Andrew J 106f 116, 135, 142f,
Murray, Jean 122
Murray, Dr Kenneth 197
Murray, Violet (Mrs MacArthur) 82

Naismith, Ann (Mrs McCulloch) 123
Nesbitt, Julian 69, 193
Ness, David 194
Ness Thomas P 194f, 196, 197
Ness Walter 194
Newte, Thomas 6, 7, 10
Newton, Robert 30
Nicholson, Dan 197
Nicholson, Norman 151
Nicol, John 180
Nicol, Mary 137
Nicol, Peter 190
Niven, Duncan 119

Ogilvie, Campbell 193
Ogilvie, Professor R M 10
Ogilvie, W Alasdair 192, 193
Owen, C H 40f

Pacey, Gordon 117
Page, David 123
Page, James 104, 135, 172
Paget, Judith 162

Palmer, Colin 193, 196
Paterson, James 43
Paul, Charles 157
Pearson, Drum Major S 164
Pennant, Thomas 5
Powell, David 150

Ramsey, David 104, 110
Reid, Robert A 114, 118, 144
Reid, Rev 28
Renfrew, Alasdair 123
Rhodes, Joe 155, 173, 187
Ritchie, Derek, 190
Robb, R 160
Robertson, Alex 32, 42, 44f, 55, 64
Robertson, Alexander C 43
Robertson, Archibald 138
Robertson, Boyd 162, 163
Robertson, Bruce 28f
Robertson, Charles 160, 161, 186-188 *passim*
Robertson, Duncan 192
Robertson, Elma 107
Robertson, Marie-Claire 189
Robertson, Nicola 177
Robertson, Peter (Pat) 121, 137
Rose, Jessie 86, 113f
Rosebery, Lord 28
Rosling, Rev 28
Ross, Stuart 123, 137
Roxburgh, Morag 197, 198

Sargent, Michael 181f
Scott, Mrs Ann 182
Scott, Betty: see MacClure
Scott, Donald 119
Scott, Captain 72
Scrimgeour, W 70, 74, 75, 77, 195
Seddon, Fred 87, 96, 109
Seggie, Robin 162
Shairp, Alexander 26, 28, 80
Shairp, Mr (factor for MacFie) 39
Sharples, John 153, 172
Shaw, Donald 163

Shepherd, William 96, 102
Silkowski, Henry 133
Sim, J Fraser 24, 25, 26
Simpson, Angus 179
Skinner, Alistair 196
Skinner, Provost Donald M 98, 100 122
Skinner, Donald M 122, 195, 197, 198
Skinner, Hugh 20, 21, 24, 26, 27, 36, 37, 42f, 51, 53, 93
Skinner, Mary Ann 51, 87, 93f, 113
Slater, G Y 160, 197
Smith, A C P 142
Smith, Alex 190
Smith, Andrew 189f
Smith, Annie 139
Smith, Chris 189
Smith, Sir Donald A, of Glencoe 28
Smith, Donald 101
Smith, Iain Crichton 106, 116, 140, 155
Smith, Isabel 162
Smith, John MP 139
Smith, John A 192
Smith, Mrs Kathleen 182
Smith, Mary 139
Smith, Moira 192
Smout, Professor T C 2, 3, 4, 5, 6, 8, 10, 11
Smyth, Ian 140
Spalding, Mr 135
Speed, Davina 86
Spence, E T F 85, 93, 94, 111, 119, 132f, 140, 145, 171
Spence, Erik, 197
Starling, Stephen 150
Stevenson, Hugh 7
Stevenson, John 7, 11
Stevenson, T 70
Stewart, Mrs 110, 141
Strachan, David 131
Strachan, Eric 179, 180
Strathern, Miss 26
Stuart, Patricia 113, 114
Sutherland, J D 28
Sutherland, William 28
Swanson, Edward 193

Taylor, Alexander L 43
Thom, Steven 149
Thomson, Donald 85, 87, 90, 92, 95, 103,
111, 119, 137, 140, 163, 171, 172, 196
Thomson, Fay 101
Thomson, Harry 183
Thomson, Ian D S 160, 176, 183f, 187, 188
Thomson, John 155
Thomson, Mairead 137
Thomson, Peter 15, 52
Thomson, William 155, 160, 187, 190
Thornton, John 87
Tindall, Maureen 162
Troup, James W 86f, 88, 96, 107f, 113,
138, 141
Turner, Nicholas 189
Turner, Mr 135
Twatt, Amanda 150
Twatt, Terence 145-150 *passim,* 154, 156-
160 *passim,* 163, 167, 169, 171, 177f, 196

Vallance, Mr (school board) 55, 57
Vass, Mrs 32
Vincent, Colin A 114

Waddell, Annie 49
Waddell, Miss (Children's Theatre) 85f,
Walker, Henry and Son (Messrs) 26
Waltho, David 177
Warwick, Penny, 162
Watson, W J 1, 9
Watson, Mr (of 1897) 28
Watt, Mrs Peter 186
Westmacott, Mr (benefactor) 39
Whyte, Janet 87, 112
Whyte, Martin 97
Wilkinson, Rev Brian 170
Wilson, Norman K 93
Wilson, Dr R 87
Withrington, Donald J 8, 10, 11
Wood, Dr Alex 87, 88, 91, 92
Wood, Irene 189, 190
Wood, Jackie 189

Wood, J 70, 73, 74, 79
Wynne, Mgr Thomas 147

Young, Alexander 193
Young, Ian 193
Young, Rev John 193
Young, Robert 43
Young, Rev William 193

(ii)

Oban High School
and Education Generally

Academic Record, 37f, 45 51, 53, 62, 68,
70, 72, 73, 90, 91, 92, 93, 94, 107, 109,
111, 112, 113, 118, 123, 143, 150, 151,
167, 179
Air Training Corps, 88f, 93, 104, 148
Argyll County Council/Education Authority or Committee, 73, 75, 94, 103, 105,
110, 145
Army Cadets 72, 75f, 79, 88, 94, 104,
134f, 147, 172,
Attendance, 15ff, 30, 40, 47, 48f, 54f, 56-
58, 60f, 68, 72, 84, 85, 88, 89, 92, 94, 130

Badge, 114, 122
Boys Brigade, 148
Burnside Cottage, 59

Canteen and School Meals, 90, 91, 92,
131, 136, 139, 146, 171, 176
Campbeltown Grammar School, 52, 71,
75, 97, 126
Campbeltown School Board, 42
Captains: see Prefects
Choir(s), 94, 95, 97, 109f, 136f, 148, 155,
163
Clans, 76, 79, 101, 133, 136, 154
    Diarmid, 79, 136
    Fingal, 76, 154

Ossian, 76, 136
Somerled, 76, 136, 154
Class Size, 55, 70, 84, 90, 91, 92, 95, 102, 126, 146
Clubs: Boys' 69, 75
Girls' 69, 75
School, 127, 129, 134
Concerts and Productions, 71, 96, 109, 136, 137, 150f, 153f, 156, 178f
Corporal Punishment, 17f, 68, 102, 146, 195
Crieff, Morrison's Academy, 45
Curriculum: see Departments

Dances and "Musicals", 98, 112, 117f, 120, 128, 129, 136, 151-153, 178
Debating, 75, 134, 142, 147, 154
Departments and Subjects:
Agriculture 37, 42, 47
Art (and Design) 98, 110, 136, 146, 150, 151, 161, 177-180
Drawing, 32, 33, 38, 39, 47
Civil Service, 47
Classics 38, 101, 102, 108, 139, 180
Greek, 12, 30, 37, 38, 47, 51, 62, 95, 118, 143, 174
Latin, 12, 30, 37, 38, 47, 48, 51, 62, 83, 95, 118, 124, 143, 174
Commercial/Business Studies, 83, 120, 124
Bookkeeping, 32, 38, 47, 54, 62
Shorthand, 32, 54, 62
Computing, 138, 174
Dairy Work, 42
Domestic Science/Home
Economics, 37, 83, 96, 98, 112, 120, 136, 146, 161
Cookery, 30, 32, 42, 54, 112
Dress-cutting, 54
Laundry, 30, 42
Needlework/Industrial Work, 31f, 62, 112
See Also Leisure Activities
English, 12, 35, 37, 38, 47, 62, 83, 105f, 118, 151, 199
Composition, 31
Grammar, 31
See also Reading, Writing and Arithmetic
Fishing, 42
Food Education, 124
Gaelic, 2, 3, 4, 5, 30, 32, 35-37, 38, 54, 77, 80-82, 83, 91, 101, 102, 103, 114, 115f, 118, 121, 124, 126, 136f, 138, 140, 143, 162f, 165, 172, 195
Gardening, 30
Geography, 31, 37, 51, 135, 146
Handwriting/Penmanship, 31, 47
See also Reading Writing and Arithmentic
History, 31, 37, 51, 106f, 116, 142
Language Laboratory, 146
Mathematics, 37, 38, 39, 42, 47, 51, 62, 80, 83, 104, 141, 199
Arithmetic, 4, 12, 30, 31, 38, 39, 47, 62: See also Reading Writing and Arithmetic
Conics, 37
Dynamics, 37
Mechanics, 42, 47
Modern Languages, 38, 51, 83, 102, 107, 145
French, 30, 33, 36, 37, 38, 47, 62, 118, 124
German, 30, 33, 36, 37, 38, 47, 62
Music, 31, 32 44, 51, 83, 109f, 120, 137, 146, 151, 176
Singing, 31, 47, 54, 62
Navigation, 30, 42, 54, 139, 178
Physical Education/Drill, 30, 33f, 40, 41, 47, 54, 62, 90, 110, 111, 132, 146
Callisthenics, 32
Physiography, 42
Reading Writing and Arithmetic 4, 30, 35

Religious Education, 4, 12, 40, 42, 47, 102, 113, 138
Science, 33, 38, 39, 62, 83, 139, 146
  Botany, 47
  Nature Study, 30
  Physics, 42, 47
Technical, 83, 96, 111f, 120, 136, 140, 178
  Building (Construction), 54, 124
  Engineering, 124
  Metalwork, 112, 174
  Technical Drawing, 112
  Wood carving, 42
  Woodwork, 112, 174
  See also Leisure Activities
Discipline, 16, 17, 30, 48, 52f, 83, 86, 97, 102, 108, 128, 130, 141, 176, 177
See also Corporal Punishment
Dublin, Blessed Oliver Plunkett Secondary School, 159
Duke of Edinburgh's Award, 135, 148, 149
Dundee, Grove Academy, 86
  Harris Academy, 86
Dunoon Grammar School, 52, 75, 92, 94, 126, 173, 187
Dunoon School Board, 42
Dux Medal and Medallists, 39, 90, 92, 123, 125, 204-206

Edinburgh, Royal High School, 125, 162, 173
Education Act 1496, 2, 10
Education (Scotland) Act, 1872, 2, 7-9, 13, 37, 147
Education Act 1944, 91
Education and Local Taxation Relief (Scotland) Act, 1892, 37
Education in the Highlands, 1-5
Elgin Academy, 96
Evening School/Classes and Extra-Mural Classes, 36, 53f, 66, 141, 158f

Fees, 9, 14f, 16, 43, 58, 66, 84f, 94
Former Pupils and FP movement, 74, 76, 77, 96, 97, 98, 117f, 122, 192-198
Fort William, Lochaber High School, 123, 183
Free Church of Scotland Schools, 4, 12, 13, 19f, 51, 93
Fund Raising, 70, 71, 77, 89, 90, 91, 95, 154, 155-158

Games: see Sport(s)
Girl Guides, 75, 147
Greenock Higher Grade (High) School, 64, 67
Guidance and Careers, 147

Health, epidemics, closures, 55, 56-58, 68f, 72, 73, 74, 85, 89, 90, 92, 93, 102
Holidays, 40, 68, 72, 74, 75, 82-83, 88, 92, 95, 100, 101, 118
HORSA Huts, 88, 95, 146, 201
Hostels, 69, 75, 126f, 130, 131, 134, 145, 165-170, 173, 183
  Craigard, 75, 77, 78, 90, 98, 117, 126, 127f, 129, 168, 169, 170, 183
  Glencruitten, 127, 130, 131, 168, 169, 170, 183
  Kilbowie, 115, 117, 119, 126, 127, 128-130, 131, 134, 135f, 168, 169f, 183
Howie Report, 124, 199

Invergordon Academy, 64, 67, 94
Inverness schools, 67, 101, 137
Islay school 123, 183

Junior Students, 52, 67, 73, 74

Lavatories, 59f, 176
Leaving Certificate, 9, 35, 37f, 52, 85, 103, 120, 123f, 158, 175, 180, 182, 199: See also Academic record, SCOTVEC
Leisure activities, 125, 147. See also Sport(s)
Library, 47, 67, 181f

Lochgilphead Schools, 91, 123, 168, 183
Lodgers and lodgings, 63, 68, 69, 72, 75, 77f, 98, 102, 113, 119, 126f, 130f, 165-167, 168, 170, 173

Motto, 114, 115f

Oban, Schools in 5, 7, 12f, 14, 18, 19f,
Oban High School:
  Name conferred, 21
  Rockfield Road, building of, 19-21; building at, 22, 29; separation from OHS, 121
  Soroba Road, building of, 22-27; building at, 27-29, 39, 73, 88, 95, 96, 111, 120, 126, 178, 200f
Oban School Board, 13-30 *passim*, 32-37 *passim*, 39, 40, 43, 44, 49, 51-56 *passim*, 58, 60-64 *passim*, 67, 68, 70, 73
Orchestra, 148, 151, 155, 156, 176
Outings/Trips/Visits, 69, 71, 83, 93, 95, 117f, 135, 137f, 142, 147f, 153, 173, 177, 180, 184f

Parent Teacher Associations, 145
Prefects and Captains, 101f, 118, 139, 143, 192, 198, 202f
Prizes and Prizegiving (not Sports) 35, 37, 39, 40, 69, 86, 90, 97, 120, 171, 172 See also Dux Medal
Pro-Cathedral School, 42
Pupil Teacher Scheme, 57f, 93

Rector: Title conferred, 43,
Rothesay Academy, 45

Salaries, 49f
St Andrews, Madras College, 43, 45, 96
St Columba's School, 14, 18f, 20, 70, 84, 146, 169
St John's School, 14, 18, 70, 84
School Boards, 9, 13, 14, 19, 49, 58, 73, 125, 145, 174, 200 See also Campbeltown, Dunoon and Oban School Boards

School Council, 125
SCOTVEC, 175, 199
Scouts, 148, 181,
Sea Cadets, 147
Secondary Education, beginning of, 42; opening of 44f
Sex Education, 105
Sport(s)
  County Youth Sports, 95, 97, 133
  Festival of Sport, 111
  School Sports, 40f, 77, 79, 80, 93, 111 133, 154, 155
  Sports prizes, 41, 77
    Rector's Cup, 77, 93
    Rosebowl, 77, 93
    Tenga Cup 77
  Athletics, 41, 91, 111, 133, 134, 148; Athletics Club 42; Athletic Association 93
  Badminton, 134, 147, 162
  Basketball, 134, 148, 162
  Boxing, 95
  Canoeing, 147, 169
  Climbing, 134, 135, 142, 169
  Cricket, 41, 42, 69, 77, 162
  Football, 41, 42, 71, 76, 91, 111, 118f, 125, 129, 132f, 134, 147, 162
  Golf, 42, 125, 134, 147, 162
  Gymnastics team, 134
  Harriers, 42
  Hill-walking, 148, 183-185
  Hockey, 76, 95, 119, 125, 132, 141, 147, 162
  Netball, 125, 132, 162
  Rowing, 73, 119, 134, 135f
  Rugby, 125, 132, 133, 147, 160f, 186-188
  Sailing, 104, 119, 134, 147, 157, 162, 169
  Shinty, 76, 102, 111, 119, 125, 132, 133, 147, 159f, 185f
  Ski-ing, 134, 147, 153, 162, 169
  Squash, 189f

Swimming, 34, 40, 41, 42, 73, 147, 157, 162, 169
Targette, 42
Tennis, 41, 42, 76, 77, 134, 148, 162, 189f
Volleyball, 147, 162
ubjects: see Departments
tornoway, Nicolson Institute, 67, 137, l67

'arbert School, 183
'iree School, 183
'obermory School, 183
'ravel and travelling pupils, 63f, 68, 75, 7, 87, 90, 92, 95, 97f, 119, 131f, 165-67, 170f, 173

Jniform, 138, 139, 154

Vick High School, 173

(iii)

Etcetera

.chnacloich, 132
.ppin, 132, 171
.rdchattan, 1, 193
.rdnamurchan, 63

.allachulish, 63, 75, 97, 119, 123, 127, 31, 132, 170, 192
arcaldine, 132, 170
arra, 63
eauly, 1, 2
enderloch, 98, 104, 132, 170, 192

eltic Church, 1
hurch of Scotland, 2, 3, 4, 5, 8, 13, 51, 92
oll, 63, 123, 166
olonsay, 123, 137

Connel, 47, 89, 132, 167
Creagan, 132

Dalavich, 167, 170
Dalmally, 64, 75, 97, 170, 198
Darjeeling, 63
Dunard Castle, 71
Dunstaffnage, 95
Dingwall, 3
Duror, 123, 132

Easdale, 170

Fearn, 1
Fort William, 63, 123, 183
Free Church of Scotland, 4, 12, 13, 19f, 51, 93, 103

Gaelic: see Index (ii) under Departments and Subjects
Gaelic Society of Edinburgh, 4
Gaelic Society of Glasgow, 4
Gaelic Society of Iverness, 4, 5
Gigha, 123
Glen Coe, 63, 123
Glen Etive, 63
Glenorchy, 3

Hebrides, 71
Hesperus, NLS, 71

Inveraray, 3, 63
Inverchaolin, 3, 4
Iona, 71, 72, 166, 198
Islay, 63, 95, 123, 183, 195

Jura, 63, 123

Kentallen, 132
Killin, 63
Kingussie, 1
Kinlochleven, 76, 123, 132
Kinloss, 1
Kirkwall, 2

Lewis, 63, 67, 98, 137, 167
Lismore, 123, 173
Lochgilphead, 63, 76, 91, 123, 168, 183
Luing, 166, 173

Morvern, 123, 171
Mull, 63, 72, 91, 96, 123, 142, 166, 183,
 196

Northampton, HMS, 42
North Uist, 63

Oban, 1, 5-7, 10, 12f, 14, 18, 19f, 67, 71f,
 73, 74, 76, 77, 78f, 83, 85, 86, 87, 88, 92,
 94, 103, 104, 109, 110, 111, 127, 129, 132,
 134, 137, 138, 139, 140, 150, 154, 156,
 157f, 158f, 173, 179, 185, 186, 187, 188

Patagonia, 63
Plover, 71

Raasay, 137
Robert Smith, HMS, 71
Roman Catholic Church, 1, 3, 8, 18, 19
Rosemarkie, 1, 3

St Kilda, 169
Scottish Episcopal Church, 13, 18, 86
Skye, 63
Society for the Propagation of Christian
Knowledge, 3f
South Uist, 63

Tarbert, 91, 168, 183, 192, 196
Tiree, 63, 78, 95, 105, 123, 166, 183, 192,
198

Uganda, SS , 173
Ullapool, 63, 69
Ulva, 166